Also by Dan Kurzman

SANTO DOMINGO: *Revolt of the Damned*

GENESIS 1948: *The First Arab-Israeli War*

MIRACLE OF NOVEMBER: *Madrid's Epic Stand 1936*

SUBVERSION OF THE INNOCENTS

DAY OF THE BOMB: *Countdown to Hiroshima*

KISHI AND JAPAN

A KILLING WIND: *Inside Union Carbide
and the Bhopal Catastrophe*

LEFT TO DIE: *The Tragedy of the USS* Juneau

FATAL VOYAGE: *The Sinking of the USS* Indianapolis

THE BRAVEST BATTLE: *The 28 Days of the
Warsaw Ghetto Uprising*

BEN-GURION: *Prophet of Fire*

THE RACE FOR ROME

# BLOOD
### AND
# WATER

## SABOTAGING HITLER'S BOMB

# DAN KURZMAN

A JOHN MACRAE BOOK

HENRY HOLT AND COMPANY ▪ NEW YORK

ISBN 0-8050-3206-1

Designed by Victoria Hartman

Printed in the United States of America

*To my dear wife, Florence—*
*whose radiance could thaw even*
*the coldest Norwegian winter*

# CONTENTS

# CONTENTS

# *PREFACE*

**WHEN NAZI GERMANY** invaded Norway in April 1940, Adolf Hitler had good reason to believe that his country would devour all remaining European Allies and dominate the world. Great Britain would soon be reeling under a rain of rocket bombs. France would shortly learn that no Maginot Line could stop a blitzkrieg. The Soviet Union was busy digesting the half of Poland it had swallowed up under a partition agreement with Germany. And the United States had only a few divisions fit for combat and hardly enough ships to ward off enemy submarine attacks, reflecting the mood of a nation rife with cries to stay out of a war that seemed to pose no immediate threat to national security.

But at least one group of people in this country realized these cries rang false—the nuclear physicists. For they knew that German scientists Otto Hahn and Friedrich Strassmann had unlocked the secret of atomic fission in December 1938, and that this discovery could give birth to an atomic bomb that would annihilate entire cities and win the war. Their German counterparts, they feared, might well accomplish this feat—if the Allies didn't build the weapon first.

And the tension grew when, in spring 1940, British intelligence revealed that Norsk Hydro, a large complex of hydroelectric and electrochemical plants that the Germans had taken over in southern Norway, was turning out increasing quantities of deuterium oxide, known as "heavy water," an important ingredient for a nuclear reactor.

This is an apparatus in which a chain reaction of fissionable material is initiated and, if uncontrolled, could spark an atomic explosion.

Since heavy water was useful only for the generation of nuclear power, Allied scientists concluded that the Germans were forcing Norsk Hydro, the world's only commercial producer of the substance, to supply them with enough for a reactor. Here was, it seemed, the first concrete evidence that Hitler was building an atomic bomb.

Thus, escalating fears helped to kindle a massive effort by the United States and Britain in 1942 to build a bomb. At the same time, Allied leaders decided that the heavy-water plant in Norway had to be destroyed—at any cost in blood or money.

This is the story of the desperate Allied campaign to demolish the plant, a story of extraordinary courage, idealism, and sacrifice. Though the campaign may have been the most daring and sustained clandestine action in World War II, the secrecy surrounding it during wartime in large degree spilled over to peacetime, and little has been written about it until now. Much of the research material used in this book was only recently declassified.

In gathering information, I scoured libraries, research institutes, and military archives, and I personally interviewed scores of people in the United States, Norway, Britain, France, and Germany. I spoke with statesmen, atomic scientists, war historians, military leaders, intelligence agents, saboteurs, flyers, soldiers, factory workers, engineers, bombing victims, farmers, and others caught by circumstance in the deadly web of this momentous secret undertaking.

All quotations, thoughts, and feelings presented here appear precisely as these individuals expressed them to me, or as they have recorded them in their diaries, memoirs, letters, or war records. Let me stress that nothing in this book is fictionalized. The sources of all quotations and important facts not indicated in the text can be found in the Notes, and all persons who granted me interviews or otherwise helped me are listed in the Bibliography or Acknowledgments.

—Dan Kurzman
Rjukan, Norway, 1993

# ACKNOWLEDGMENTS

I OWE MUCH to my wife, Florence, for her invaluable contribution to this book. She edited it, rewrote numerous passages, and helped to infuse life into an important, little-known chapter of history.

I also wish to thank Jack Macrae, my editor at Henry Holt, and Julian Bach, my agent, for their detailed editorial advice; nuclear scientist Ralph E. Lapp for checking the manuscript for technical accuracy; nuclear scientist Arnold Kramish for his wise suggestions; and Rjukan reporter Gary Payton and Egersund historian Jostein Berglyd for their generous help.

Many others deserve my gratitude for facilitating my research:

Hilde Aaones—guide, Industriarbeider Museet, Vemork, Norway

Kurt Guija Artmann—official, German Information Center, New York

Bjorg Bjilland—guide and translator, Stavanger, Norway

Egil Bjilland—photographer, Rogaland Fylkeskommune, Stavanger

Richard Boylen—chief, Suitland, Maryland, Branch, National Archives

Robin Brook—British intelligence officer

William Colby—OSS officer

John Dancke—relative of Fritz Bornschein

Bjorn Edvardsen—director, Industriarbeider Museet

Sharon K. Fawcett—chief, Reference Services Branch, National Archives

David Giordano—archivist, Reference Services Branch, National Archives

Renée Hatche—technician, Reference Services Branch, National Archives

Thomas M. Hatfield—dean, University of Texas

Jan-Petter Helgesen—political editor, *Stavanger Aftenblad*

Per Johnsen—writer, Stavanger

Kate Johnson—archivist, Imperial War Museum, London

Janis Bjorn Kanavin—director, Norwegian Information Service, New York

Norbert Kastner—interpreter from German

Roger Kershaw—archivist, Public Records Office, Kew, Richmond, Surrey, England

Robert B. Lane—official, Historical Research Center, Maxwell Field Air Force Base

Robert Larsen—Oslo television producer

Trond Lepperod—editor, *Rjukan Arbeiderblad*

Jean Claude Levain—archivist, Centre d'Études, Fontenay aux Roses, France

Arne Finn Malme—curator, Industriarbeider Museet

Kirsten Nielsen—guide, Industriarbeider Museet

Ruth Paley—archivist, Public Records Office

Suzanne Palme—Oslo literary agent

Edward J. Reese—archivist, Modern Military Branch, National Archives

Lars Christian Sande—director, Rogaland Fylkeskommune, Stavanger

Jonny Skogstad—Norwegian television reporter

Tor Olav Sperre—Norwegian television reporter

James Taylor—archivist, Imperial War Museum

John Taylor—archivist, Modern Military Branch, National Archives

Raidar Torp—director, Norges Hjemmefrontmuseum, Oslo

Stephen Walton—archivist, Imperial War Museum

Victor S. Washington—technician, National Archives

# BLOOD

≡ A N D ≡

# WATER

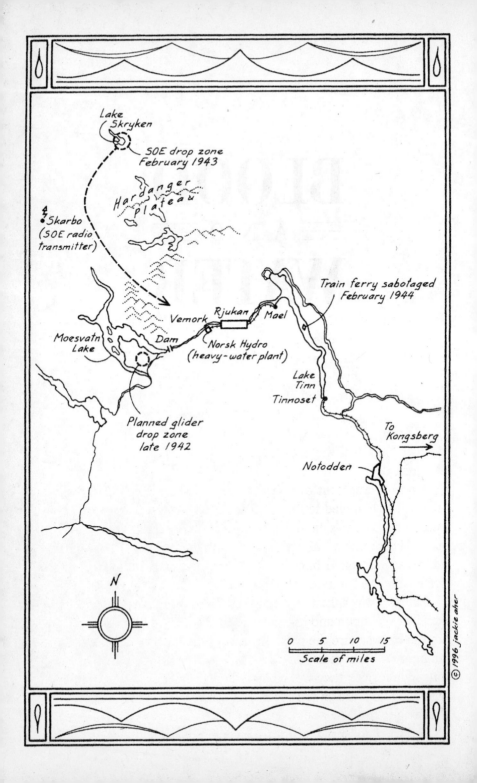

Lake
Skryken

SOE drop zone
February 1943

Hardanger
plateau

Skarbo
(SOE radio
transmitter)

Train ferry sabotaged
February 1944

Vemork    Rjukan    Mael

Moesvatn
Lake              Dam

Norsk Hydro
(heavy-water plant)

Lake
Tinn

Tinnoset

To
Kongsberg

Planned glider
drop zone
late 1942

Notodden

N

0    5    10    15
Scale of miles

© 1996 jackie aher

# PROLOGUE

MINUTES BEFORE MIDNIGHT on November 19, 1942, Martin
Selmer Sandstol rolled over in bed and awoke with a start. He
mumbled a curse. The Germans never let him sleep. If they weren't
rumbling past his house with their motorcycles and trucks looking
for people to throw into jail, they were roaring overhead in their
planes, waking up everybody in Helleland and maybe in other villages near the southern coast of Norway. And never had the roar
been as loud as it was right now. Louder than any thunder he had
ever heard.

Sandstol crept out of bed, his rugged, stubbly face a frowning
mask, and shambled to the window. As he peered toward the great
snow-streaked hills in the distance, the sky suddenly seemed to
explode over one of the peaks, as if lightning had struck. Before the
blast had dissipated into an angry echo, a great ball of fire rolled
forth from the summit.

Sandstol was aghast. A plane had just missed clearing the Benkafjellet mountain and had crashed into it. Could anyone have survived? He was sure the pilot and crew were Germans, he told me in
an interview fifty years later, and he hated them. But at this moment
of sudden shock they were simply human beings. Maybe someone
was lying up there on the snowy peak gravely wounded, bleeding, or
freezing to death.

He tried to shrug off such feelings. After all, since invading

Norway in 1940, the Germans had ruined the country, forcing people to work for them, stealing the sheep, pigs, and chickens of poor farmers like himself, frightening teachers into spreading Nazi propaganda in the schools, hunting and killing people who dared speak out against them. What business did they have in Norway, in Helleland, where his family had peacefully plowed the crusty earth for generations?

Sandstol went back to bed but couldn't sleep. The great ball of fire burned through his mind as if someone had suddenly turned on the light. Yes, they were Germans, but did he have to succumb to their standards? He would climb the mountain to see if he could find any survivors. He quickly dressed, told his wife where he was going, and strode into the rainy darkness.

With his flashlight glowing, he followed a tortuous path that led to the mountain and began to climb, stumbling over snow-covered rocks, crawling through thorny brush, slipping across patches of solid ice. After almost two hours, he was exhausted and wished he were back in his warm bed. But he breathlessly trudged upward toward a summit that never seemed to get closer.

Finally, half an hour later, Sandstol made a last thrust up an ice-laden boulder and stood atop Benkafjellet mountain. In the glare of his flashlight, he was appalled at the scene that stretched before him. There, yards away, sprawled the blackened wreckage of the plane, which had shorn away the upper layer of rocky earth like a knife slicing off the top tier of a tall wedding cake. The floor of the plane had been ripped away and the four motors together with other twisted metal lay scattered in the snow.

As Sandstol poked his head through a broken window of the plane, he saw lying on the ground inside the fuselage the shattered bodies of five men, some missing limbs, most with their intestines strewn about the cabin. Just outside the fuselage he stared into the strange, lacerated face of a leather-jacketed man. A black man. Sandstol had heard about such people, but he had never seen one of them before. They came from Africa, he knew, and some lived in other countries like France and England. But he doubted there were any in Germany; the German soldiers he saw in Norway were all white. The dead men, he guessed, must be British. Britain, he knew, had helped Norway fight the Germans before the occupation and wanted to liberate his people.

Near the plane Sandstol found another corpse, and then another, or at least the parts of one. This man had been cut in half; his torso was grotesquely nestled in a crescent of three stones, with a dark sweater pulled up over his face. Sandstol reached into the man's shirt pocket and removed the photo of a beautiful, smiling young woman who wore ski clothes and had obviously been on vacation at some happy time. He lamented that her joy would be cut short by news of this tragedy.

Sandstol also found a pamphlet on the body with a letter from exiled King Haakon VII to his people promising that they would soon be free. It appeared that these seven British airmen, all of whom were dead, had come to bring the Norwegians freedom. But Sandstol was puzzled. Were they attacking Norway all by themselves? And what was their target?

With his flashlight shakily searching the scene, Sandstol followed the beam as it danced from one snow-soaked item to another—a pistol, a radio part, an article of clothing. Also a wrinkled silk handkerchief, curiously with a map of Norway printed on it. One place was circled in blue—a town named Rjukan.

# 1

## "A DELIGHTFUL PLAYTHING"

### *September 1942*

RJUKAN.

Two months earlier, Brigadier General Leslie R. Groves had apparently never heard of this town, a quaint, isolated, oversized village darkly nestled amid snow-splashed mountains about seventy-five miles west of Oslo. Even after he settled into his Washington office in late September 1942 as commander of an ultrasecret venture called the Manhattan Project, he wasn't quite sure how to pronounce the name (Rookan). But in his mind it soon became a code word for possible global catastrophe.

Rjukan, in fact, turned the Manhattan Project—a colossal effort by nuclear scientists to build an atomic bomb that could end World War II swiftly—into a labor of near desperation. For perched at the edge of a cliff overlooking the Rjukan Valley, in the suburb of Vemork, was the Norsk Hydro hydrogen-electrolysis plant, which since 1943 had been turning out a unique product, deuterium oxide, or heavy water, as a by-product of chemical fertilizer. The Germans, on invading Norway in April 1940, found that a vital ingredient of an atomic reactor had fallen into their hands.

Heavy water looks and tastes like ordinary water, but it is chemically different. Composed of the hydrogen isotope deuterium and oxygen, it has twice as many hydrogen atoms as ordinary water and is 10 percent heavier. The extra weight works as a slow-motion mechanism, moderating the speed of the neutrons set free in a nuclear reactor and permitting these elementary atomic particles to split uranium atoms in a chain reaction and produce plutonium, a fissionable element that could be used in a bomb.

When American chemist Harold Urey discovered the deuterium nucleus in 1932, he could not imagine that in a few years the atom would be split, launching the nuclear age. Nor could he envision history ordaining the role that heavy water would play in the making of an atomic bomb and the conduct of a world war. An intense, idealistic man who won a Nobel Prize in 1934 for his feat, he called heavy water "one of the most delightful playthings for physicists."

Urey viewed the simple deuterium nucleus mainly as an "atom gun" for bombarding the heart of more complex atoms to permit a deeper probe of their structures and properties. He also thought that experiments with heavy water could "be valuable in understanding more of living processes." It might even help in cancer research, he figured, since some biologists found that yeast cells multiplied much more rapidly in ordinary water than in heavy water, a quality largely shared by cancer cells. But Urey would learn, to his regret, that his "delightful plaything" would prove useful not as a tool for studying any living process but—aside from its role in atom probing—as an instrument for implementing the killing process.

During World War II, Urey served under Groves, seeking through the process of gaseous diffusion to separate the isotope U-235, the 1 percent of uranium that could undergo fission, from U-238, the 99 percent that could not. Separation, it was believed, could be achieved by physical means—electromagnetism or centrifuge as well as gaseous diffusion—but more easily and cheaply by chemical means, with an atomic reactor yielding plutonium.

After the war, Urey would reveal his disillusion with nuclear science and his fear for the future in an article aptly entitled, "I Am a Frightened Man." But history would remember him mainly for his special contribution to this science. His discovery, in fact, stirs our imagination even today. In Joseph Heller's novel *Closing Time*, a character becomes a valuable military resource because he can urinate heavy water. Equally fanciful was a 1935 murder mystery in which a murderer induces his victim to swim in a pool filled with the "lethal" fluid.

"It is the most expensive murder on record," one scientist wryly commented in the *Columbia Quarterly* after reading the book. "A computation shows that, at the present costs, that pool of heavy water would have cost about two hundred million dollars."

The price of heavy water was actually so high and its production so difficult that Urey's discovery, though proving useful for studying the atom before the war, did not send scientists scrambling to the few laboratories in the United States that supplied small quantities of it. Only Norsk Hydro manufactured it commercially, and this firm supplied mainly French and German scientists. In 1939, however, when a chain reaction seemed possible, the demand among the powers suddenly soared.

• • •

With the German seizure of Norsk Hydro in the spring of 1940, heavy-water production jumped even more dramatically. And when General Groves took over the Manhattan Project two and a half years later, Norsk Hydro was shipping out ten times the normal number of heavy-water canisters, or about 100 kilograms (220 pounds) a month.

Some of Groves's top scientists believed at this time that Germany might already have a reactor, with its first bomb only months away. The United States, on the other hand, did not yet have a reactor and would not test one until December 1942. The general had barely started on his job, and Hitler, it seemed to him, could be on the verge of winning the war with the atomic bomb.

Groves knew that Otto Hahn and Friedrich Strassmann had discovered fission in 1938—and hadn't Hitler been warning since the war started a year later that he would unleash a cataclysmic weapon? One had to assume that the most competent German scientists and engineers were transforming theory into deadly reality with the full support of their government.

"Our chief danger," Groves would write in his memoirs, "was that they might come up with relatively simple solutions to the problems we were finding so difficult."

And many of his own scientists agreed, for they knew the genius of their German counterparts. And they knew that in the summer of 1941 in Britain, Rudolf Peierls and Otto Frisch found that it was possible to separate a sufficient quantity of uranium 235 to make a bomb. The Germans may have made the same discovery, and, in fact, word had come on June 1, 1942, that the Germans had already "got a chain reaction going."

Hungarian scientist Leo Szilard claimed he was told this in a letter from an anti-Nazi German colleague, Friedrich Houtermans, who was then living in Switzerland, though it has never been established that Houtermans went beyond saying that a chain reaction seemed possible.

Szilard passed on his questionable interpretation to Arthur H. Compton, who directed atomic research at the University of Chicago, ominously telling him: "It might be argued, of course, that if we are going full speed ahead anyway, there is not much point in trying to find out what the Germans are doing since there is no possibility of any defenses anyway."

After consulting his own sources, Compton wrote on June 22, 1942, to Vannevar Bush, director of the Office of Scientific Research and Development: "We have just recognized how a chain reaction started with a small heavy-water plant can quickly supply material for a high power plant for producing [fissionable material]. If the Germans know what we know—and we dare not discount their knowledge—they should be dropping fission bombs on us in 1943, a year before our bombs are planned to be ready."

And on August 31, Bush, in turn, wrote to Major General George V. Strong, assistant chief of staff, G-2 Intelligence, in the War Department: "A plant at [Rjukan] Vemork is producing 120 kilograms per month of one of the essential materials [for a bomb] and shipping it to Berlin, and it then goes into the hands of Dr. [Werner] Heisenberg, the distinguished physicist."

These reports seemed to confirm fears generated by news filtering in from Danish intelligence that Niels Bohr, the great Danish nuclear physicist, had met with Heisenberg in the garden of Copenhagen's House of Honor in October 1941. Carl von Weizsaecker, another leading German nuclear scientist at that time, recently told me at his home near Munich that he had pressed Heisenberg to see Bohr in order to propose "an agreement between the scientists on both sides not to build an atomic bomb." According to a letter from Heisenberg to author Robert Jungk, the dialogue went like this:

BOHR: Do you really think that uranium fission could be utilized for the construction of weapons?

HEISENBERG: I know that this is in principle possible, but it would require a terrific technical effort, which, one can only hope, cannot be realized in this war.

Whatever Heisenberg actually said, Bohr was reported to have felt that the German's statement may have been intended to intimidate the West by implying that Hitler was in fact building a bomb.

* * *

Alarmed by such omens, General Groves viewed himself as a potential messiah. And his stern, taut expression reflected his iron will. He was a vigorous, stocky man of forty-seven with piercing blue eyes, a neatly trimmed mustache bordering thin, unsmiling lips, and shiny, dark brown hair that had earned him the nickname "Greasy" at West Point. It was up to him to stop Hitler from conquering the planet.

Hans Bethe, who was one of Groves's top scientists, told me: "Groves would have been disappointed if the war had ended before the bomb could be used."

He must not only drive his scientists and workers mercilessly, the general thought, but must knock out the Rjukan-Vemork heavy-water plant, which constituted the most compelling evidence that the Germans were making a bomb. He must make one first, before they could ravage humanity, not to mention his own impeccable reputation for succeeding at every task he undertook.

No problem was insoluble in Groves's view. He was determined to prove himself worthy of his martinet father, who had been a heroic army chaplain in the Spanish-American War. Nor would he ever forget that his father, a descendant from French Huguenots who had settled in America in the mid-seventeenth century, loathed George III for reasons never made clear, a hostility that would apparently color the son's relations with the British.

In any case, Groves's compulsion to please his father, it seems, was nurtured by a feeling of inadequacy fed by the elder man's favoritism toward his two other sons. This feeling may have nourished the general's aggressive attitude and would come to the fore most virulently when he would seek to convince the geniuses working under his direction that he was their intellectual equal. On one occasion, in his University of Chicago laboratory, he told them, according to a letter he wrote to an acquaintance: "You may know that I don't have a Ph.D . . . But . . . I had ten years of formal education after I entered college. . . . That would be the equivalent of two Ph.D's, wouldn't it?"

The statement was greeted by an embarrassed silence.

But Groves was not easily embarrassed. Symbolically tacked to a wall of his office was the drawing of a turtle with its neck stretched forward. The caption read: "Behold the turtle! He makes progress only when his neck is out."

Groves, whose neck was perpetually out, managed, despite enormous difficulties, to organize the greatest scientific project ever undertaken. And he had the full support of General George C. Marshall, the army chief of staff, who handed over virtually all his authority to him on matters related to the bomb.

General Groves, however, found that his scientists did not easily submit to authority. A few found him a tough but fair commander; one such supporter was J. Robert Oppenheimer, who headed the barbed wire–enclosed research center at Los Alamos, New Mexico, where the bomb was being built. Many others, however, especially Leo Szilard, deeply resented him for making them conform to military regulations and daring to tell them how to conduct their research. He was, they charged, an egomaniacal, whip-wielding dictator.

• • •

When Groves took over as project chief, Szilard was working with Italian scientist Enrico Fermi on an atomic reactor at the University of Chicago after having experimented with the use of heavy water at Columbia University. What did a chest-thumping military man like Groves know about atomic energy? Szilard would caustically remark to Eugene Wigner, also a scientist from Hungary, scoffing at the general's engineering and scientific training in college. "How can you work with people like that?"

Wigner agreed that it was not easy, and refused to let Groves turn him against Szilard with attacks on Szilard's ability and character.

"Within ten minutes," Groves would tell an interviewer with exasperation, "[Wigner] would be down in Szilard's office or Szilard would be in his office, talking to him in Hungarian Yiddish, convincing Wigner that I didn't like scientists, that I hated physicists above all else . . . and I disliked particularly Hungarians and I had no use for Jews."

Groves finally implored scientist James B. Conant, president of Harvard University, to offer his nemesis a job at Harvard, promising to reimburse the institution "for all its expenditures in connection with his employment." No, Conant said, he wouldn't agree even if the general endowed the university for life.

But if the clash between Groves's pragmatic authoritarianism and Szilard's visionary iconoclasm left little room for accommodation, the two men shared one strong emotion: a chilling fear that Hitler might build a bomb first. Szilard felt that the letter he had received from Friedrich Houtermans, which he interpreted as saying that the Germans had "got a chain reaction going," proved that they were ahead. And it appeared that the Rjukan heavy-water operation had made this possible.

Still, even in this period of anxiety, Szilard, a rotund, forty-seven year-old physicist with a round, pixyish face, saw humor in life and would not let adversity dilute his unlimited faith in the human spirit. A pair of horn-rimmed spectacles magnified the quizzical glint in his eyes, which mocked anyone cut from a more cynical mold. They also reflected obsession. He had to rescue the world.

In fact, Szilard had been preparing himself for this mission ever since the age of ten, when, as a student in Budapest he was overwhelmed by Imre Madach's Hungarian classic, *The Tragedy of Man*. As he would later describe the book: "The devil shows Adam the history of mankind, with the sun dying down. Only Eskimos are left and they worry chiefly because there are too many Eskimos and too few seals. The thought is that there remains a rather narrow margin of hope."

Szilard's awareness of the narrow margin helped to stir his intense early interest in physics, which he firmly believed held the key to whether the margin would disappear altogether. The secrets of the universe could, when revealed, be used either to ravage or to rescue humanity. He would learn the secrets so that he might rescue it, an obsession that intensified after Hitler came to power in Germany in 1933.

Szilard kept two suitcases packed in his room at the faculty club of the Kaiser Wilhelm Institute in Berlin, where he conducted nuclear research, and was ready to go "when things got too bad." He would keep his suitcases packed, literally, for much of his life, as he found himself fleeing from one crisis after another, real or imagined, and finally from the monster that he himself would help to create but could not control. During the 1962 Cuban missile crisis, he would flee Washington, believing it was about to be incinerated. "When Szilard fled," one acquaintance of the scientist said, "he quivered in every muscle like a thoroughbred horse in the starting stall."

The monster that would ultimately pursue Szilard was conceived during a moment of inspired reverie on a gloomy London day in September 1933, while Szilard, according to his memoirs, was waiting at a street corner for the light to turn green. He was pondering a newspaper article he had just read in which Lord Ernest Rutherford, the most distinguished British physicist, was quoted as saying that anyone who talked about the liberation of atomic energy on an industrial scale was talking "moonshine."

Szilard was not so sure. Some months earlier, he had been captivated by an H. G. Wells novel, *The World Set Free*. In this 1914 book, the author foresaw the massive release of atomic energy, the development of atomic bombs, and a nuclear world war in which major cities would be destroyed.

As the thought of such a catastrophe sped through Szilard's mind, the traffic light flashed green, and it turned out to be a signal of revelation. Albert Einstein had shown that vast stores of energy were trapped in the atomic nucleus, but no one had yet found a way to release this dormant energy. Szilard now thought of the neutron, which British scientist James Chadwick had discovered only a year earlier, in 1932.

Each atom was composed of electrically charged particles—positive (protons), negative (electrons), and neutral (neutrons). All these particles remained firmly in place in most elements, but in radioactive ones that were in constant flux, the neutrons, acting like bullets, were capable of piercing other atoms and splitting them apart with tremendous energy.

At this obscure but key moment in human history, Szilard suddenly perceived a way to make a chain reaction. He had to find an element composed of atoms that, when split, would emit more than one neutron for each neutron absorbed. Then, each neutron released would split another atom in a chain reaction. Should this process be allowed to escalate out of control, a huge explosion would occur, just as H. G. Wells had foreseen.

By the time Szilard reached the opposite curb, he was as horrified as he was excited. What if Hitler, who had just come to power, found the element first? He moved into the Strand Palace Hotel in London, preferring the transient nature of hotel living to the frightening permanence of a home, which he could less easily abandon at a moment's notice. And hardly had he put down his suitcases when he tore off his clothing, ensconced himself in a tub of hot water, and soaked for hours just thinking, interrupted only by a troubled chambermaid who would knock on the door occasionally and ask, "Are you all right, sir?"

Szilard was all right, but he had plenty to think about. How would he achieve a chain reaction before Hitler did? Where would he get the money for research? He stayed locked in the hotel room for a week, nibbling on food sent up to him, snatching a few hours of sleep, then returning to the bathtub to continue his silent dialogue with himself. Finally, he stumbled out of the tub, dressed, and left, determined to explore every possible road to success. In 1938, he departed for the United States.

Shortly after Hahn and Strassmann discovered fission that same year, Szilard joined Italian scientist Enrico Fermi and Herbert Anderson in experimenting at Columbia University on a reactor project using heavy water. At the same time, he urged the U.S. government to finance the building of a bomb and visited Einstein at his summer home in Peconic, Long Island, to seek his help. Dressed in undershirt, rolled-up pants, and slippers, Einstein warmly greeted Szilard and Eugene Wigner and led them onto a screened porch, where he lit up his pipe and listened to Szilard's story of the great nuclear peril. By the time he departed, Szilard had typed out the draft of a letter Einstein would have someone deliver to President Franklin D. Roosevelt. It read in part:

> In the course of the last four months it has been made probable—through the work of [Frédéric] Joliot [-Curie] in France as well as Fermi and Szilard in America—that it may become possible to set up nuclear chain reactions in a large mass of uranium, by which vast amounts of power and large quantities of new radium-like elements would be generated. Now it appears almost certain that this could be achieved in the immediate future. . . .

Hitler, the letter warned, had stopped the export of uranium from Czechoslovakia and his scientists were probing into the atom. The United States had no time to lose, Einstein made clear. It must build a bomb. On October 13, 1939, Roosevelt agreed to do so.

Szilard was jubilant, especially since he desperately needed government support after suffering a major setback in his research. He and his partners at Columbia University lacked enough heavy water to carry on their experiments, while the Germans were getting a steady supply from Norsk Hydro.

Actually, this failure might have helped assure an Allied victory in the war, for Szilard was now forced to seek another possible moderator—the more readily available graphite. Since government funds were unavailable, Szilard solicited help from the Union Carbon and Carbide Company, ignoring the sneers of officials who were upset that he, rather than the better-known Fermi, turned up at a meeting.

Who was this rather odd man who seemed to be asleep while others talked, then suddenly sprang to life with aggressive questions? What did he want?

About two thousand dollars' worth of graphite to achieve an atomic chain reaction, Szilard replied, expecting a skeptical response.

His expectations were met.

"You know," the company's director of research said, "I am a gambling man myself, but you are now asking me to gamble with the stockholders' money, and I am not sure that we can do that. What would be the practical applications of a chain reaction?"

It was really too early to say, Szilard replied, unable to reveal the most closely guarded secret in history.

And so the meeting failed.

But then came the White House reply to Einstein's letter, followed by the presidential appointment of a Uranium Committee. Members, including Szilard and other scientists, met on October 21, 1942, and were asked by Lieutenant Colonel Keith F. Adamson, the army representative:

"How much money do you need?"

About two thousand dollars for graphite, Szilard replied once again, though more hopefully this time. And perhaps later, another four thousand dollars for a few experiments.

But his hopes plunged anew when Adamson seemed as skeptical as the Union Carbide man had been. Atomic research should be left to the universities, the colonel felt. It was naive to believe that a new explosive could make a significant contribution to defense. Once, he was outside an ordnance depot when it blew up and "it didn't even knock me down." Besides, when a new weapon was created, it usually took two wars before one could know whether the weapon was any good or not. In the final analysis, it was not weapons but troop morale that won wars.

Szilard was distraught. How often had he heard those arguments? But then Adamson said, his tone magnanimous: "As far as the two thousand dollars is concerned, you can have it."

Silence prevailed for a moment, as if there were need to adjust to a new era, perhaps a new universe. But nobody could imagine that the two thousand dollars would ultimately snowball into two billion.

The cost of building a bomb began to snowball on June 15, 1940, the day Paris fell to Hitler, underscoring the possibility of an Allied defeat. Roosevelt urgently formed a committee of executives, engineers, and economists who would supervise all technical defense projects: the Office of Scientific Research and Development under Vannevar Bush and his deputy, Harvard's James Conant.

Columbia University was now granted forty thousand dollars to complete research on a chain reaction. Thus, on November 1, 1940, Szilard went on the Columbia payroll for the first time. He was no longer an unpaid "guest," as he had been. Two years later, in 1942, he would be helping to build a graphite reactor in Groves's atomic program at the University of Chicago, almost pining for those days when he could soak in a hot tub and contemplate building a bomb, without the raspy voice of a general telling him how.

• • •

Whatever Szilard and the other scientists thought of Groves, the general listened to their views. Even before he officially took over the reins of the Manhattan Project, Groves conferred with them about German nuclear progress. Intelligence reports revealed that Germany, upon occupying Europe, had seized 3,500 tons of uranium from Union Minière in Belgium. In addition, it controlled the uranium deposits of Czechoslovakia. It had top nuclear scientists, fifteen of whom were known by British intelligence to be working on atomic research. It had the best chemical engineering industry in the world. And, perhaps most significantly of all, it had the heavy water of Rjukan-Vemork and was drastically boosting production.

Groves listened with special interest to Arthur Compton, who chillingly calculated in his letter of June 22, 1942, addressed to Bush, that the United States must:

> 1. Complete domination of Germany before about June 1943.
>
> 2. [Destroy] their fission plants by sabotage, air, or commando raids.
>
> 3. Speed our schedule to beat theirs.

"At best," Compton added, "I do not see how we can catch up with the Germans unless they have overlooked some possibilities that we recognize, or unless our military action should delay them."

Groves accepted this assessment and immediately contacted General Strong, the U.S. intelligence leader, to suggest he get in touch with General Dwight D. Eisenhower, the Allied Supreme Commander in Europe. Eisenhower, he said, should be asked either to bomb or sabotage the Norwegian heavy-water plant.

Strong conferred with General Henry H. Arnold, the Army Air Force chief, and Major General Thomas T. Handy, head of the Operations Division, War Department. And on September 8, 1942, Strong wrote to Eisenhower that

> whichever nation can put fission bombs . . . in use will have a destructive agent which may determine the final outcome of this war. It seems obvious that since there can be no production or development along this line without heavy water, that the designation of Vemork as a bombing objective from the air, or crippling of the plant by sabotage, should seriously be considered.

Groves was proud that he had set in motion the machinery that could stifle the German nuclear threat. He would deprive the Germans of heavy water while churning out the substance for his own program. He was already planning to build the continent's first heavy-water plant at Trail, British Columbia, though he had decided to use the water only if the more accessible graphite proved unsuitable. The general hoped the Germans didn't realize that graphite would probably be a satisfactory substitute.

Meanwhile, he would finish the job in Norway that the French had started. . . .

# 2

## THE JOURNEY OF PRODUCT Z

*February–June 1940*

ON THE FROSTY MORNING of February 14, 1940, as France nervously prepared to thwart an expected German invasion, French Lieutenant Jacques Allier breathlessly rushed up the stairs of the Hotel Majestic on Avenue Kléber in Paris. An agent of the Deuxième Bureau, France's intelligence agency, he was to meet secretly with Minister of Armaments Raoul Dautry and nuclear scientist Frédéric Joliot-Curie for an urgent discussion that could help determine the course of the war that had begun the previous year.

Allier had met a month earlier, on January 14, with Bjorne G. Eriksen, a director of Norsk Hydro, who was visiting Paris on business. At this meeting, the Frenchman was acting not in his capacity as a spy but as an official of the Banque de Paris et des Pays-Bas, which held the majority financial interest in the Norwegian company. Business was good, Eriksen indicated—perhaps too good.

Allier was puzzled. How could business be too good?

A few days earlier, Eriksen said, a representative of the giant German combine, I. G. Farben, which held 25 percent of the shares in Norsk Hydro, had visited plant headquarters in Oslo and made a strange demand. Farben wanted to buy the entire stock of heavy water and proposed that production jump tenfold so that Germany could buy another 100 kilograms (220 pounds) a month.

For how long?

Indefinitely.

Allier was stunned by the implications of this German demand.

Norsk Hydro had a stockpile of almost 200 kilograms (440 pounds), worth about $128,000, and it was turning out about ten kilograms (22 pounds) per month, all of this sold abroad to scientists in their experimental search for nuclear power.

The search began almost immediately after Hahn and Strassmann had induced fission in late 1938 by bombarding the nucleus of uranium with neutrons. Even the two scientists did not know the full implications of fission until Hahn's former assistant, Lisa Meitner, and her nephew, Otto Frisch, proved that the nucleus of a uranium atom that absorbs a neutron will split into two nearly equal parts. They had solved the mystery: a chain reaction was possible.

In France, Joliot-Curie and his assistants rushed to the patent office to file five patents covering the use of nuclear energy, including one for the construction of a uranium bomb. In Britain, government leaders speeded up atomic research and dock workers unloaded crates of uranium from the Belgian Congo, where mine operators had promised British officials in mid-1939 that they would not sell any to the Germans. And in Berlin, at about the same time, scientists at the Kaiser Wilhelm Institute produced fission and drew up plans to build a "uranium device."

• • •

In March 1939, Joliot-Curie and his helpers at the Collège de France in Paris published in the scientific journal *Nature* an article headed "Liberation of Neutrons in the Nuclear Explosion of Uranium." When a neutron splits a uranium atom, the scientists wrote, the reaction causes new neutrons to spew out of the atom at high speed. The authors would now seek to achieve such a reaction by producing one neutron for each fission.

By coincidence, Szilard and Fermi made the same finding at about the same time at Columbia University, but they did not publicize it. Enraged by Joliot's breach of security, Szilard wrote and then wired the Frenchman urging him to keep all future developments secret:

In certain circumstances, [a chain reaction] might lead to the construction of bombs which would be extremely dangerous in general and particularly in the hands of certain governments. . . . We all hope there will be no or at least not sufficient neutron emission and therefore nothing to worry about.

Szilard thus indicated he was willing to forgo the glory and satisfaction of succeeding in the most important experiment in history—not to mention the huge benefits that nuclear power could bring to the world—so that mankind would not fall victim to this power. But Joliot was clearly not willing to do so. After a long silence, he finally spurned Szilard's idea, arguing that word had leaked out anyway and it was too late to stop the leak. A colleague of Joliot would later explain that "France's reputation was for women's fashions and the niceties of life. Joliot wanted to change that."

Perhaps, but Joliot was right. It was too late—from the moment his article appeared. The German government, as Szilard feared, immediately set up a research project known as the Uranium Club. And among other countries spurred by the article to start bombarding their atoms was the Soviet Union.

The "leak" gradually swelled into a flood as information gushed forth from Allied research centers. And even Szilard finally had to end his campaign after being warned that he might lose his "guest" privileges at Columbia if he did not. The irony was that, in 1939, amid the nuclear machinery grinding away in Germany and elsewhere, Washington still scoffed at the "harebrained" idea of an atomic bomb—an idea being pushed by "untrustworthy foreigners." Joliot, in any event, would not be overshadowed by these colleagues.

On April 22, about six weeks after his first article appeared in *Nature*, Joliot published another one. On average, it stated, 3.5 neutrons were emitted by a uranium nucleus during fission. This clearly showed that a chain reaction was possible.

Szilard could barely suppress an explosion of his own. Would there soon be any place left to flee with his suitcases?

By the end of 1939, scientists in France, the United States, and

Germany had all confirmed that to achieve the elusive chain reaction they needed a moderator to slow down the flying neutrons. What would be the best one? They all agreed: heavy water. And so business at Norsk Hydro burgeoned . . .

But why, Jacques Allier wondered, were the Germans trying to corner the world's heavy-water market? Did they simply want to develop a nuclear reactor to generate power . . . or did they want to build a superbomb that could lay waste a city and win a war?

Hoping to find out, Allier asked Eriksen what Norsk Hydro told the Farben representative when he said he wanted to buy the plant's entire stock.

Norsk Hydro would consider it, but wouldn't give an immediate commitment, Eriksen replied.

Allier was relieved. The company, he said, should hold up the transaction until he checked with experts to see what it could mean.

The experts soon told him. It meant that Germany might shortly have the power to control the world. Norsk Hydro then reached a decision: Germany would get as much heavy water as it was already getting, and no more.

· · ·

Now, in a suite at the Hotel Majestic, Allier was meeting with the experts again, this time to find a way to funnel all the heavy water into France before the Germans could get their hands on it. Actually, Minister of Armaments Dautry was an expert only in the political arena, but political savvy would be needed to calculate the possibly earthshaking consequences of any move Hitler might contemplate.

Dautry was not a man of vision. He even doubted that the airplane was of much military value. Yet technical magic could sometimes melt his conservative armor. Unschooled in science, he once read in a newspaper that if it were possible to "disintegrate" an ordinary kitchen table, the energy locked inside it would be sufficient to demolish the world. Fascinated, though unable to understand how the energy could be mobilized, Dautry did not deny this possibility.

Nor did Dautry discount Joliot-Curie's belief that nuclear power could cause similar damage—and would first be generated by none other than Joliot-Curie. For the scientist's very name commanded respect, even awe. He was only the son-in-law of Pierre and Marie Curie, the famed scientists who had discovered radium, but few Frenchmen doubted that anyone with the name of Curie, even if acquired through marriage, could perform scientific miracles. And Joliot was in fact regarded by his peers as one of the world's finest nuclear scientists; he and his wife, Irène, a famous physicist in her own right, won the Nobel Prize in 1935 for the discovery of artificial radioactivity. Ironically, however, the scientist himself, unable to escape the shadow of his in-laws, resented people whom he sensed admired him more for his family ties than for his own brilliant work. Joliot felt he must live by the motto of William of Orange: "It is not necessary to have hope in order to undertake an enterprise, nor to be successful in order to persevere."

Thus, while he wasn't certain that his research would yield the nuclear fruit he craved, he would never stop planting seeds. And the principal seed he needed now was heavy water, which he code-named Product Z. His passion turned Dautry into a true believer, and the minister promised all possible support. He had already brought ten tons of graphite from Grenoble so Joliot could use it as a moderator for the crude atomic pile he was building. The reactor had started to work, but then petered out. Perhaps heavy water would do the job, Joliot now felt.

German pressure on Norsk Hydro to meet Farben's terms was growing, Allier reported, and France would have to act swiftly, buy-ing from the company all the heavy water it could get, especially since the Germans might invade at any time. Everyone agreed, and when the meeting ended, Dautry solicited support from Premier Éduard Daladier and then signed an order stating:

> Monsieur Jacques Allier is empowered by the Premier to negotiate with the party holding the material that is the object of his mission to assure for France the availability of the largest quantities thereof.

The order meant that Allier would go to Norway clandestinely and seek to persuade Norsk Hydro officials to let him transfer all of its heavy water to Paris. If the Germans learned of this plan, French intelligence knew, they would stop at nothing to thwart it. So Allier would travel in the greatest secrecy, with a passport identifying him by his mother's maiden name, Freiss.

He was warned that he must transport the heavy water in canisters free of cadmium, boron, gold, silver, or organic materials, for they would make the substance unusable. An aluminum canister was the preferred choice, but nickel, copper, or stainless steel would be acceptable. Each canister would contain ten liters (2.6 gallons) and be the right size to fit into a special suitcase. If Allier believed his mission was compromised, he was to contaminate all the heavy water stored in Rjukan. The French would go to any length to make certain the Germans couldn't use it.

Not even Joliot's collaborators, Hans Halban and Lew Kowarski, were trusted, since they were only naturalized Frenchmen. During the talks in Norway, the Deuxième Bureau insisted that they be "locked up." Joliot agreed to their imprisonment—with their approval—though they were finally whisked away to two different islands.

Despite the security precautions, however, the Germans were not fooled. French intelligence intercepted a German message that read: "At any price intercept a suspect Frenchman traveling under the name of Freiss."

• • •

On March 4, 1940, Allier arrived in Oslo and moved into the French legation there without revealing to the French minister why he had come. From a nearby public phone booth, he called an official of Norsk Hydro, who was an old friend. They met at a designated street corner, and the official drove him to the plant in Vemork, where they met with Axel Aubert, general secretary of the company.

Allier was a bit wary of Aubert, whom he had heard was "friendly" toward the Germans. But the Frenchman was relieved when Aubert warmly welcomed him.

He was unhappy, Aubert said, that the Germans didn't tell him why they so urgently needed large quantities of heavy water.

Was Aubert sincere, or was he simply trying to sniff out the motives of the French? Allier wasn't sure, and thus said nothing about French intentions at first. But gradually his trust in Aubert grew and, persuaded that the man was a friend of France, he would write Dautry afterward: "The first meeting was extremely cordial. . . . By appealing to his friendship for France, I gained his assent to more things than we hoped."

The "things" were considerable indeed. On March 9, after nearly a week of negotiations, Aubert agreed to deliver to France all the heavy water in Rjukan-Vemork: about 185 kilograms (407 pounds). In addition, all future production would be reserved for France.

Allier, in his joy, now revealed to Aubert "the possibly far-reaching effects of the research then being carried out in France." Aubert was "deeply affected" and declared that he was more resolved than ever to help the French "Will you please let Premier Daladier know," he said,

> that my company does not wish to receive a *centime*, until France has won, for the product you are going to take away. As for myself, I hope the experiment you have told me about will be successful. If later, by bad luck, France should lose the war, I shall be shot for what I have done today. But it is with pride that I run that risk.

After his last meeting with Aubert, Allier returned to Oslo and ordered his chauffeur to take a circuitous route around town in case German agents had been alerted; he then arranged for a local craftsman to make aluminum canisters for the heavy water in the privacy of the man's home. In the evening, Allier returned to the legation and spent the night watching a nearby building he suspected was occupied by German intelligence agents who were plotting against him behind drawn curtains.

On the morning of March 10, Allier exchanged views with fellow French agents on how to get the heavy water to Paris.

They could call for a submarine from Brest or Cherbourg, Allier suggested. It could come to some lonely part of the Norwegian coast to pick up the priceless liquid.

No, there would be too many diplomatic obstacles, someone replied.

The agents finally settled on a plan. Twenty-six canisters of heavy water, hidden in the special suitcases of two teams of men, would be trucked from Rjukan to Oslo, where a plane would be waiting to fly them to Scotland. From there the men would fly with the canisters to Paris. In order to throw pursuing German agents off the track, Allier booked seats on a plane to Amsterdam, using his real name, as well as on a plane to Perth, Scotland, using a new pseudonym.

• • •

On March 12, as the planes to Amsterdam and Perth stood side by side on the tarmac, Allier and the agents accompanying him entered the airline terminal and began speaking loudly about their trip to the Dutch capital. Shortly, a taxi sped on to the tarmac and screeched to a halt between the two aircraft, where it was shielded from the eyes of anyone watching from the terminal.

Allier and a colleague jumped out of the taxi, rushed onto the Perth-bound aircraft carrying their suitcases filled with canisters of heavy water, and trembled in their seats as the plane swooped into the sky. Minutes later, the plane to Amsterdam took off, only to be forced down in Hamburg by two German fighter planes. German security police searched every corner of the aircraft, but in vain. No heavy water.

Aboard the plane to Perth, Allier walked into the cockpit and explained the situation to the pilot. He and his companion were French army officers in civilian clothes, he said. The Germans were after them and might try to force down the plane.

The pilot gaped at Allier, but regained his composure when he suddenly sighted an unidentified plane on his tail. He swiftly changed course and headed over the North Sea in cloud cover, landing in Montrose, Scotland, rather than in Perth as scheduled. The Frenchmen loaded their ten canisters on a train for Edinburgh and the next day met there with two other agents, who had arrived with the second shipment of sixteen canisters.

The agents and their precious cargo then traveled to the English Channel, which they crossed by ferry, and arrived in Paris by train on March 16. The heavy water, virtually the world's entire supply, was stored in the cellars of the Collège de France while workers built a special air-raid shelter that would protect it even from 1,000-pound bombs.

The chase, however, did not end. For Paris was not beyond the Germans' reach. They invaded France on May 10.

• • •

Six days after the invasion, on May 16, Henri Moureux, deputy director of the Nuclear Chemistry Laboratory at the Collège de France, answered his phone and heard the excited voice of his friend, Joliot-Curie:

"Henri, please come to my office immediately!"

When Moureux arrived, Joliot told him that the front had been penetrated near Sedan.

"Dautry has just telephoned me," he said. "The heavy water will have to be taken to a safe place at once. I give you the job. Absolute secrecy. You have a free hand."

Two hours later, after some frantic phone calls, Moureux won agreement from the Clermont-Ferrand branch of the Banque de France to store the mysterious canisters in its vaults. That night he loaded his laboratory truck and lurched through the crowds beginning to flee Paris. At 5 A.M., May 17, he chugged into Clermont-Ferrand in central France, drew up to the bank, and helped carry the containers of Product Z to the vaults. Safe at last! And Moureux finally relaxed. But soon after he returned to Paris, German tanks smashed through the French defenses and ground toward the capital. They could be days away from Clermont-Ferrand.

The bank manager hiding the heavy water panicked.

"Get Product Z out of the bank before the Germans find it here and kill me!" he demanded.

Moureux, desperate on learning of this demand in Paris, called a friend, Dr. J. J. Trillat of the Faculty of Sciences at Besançon, who was responsible for protecting France's stock of radium and came from the Clermont-Ferrand region. Without hesitation, Trillat advised: hide Product Z in the Central Prison in the nearby town of Riom.

Within an hour, orders came down the "chain of command." The minister of armaments called the police chief of Riom, who, in turn, called the prison warden, and a truck carrying the containers of Product Z was soon roaring toward the jail in Riom. There the containers were carried to the barricaded and isolated death cell—the most secure place in the prison—by the dislodged convicts themselves.

Meanwhile, Joliot's two assistants, Halban and Kowarski, fled Paris for Clermont-Ferrand with 800 kilograms (1,760 pounds) of equipment. Joliot and Moureux would follow on June 12—three days before the Germans would enter Paris. Surely the French army, they believed, would turn back the Germans before they reached central France, as it did in World War I. France simply could not afford to fall behind other countries in nuclear research. French prestige—and their own—was at stake.

But hardly had the team arrived in Clermont-Ferrand when bitter reality set in. On June 16, as Joliot and Moureux were strolling in the town, a Simca ground to a halt beside them and Allier jumped out.

The French army was collapsing, he gasped, and the heavy water must be moved immediately to Bordeaux, and from there to England. The British embassy had agreed to cooperate. He had already arranged, he said, for eight tons of Congolese uranium oxide the French had borrowed from the Belgians to be rushed to Morocco and hidden in a phosphate mine there.

Joliot hurried to find his assistants, Halban and Kowarski, and it was agreed that the heavy water would be moved to Bordeaux, then to London. Shortly, the two men, together with Allier, drew up to the Riom prison in a truck.

They had come for the heavy water, Allier told the warden.

When the warden demanded to see the military order, Allier

replied that he represented the minister of armaments and didn't need one.

Without an order, the warden snapped, he would not turn over the canisters.

Allier drew a revolver and barked: "This is my authority!"

The warden was not inclined to challenge it. He ordered his convicts to move the canisters into the waiting vehicle.

•  •  •

On arriving in Bordeaux on June 17, Halban and Kowarski were met by the Earl of Suffolk, whose job as science attaché in the British embassy in Paris was a cover for his intelligence activities. A daring, colorfully eccentric man with heavily tattooed arms, a limp, and a thick moustache, the earl resembled more a pirate than a peer. He wore hunting boots and swung a hunting crop with a swagger that left no doubt who was in charge.

After commandeering a British coaler, *Broompark*, the earl ordered the captain to take aboard more than twenty scientists and engineers, including Halban and Kowarski, together with the heavy water, a sackful of industrial diamonds, and some rare machine tools.

Joliot had been unsure at first whether he should also go to England or remain in France and somehow continue his research while helping the *Maquis*, the French Resistance. He might be able to work on atomic energy in England, but perhaps not, since his communist leanings were no secret. In any case, he didn't want to be subservient to Anglo-American scientists. Nor did he wish to abandon the cyclotron he was building, the first in Western Europe, though he wasn't sure how he could keep it out of German hands. Joliot decided to remain in France.

The crew had been waiting for the Joliot party, with or without Joliot, for hours, and the captain, fearful of enemy bombs, had wanted to shove off without it. But the earl, to keep crew members in check, had drenched them in champagne, and they were too drunk to rebel.

They had good reason to get drunk, for the odds, by the earl's reckoning, were about even that their ship would be sunk before it reached England. Should this happen, a raft laden with explosives and the canisters of heavy water would be set free and a blast would shower the sea with this treasured liquid.

Halban and Kowarski finally arrived and, after high officials of the Ministry of Armaments helped load the heavy water and other paraphernalia aboard, the vessel was soon steaming toward England. But hardly had the *Broompark* set sail when a tremendous explosion shook a nearby ship, and it sank in a smoldering black cloud of smoke. Had it struck a mine, or had German agents sabotaged it, mistaking it for the ship carrying the heavy water?

The *Broompark* thrashed across the perilous waters and finally, on June 21, sailed undamaged into Falmouth Roads. The heavy water was stored at first in a London prison, then in Windsor Castle. Drawing from this precious reservoir, Halban and Kowarski would help to build up Britain's own nuclear potential.

But if the Germans had been outwitted by the French, they would have opportunities to compensate for their loss. They had occupied Norway in April and stormed into Rjukan in May, about a month before the *Broompark* reached Britain. And they had already started draining fresh supplies of heavy water into Hitler's nuclear laboratories.

# 3

## THE TURNING POINT

*June 1942*

TENSION RIPPLED THROUGH Harnack House, headquarters of the Kaiser Wilhelm Institute in Berlin-Dahlem, as Germany's top military leaders and scientists gathered there on June 4, 1942. They were meeting to determine priorities among competing demands for money needed to escalate war production in preparation for an all-out war drive.

All eyes were fixed on the speaker at the podium, Werner Heisenberg, the country's leading nuclear physicist, who exuded confidence in his expertise as he described the vast power compressed in the atom. He was, however, clearly uncomfortable when the generals and admirals sitting in a semicircle around him began tossing questions at him as if they were live grenades.

Heisenberg was probably tempted to ask for billions of marks to pursue nuclear research; after all, he and his colleague, Robert Doepel, had managed to build an atomic reactor in their Leipzig laboratory some weeks earlier using 140 kilograms (308 pounds) of heavy water as a moderator. In joy he had reported to the War Office only days earlier: "We have at last succeeded in building a pile configuration that generates more neutrons than it absorbs."

If the reactor could be enlarged to include approximately five tons of heavy water and ten tons of solid uranium metal, the two scientists concluded, they could build the world's first chain-reacting pile. Occupied Belgium and Czechoslovakia could provide the uranium and Norway, the heavy water. Norsk Hydro, which had stocked about one and a half tons of the fluid since the Joliot-Curie "heist" in mid-1940, was ordered by Berlin in early 1942 to raise annual production to five tons. Thus, Germany might have enough heavy water to build a reactor in a few months—if its scientists could find a way to meet this production target.

· · ·

These scientists, led by Heisenberg, had come a long way since 1939, when the government decided to support a program to exploit atomic power. In September, Paul Harteck, a chemist at the University of Hamburg, was chatting with a colleague, Hans Suess, about a possible design for a uranium reactor when Suess offered a suggestion Harteck had never considered.

Couldn't heavy water be used as a moderator? Suess asked.

Harteck was dismayed. He should have thought of this himself. Especially since he had worked with heavy water five years earlier as an assistant to Ernest Rutherford at Cambridge University's Cavendish Laboratory. For several weeks, he had passed an electric current through gallons of water in an electrolytic cell and found that only a minute residue of water remained—virtually pure heavy water.

Still, Harteck realized, a reactor would require not just a few pounds of the liquid but tons of it. And the cost of producing it would be monumental. Would the government agree to such a venture? On January 15, 1940, he wrote Heisenberg, arguing that it was as important to produce heavy water as it was to obtain uranium for their experiments. He didn't wish to depend on imports from Norway. "As the burden of the execution of these experiments is to fall upon the shoulders of us poor experimenters," he wrote,

> may I ask you who—if anybody—is working on the production in Germany of heavy water? . . . From my own experience in our War Office, the production of large quantities of heavy water will certainly take several years if we leave it to

them; but I can well imagine that if I personally take this up
with the right gentlemen in our heavy industry the time could
be cut to a mere fraction of that.

Actually, nine days earlier, on January 6, 1940, Harteck and
Heisenberg had attended a government conference on heavy water
in Berlin, at which Harteck outlined his views on its use. He
expressed confidence that heavy water could facilitate a chain reaction, warning, however, that the uranium fuel and the moderator
should not be mixed in the reactor but should be separated in alter-
nate layers to avoid an explosion—a warning that would shortly
resonate in the shaping of history.

As Harteck had feared, officials were cool to the idea of spending
large sums to produce a mysterious fluid that might or might not
work. Especially since scientists would have to use steam-generated
electricity to electrolyze water—a process that, to produce a ton
of the fluid, would require a costly one hundred thousand tons of
coal. But the officials nevertheless asked Heisenberg to investigate
whether a chain reaction was possible so they could better judge
whether to risk the gamble proposed by Harteck.

. . .

Now, almost three years later, Heisenberg was on the verge of
achieving a chain reaction, hewing closely to Harteck's prescription.
The government had finally given him enough money to build a
small reactor using modest quantities of U-235 from Belgium and
heavy water from Norway.

Even so, at the meeting in Dahlem the problem for the scientists
was still money. But now they were afraid to ask for much more.
Nuclear scientist Carl von Weizsaecker explained their rationale to
me at his home near Munich. In early 1941, Weizsaecker said, he
suggested to supervising scientist Erich Schumann: "Wouldn't it be
wise to approach Rudolf Hess about the possibility that our research
could lead to an atomic bomb?"

Schumann, according to Weizsaecker, was reluctant to discuss
the matter with one of Hitler's closest associates.

"We shouldn't do it," he replied. "If the Fuehrer learned that an atomic bomb was possible, he would give us six months to make one. If we couldn't do it, you can imagine what he would do to us."

And this fear of what Hitler might do was expressed even more succinctly by physicist Erich Bagge, who, despite his apprehension, had pushed especially hard to build a bomb. Conversations secretly recorded by British agents while the German scientists were being held captive in England after the war reveal that Bagge had told his colleagues: "If the Germans had spent ten milliard [ten billion] marks on it and it hadn't succeeded, all physicists would've had their heads cut off."

Thus, the fear-ridden scientists, Weizsaecker told me, never informed top German leaders before the Dahlem meeting that their research could blossom into a bomb and therefore did not dare ask for funds sufficient to build one. These leaders, including Hitler, believed the research might simply yield a "uranium furnace," a machine that could power submarines. But Heisenberg clearly knew better. He knew that the atomic research would inevitably lead to a bomb, though only after he could ask Hitler for sufficient funds without risking the fuehrer's deadly ire should he fail.

Heisenberg—and colleagues who shared his fears—would tell a different story after the war, claiming they had deliberately tried to hamper Germany's nuclear effort or did little to advance it. And this is probably true for some of the scientists, those who were disturbed by a feeling of guilt or who worked in the laboratory simply to avoid service at the front or to prevent interruption in wartime scientific research. Otto Hahn, the discoverer of atomic fission, Weizsaecker told me, declared that "if our work leads to a bomb, I'll commit suicide." Also, the recordings made secretly in England reveal that Weizsaecker himself told his colleagues they didn't succeed in building a bomb "because all the physicists didn't want to do it, on principle."

But this statement was refuted by Erich Bagge, who replied: "I think it is absurd for Weizsaecker to say he did not want the thing to succeed. This may be so in his case, but not for all of us."

Apparently not for Heisenberg, anyway. When he returned from a visit to the United States just before the war and was invited by Weizsaecker to join the atomic research group, he eagerly agreed.

"You realize, of course," Weizsaecker said, "that our research could result in a bomb."

Heisenberg replied that he did, according to Weizsaecker.

After the war, he would confirm that "it was from September 1941 that we saw an open road ahead of us, leading to the atomic bomb."

Heisenberg's eagerness to join the atomic research group reflected his hard nationalist mentality. The United States, he suspected, was working on a bomb, so Germany, he apparently felt, could hardly do less if it wished to avoid possible destruction. During a visit to the United States just before the war, he rejected an offer of a plum research job at Columbia University in favor of returning to his homeland. He explained to some colleagues that he was indeed a German nationalist and believed, despite moral reservations about Hitler's extremism, that some kind of authoritarian government was needed. Thus, he would tell Dutch scientist Hendrik B. G. Casimir in October 1943, bridling at the thought of Germany losing its grip on Europe:

> History legitimizes Germany to rule Europe and later the world. Only a nation that rules ruthlessly can maintain itself. Democracy cannot develop sufficient energy to rule Europe. There are, therefore, only two possibilities: Germany and Russia, and perhaps a Europe under German leadership is the lesser evil.

And Germany obviously could not rule Europe if the democracies had a bomb and his country was at their mercy.

. . .

Now, in Dahlem, Albert Speer, the minister of armaments and war production, bluntly asked Heisenberg: How could nuclear physics "be applied to the manufacture of atomic bombs?"

No doubt surprised by this reference to a bomb he had apparently never discussed with political leaders, Heisenberg replied, according to Speer in his memoirs:

> The scientific solution [has] already been found and . . . theoretically nothing [stands] in the way of building such a bomb. But the technical prerequisites for production would take years to develop, two years at the earliest, even provided that the program was given maximum support.

Then Heisenberg warned that the Americans might have a uranium pile shortly and a uranium bomb in two years—the same period of time he predicted it might take Germany to build one.

"How big must a bomb be in order to reduce a large city like London to ruins?" asked Field Marshal Erhard Milch, deputy commander of the Luftwaffe under Field Marshal Hermann Goering.

"About as big as a pineapple," Heisenberg answered, cupping his hands in front of him to demonstrate its size. A wave of muttering swept through the audience. A "pineapple" could also wipe out Berlin.

Actually, Heisenberg's statement reflected his limited knowledge of bomb making at that time; the bomb that would be dropped on Hiroshima, after all, was ten feet long. In any case, the implication of Heisenberg's remarks appeared clear: Germany would have to start working on its own bomb or risk being destroyed by an American one.

But the scientists' lack of enthusiasm apparently masked a subtle delaying tactic. Heisenberg had to achieve a chain reaction to prove a bomb was possible before he would dare approach Hitler for enormous sums of money. He needed, however, five tons of heavy water in order to get a chain reaction.

Thus, Heisenberg seems to have felt, he had created the right balance. By frightening the political and military leaders into thinking that the Americans might forge a bomb first, he assured government support for constantly feeding his nuclear research, including the effort to boost heavy-water production. At the same time, he avoided sparking a Hitler directive demanding that his scientists build a bomb in six months—or else!

So when Albert Speer asked Heisenberg how much money he would need to develop a weapon, the scientist replied: a hundred thousand marks would be sufficient. Weizsaecker then suggested another ten thousand marks for "construction."

Speer was amazed. What could the scientists do with so little?

If an atomic bomb really could be built, he responded to the meager requests, the government would pour millions of marks into the project.

It isn't clear whether Speer was offering enough funds for a German Manhattan Project, but this was not what Heisenberg wanted to hear—at least not yet. He was grateful for the offer, he said, but he didn't need that much money.

The government delegates were dumbfounded. Who in his right mind would turn down funds for research? But Heisenberg was unfazed. When he finally had enough heavy water to achieve a chain reaction, he could more easily take the risk of telling the fuehrer that a bomb could be built and of requesting large-scale financial support.

As Heisenberg would tell his colleagues after the war in reference to the bomb, according to the British secret tapes: "We wouldn't have had the moral courage to recommend to the government in the spring of 1942 that they should employ one hundred thousand men just for building the thing up."

On June 23, shortly after the Dahlem meeting, Speer would write in his diary with all the enthusiasm of a bureaucrat reporting on the garbage-collection budget: "Reported briefly to the fuehrer on the meeting concerning atomic fission, and on the assistance we have rendered."

Since the assistance was so little, Hitler could hardly have expected his scientists to make much headway toward an atomic bomb. Especially since his military leaders were not pressing for the project. They were no less fearful of asking for large sums of money than were the scientists, as Field Marshal Milch would admit after the war. He reserved requests for investment in the simple flying bombs that the fuehrer could see were ripping up London.

Nor was the fear of the scientists and military leaders eased when, on June 23, 1942, the same day Speer reported to Hitler, a disaster blocked the way to a bomb, at least temporarily.

• • •

Robert Doepel, Heisenberg's partner, was working in the Leipzig laboratory where atomic pile L-IV had almost reached criticality when suddenly it began to emit bubbles. Testing the bubbles, Doepel found them to be mainly hydrogen, suggesting a chemical reaction between the uranium and the heavy water, which, as Harteck had warned, were chemically incompatible. The heavy water had apparently leaked into a sealed-off shell of uranium.

Doepel ordered a technician to unscrew an inlet so he could determine the extent of leakage. But when the inlet cap was loosened, air suddenly rushed in and a stream of hot gas escaped, aglow with bits of burning uranium. A flame then shot out of the opening and more uranium was set afire.

In panic, Doepel dumped a bucket of water on the flame and it soon sputtered out, but now smoke poured out of the pile. Doepel rushed to the phone and called Heisenberg.

Come quickly, he cried, and he described what happened. The pile was getting hotter and hotter.

Heisenberg arrived momentarily and the two men, wielding a chisel, were about to open the uranium shell at several points to reduce the pressure inside when it began to shudder and swell. The two men exchanged horrified glances and lurched out the door and into the street—seconds before the laboratory blew up and vanished in a shower of burning uranium. Minutes later, the Leipzig fire brigade arrived, but it wasn't able to put the fire out for two days.

Heisenberg was shattered by this setback. He had been so close to achieving what he thought would be the world's first chain reaction. Now he would have to start building a new reactor and scrounge the necessary heavy water for it. Meanwhile, he feared, Allied scientists might construct one first.

What Heisenberg didn't know was that Fermi and Szilard had come close to achieving a chain reaction at about the same time that he did. If he had known, more than bad luck would probably have disturbed him. For he and Fermi, each of them a Nobel laureate at an early age, had long competed for professional honors, though the German was essentially a theorist and the Italian an experimentalist.

While the two respected each other's genius, they had little in common other than a passion for physics. Heisenberg, a tall, blond-haired man with a high forehead, straight-back pompadour, and handsome face often graced with a shy smile, was cultured, polished, and rather aloof. Fermi, short, olive-skinned, his balding scalp patched with curly dark hair, could have been taken for an unschooled peasant, and in fact demonstrated little interest in any sphere of life outside science.

Their differences, moreover, extended to the moral level. As Heisenberg's comment to B. G. Casimir apparently condoning Hitler as the "lesser evil" in Europe suggested, the German scientist was not entirely enamored of democracy. Fermi, on the other hand, had fled to the United States from fascist Italy and, unlike Heisenberg, intended to stay and fight his totalitarian homeland.

The destruction of Heisenberg's reactor was a turning point in the nuclear race. Before it happened, Germany had kept pace with the Allies in nuclear research. But now its atomic schedule would be delayed while America's would advance swiftly. For with the certainty that a chain reaction was possible, Washington would start to funnel $2 billion into the Manhattan Project.

Similarly, Hitler might have given full support to a nuclear program had he been convinced that a bomb was feasible.

. . .

Actually, the scene had been set for Hitler's defeat even before the Dahlem conference. In January 1941, one of the more egregious scientific errors in history was committed—in part, it seems, because heart triumphed over mind. In the United States, Szilard had discovered that purified graphite could be used as a moderator in an atomic reactor, and that the much less plentiful heavy water was therefore not essential, though more reliable. And graphite would, in fact, be successfully used in the American reactor.

The German scientists, on the other hand, were convinced they had to depend on the relative trickle of heavy water from Norsk Hydro for a moderator because of a fatal miscalculation by a top German physicist, Walther Bothe. In June 1939, Bothe, while sailing to the United States for a meeting in Chicago, met a young woman, Ingeborg Moerschner. According to his diary, they became romantically involved and, when their liner docked, visited the San Francisco and New York world's fairs. Finally, Bothe returned to Heidelberg to resume work on the nuclear qualities of graphite.

But the scientist often found himself dwelling on the qualities of Ingeborg instead, and on the first anniversary of their meeting he wrote her: "Ingeborg, I must once again write you a letter. Tomorrow, it is a year that you came into my life. . . ." He spoke of his dreams and admitted to feeling like a "drunken teenager." Two weeks later, Bothe wrote that he had been "speaking of physics the entire day, while thinking only of you."

The physics he had been speaking of concerned the nuclear constants of graphite, and apparently in part because his thoughts were elsewhere, he wrongly concluded from his experiments that graphite, however pure, could not be used as a moderator.

Thus, he stopped all further experimentation with graphite. Why waste time and money on an unworkable substance? And his colleagues accepted his assessment and did no further research either—until scientist Karl Wirtz discovered the error too late in the war to have any effect.

• • •

Fatefully, if not for a laboratory explosion and the mistake of a lovesick scientist, Germany might have beaten the United States to a reactor and perhaps to a bomb. Now, instead, it would fall behind in the nuclear race. Heisenberg would work on a new heavy-water reactor and on plans for building new heavy-water facilities in Norway and Germany. But that would take time. Indeed, Heisenberg, still fearful of failure like many of his colleagues, postponed constructing a plant in Germany, apparently until Hitler would be able to hear the vibrations of a chain reaction.

Meanwhile, he and the other scientists, while unaware that the Americans were surging ahead, knew that to stay in the race they would have to act swiftly. Thus, Harteck and some of his colleagues worked frantically on a centrifuge method of separation, while Heisenberg and others set out to turn the trickle of heavy water from Norway into a rushing stream.

The Allies did not know of Germany's decision to rely on heavy water alone. And even if they had known, they might not have realized at this early stage of nuclear research that this decision would slow up Germany's nuclear progress. What was clear to them was that the Germans were operating the only commercial heavy-water factory in the world. And that was ominous.

# 4

## DIVIDED THEY STAND

*August 1941–September 1942*

"HEAVY WATER? Who ever heard of such a thing?"

Lieutenant Commander Eric Welsh, chief of Britain's Secret Intelligence Service (SIS), Norwegian Section, reacted as if this rare liquid must be some exotic compound from a faraway planet. He stared at the wire from the Norwegian underground that R. V. Jones, an intelligence officer, brought him one day in August 1941.

Ever since the Germans captured the Norsk Hydro complex in May 1940, the message said, they had been turning out heavy water at a feverish pace.

"A ruddy funny telegram," Welsh remarked.

Welsh, described by one colleague as "a little man with a big head," was actually quite familiar with heavy water, and he didn't think the message was funny at all. He had been a secret agent in naval intelligence since World War I, and was sent to Norway in 1919 to spy on German naval and industrial activities in Scandinavia. He had joined the International Paint Company in Bergen as a cover, studied chemistry, and when Norsk Hydro began producing heavy water in 1934, he made the special floor tiles that would prevent leakage of the liquid in the processing rooms of the plant.

Welsh soon learned everything there was to know about heavy water. But he was so secretive about security matters that he didn't want to share his knowledge even with his own men. Like General

Groves at the Manhattan Project, he trusted no one and would ruthlessly make any sacrifice to achieve success. For example, as the official SIS history would note, when the Germans invaded Norway, Welsh "even left his wife and family in [the country] with false papers. They became an asset to SIS," spying for the British. Welsh himself fled to Britain by submarine and in summer 1941 was appointed chief of the SIS, Norwegian Section.

A few months earlier, in spring 1941, Prime Minister Winston Churchill's scientific adviser, Lord Cherwell, had received a suggestion from British physicist G. P. Thompson that "someone with knowledge of physics and especially of the personalities and specialties of German physicists" be asked to study what the Germans planned to do with the heavy water they were buying from Norsk Hydro.

Soon, scientist Rudolf Peierls was busy drawing up a list of sixteen German nuclear scientists, headed by Werner Heisenberg, and perusing articles in German scientific journals. He found that Heisenberg had written no recent pieces and was no longer teaching at any university.

"I wondered what Heisenberg was doing," Peierls told me when I visited him at his home in Oxford. "He seemed to have disappeared. I thought he might be working on an atomic weapon."

Welsh knew that Germany must be wondering whether the Allies were working on one, too, and hatched a plot to make it appear that they were not. He called in a Norwegian atomic scientist, Helmer Dahl, and asked if he wouldn't mind being "kidnapped."

By whom? Dahl asked.

By the British. They would supposedly "force" him to work in an atomic laboratory, and then send him back to Norway on a "secret mission" involving heavy water. He would soon "defect" to the Germans, assuring them that Britain was making little progress in the nuclear field. This daring plan, however, went awry when, in October 1941, the Gestapo arrested Dahl and held him until February 1942. Welsh then arranged for him to be bundled off by sea to England.

Now the SIS chief listened to R. V. Jones explain the importance of heavy water. Welsh didn't mention that the cable from the Norwegian Resistance was in response to one he had sent some days earlier. It had read:

> FOR HEAVENS SAKE KEEP THIS UNDER YOUR HAT STOP TRY
> TO FIND OUT WHAT THE GERMANS ARE DOING WITH THE
> HEAVY WATER THEY PRODUCE AT RJUKAN STOP
> PARTICULARLY FIND OUT WHAT ADDRESS THEY SENT IT
> TO IN GERMANY STOP *GUD SIGNE NORGE*

*Gud signe norge,* meaning "God bless Norway," was Welsh's code expression for "strictly limited" distribution.

Welsh now wired back the Norwegian underground contact requesting more information. A reply soon arrived:

> IF YOU CAN ASSURE US THAT IT IS OF IMMEDIATE
> IMPORTANCE TO THE PRESENT WAR WE WILL GET THE
> INFORMATION YOU REQUEST AT ONCE STOP IF IT IS ONLY
> FOR THE ICI [BRITAIN'S IMPERIAL CHEMICAL INDUSTRIES]
> THEN PLEASE REMEMBER THAT BLOOD IS THICKER EVEN
> THAN HEAVY WATER.

No organized national underground had been developed in Norway yet, but various groups worked with the British, and the members of one of them, code-named Skylark, operated radio stations out of Oslo and Trondheim, an important German naval base. It was Skylark that had cabled SIS. An organized Resistance called Milorg (Military Division of the Home Front), embracing about thirty thousand people, would gradually form and harass the Germans, paving the way for an Allied invasion of Norway. In this early period, however, small teams like Skylark acted independently, hiding arms they had fought with during the German invasion, cutting German military telegraph cables, immobilizing military vehicles, blowing up railway lines, setting fire to German garages, and, most importantly, sending radio messages to Britain about Germany's military activities.

But Norsk Hydro posed a problem for Skylark: in peacetime, ICI competed with it in the world marketplace for chemicals, and ICI was an SIS client. Was ICI simply fishing for industrial information? Skylark finally decided that while blood might be thicker than heavy water, this fluid could be used to shed a good deal of blood. And so the team continued to cooperate with Welsh until September 1942, when the Gestapo broke it up.

The crackdown helped to place many Norwegians under suspicion, and some fled to Britain. One of them showed up at SIS headquarters that same month—an amiable man with blond hair and blue eyes that reflected a keen intelligence. Leif Hans Tronstad was the son of a poor Norwegian farmer who died when Leif was a year old. Tronstad worked at odd jobs and managed to save enough money to pursue technical studies at universities in Berlin, Stockholm, and Cambridge. Then, as one of the youngest physics professors in the country, he taught at Norwegian Technical University in Trondheim, hoping one day to find a way to probe the power of the atom.

In 1933, Tronstad was only too happy to help design the Norsk Hydro heavy-water plant in Rjukan, which opened new vistas for the study of nuclear energy. With the invasion of Norway, Tronstad joined the Resistance, but when the Gestapo broke up his cell, he skied to Sweden, from where he flew to England in a British military plane.

Tronstad, now thirty-nine, came with discouraging news. Since the Germans seized Norsk Hydro, ten times as many canisters of heavy water were rolling out of the Rjukan-Vemork plant. This could mean only one thing, the men agreed: the Germans were working on a nuclear reactor. And this was also the view of Harold Urey, who visited Britain in November and studied Tronstad's report.

Welsh no longer tried to hide his intimate knowledge of the chemistry and use of heavy water, since there was nothing he could tell Tronstad that the man didn't already know. The heavy-water plant, he told Tronstad with cool passion, was a top-priority Allied concern. Could Tronstad organize an intelligence operation in

Norsk Hydro? SIS wanted day-to-day details on what was happening at the plant.

He would do his best, Tronstad replied.

Welsh then appointed him chief of intelligence for the Norwegian government-in-exile, code-named Mikkel, or the Fox. If he didn't live up to his code name, the Fox suspected, he might learn about the destructive power of the atom sooner than he wished.

• • •

"We knew," Prime Minister Winston Churchill would write in his memoirs, "what efforts the Germans were making to procure supplies of 'heavy water'—a sinister term, eerie, unnatural, which began to creep into our secret papers. What if the enemy should get an atomic bomb before we did!"

Churchill was plagued with this alarming thought as he flew over the clouds on his way to meet with President Roosevelt at Hyde Park on June 19, 1942. It was about two weeks after the Germans, unknown to the Allies, decided to limit funds for nuclear research—at least until a chain reaction sent tremors through Heisenberg's reactor.

The prime minister would be visiting Hyde Park mainly to plan military operations for 1942–43. But "heavy on [his] mind" was the question of "Tube Alloys," the code name for British atomic research. Lord Cherwell, his adviser on technical developments, had "reported the substantial progress which was being made," and it seemed a chain reaction was now within reach. No time could be lost in building a bomb.

Both he and the president, Churchill realized, "felt painfully the dangers of doing nothing." But what role would Britain play in making a bomb? Only the United States had the money and resources to build one, he would say in his memoirs. Besides, any large-scale nuclear facilities that might mushroom in Britain could crumble under a rain of German bombs. Both sides must share all their atomic knowledge. Without such a guaranteed future exchange, Churchill feared, Britain's role in the war and in the peace to follow might be to watch the world power struggle from the sidelines.

The prime minister arrived in Hyde Park on the morning of June 19 and was greeted with the "greatest cordiality" by Roosevelt, who drove him around the family estate in his black Ford. Though the prime minister had some nervous moments as the paralyzed president, using hand levers for the brake, clutch, and accelerator, bumped along a ridge overlooking the Hudson River, he was also able to wedge in "some thoughtful moments."

The next day, Churchill, hopeful that the diplomatic road would be smoother than his ride around Hyde Park, was ready to make his pitch. After lunching, the two men moved to a little dark, dreary room on the ground floor. But the prime minister was unrestrained by the gloomy atmospherics.

There must be a tremendous effort to build a bomb, he vigorously advised, especially since the Germans were squeezing every magic drop of heavy water out of the Norsk Hydro plant in Norway.

"What if the enemy should get an atomic bomb before we do?" the prime minister would later say he asked Roosevelt. "However skeptical one might feel about the assertions of scientists, much disputed among themselves and expressed in jargon incomprehensible to laymen, we could not run the mortal risk of being outstripped in this awful sphere."

The president, who sat in lordly authority behind a huge desk, heartily agreed, especially since two days earlier, on June 17, as General Groves would write in his memoirs, Vannevar Bush pointed out in a memo to the president "that it was possible to make a nuclear weapon that . . . might be made ready in time to influence the outcome of the present war."

Bush based his conclusion on the success of an experiment Enrico Fermi conducted at Columbia University in May. Fermi's reactor had almost achieved a chain reaction, falling only 5 percent short of emitting more neutrons than it absorbed. Bush's memo would conclude: "This report and program have been approved by those with whom you instructed me to take up matters of policy on this subject. . . . If you also approve, we will proceed along these lines immediately."

Roosevelt, with a feeling of relief, jotted on the report: "VB. OK. FDR."

The Manhattan Project was launched.

The president might not have felt so relieved if he had known that Werner Heisenberg and Robert Doepel had, at about the same time, come even closer to reaching a chain reaction. Or that in mid-1942, the United States and Germany were locked in a dead heat in the race for a bomb.

But his spirits would just as surely have soared if he were aware that, even as he sat with Churchill, the smoke was still clearing from an explosion that demolished the German reactor, postponing the moment when Heisenberg would have the courage to tell Hitler, as Bush told Roosevelt, that a bomb could be built.

Churchill now urged the president to "at once pool all our information, work together on equal terms, and share the results, if any, equally between us."

He would have preferred that Britain build its own bomb, if with American help, so it could assure itself a top niche in Europe's power structure after the war, but he was a realist. It simply wouldn't be wise for Britain to deplete its resources and risk unnecessary destruction, the prime minister felt, when it must remain strong to keep postwar Europe from succumbing to Russian power—especially since the atomic program might fail. The United States, he thought, should do most of the work even while sharing all its nuclear secrets.

Roosevelt reflected on Churchill's logic, which melded with his own crystallizing vision of the future. The united world he had favored might not be possible after all, he now felt, however tempting the idea. How could he force Stalin to order his troops out of the territory they would overrun in Europe and perhaps in parts of Asia? As the president would tell a colleague in 1944: "We have no idea as yet what [the Russians] have in mind, but we have to remember that in their occupied territory they will do more or less what they wish."

No, there could not be a close Big Three relationship after the war similar to the wartime alliance. Instead, he began to view the postwar geopolitical structure as based on spheres of influence that would cooperate in maintaining a balance of power. But for the democratic world to offset Russian power, Britain, as Churchill pointed out, would have to be strong. And this meant, after so draining a war, American nuclear data must flow freely into his country.

So the United States, it was decided, would assume the Herculean task of building the bomb, while Britain would devote most of its scarce resources to fighting the war and researching the use of heavy water in Canada. Not even the window shading, it seems, could block out the sun as Churchill rose to leave the little presidential office with the happy "understanding . . . that everything was [still] on the basis of fully sharing the results of equal partners." Roosevelt, for his part, wrote Vannevar Bush on July 11 that he and the prime minister were "in complete accord."

• • •

Churchill's joy, however, was short-lived. For a few weeks later, when the British tried to integrate some of their nuclear research projects into the U.S. program, they met a growing resistance, especially from General Groves. The general was furious at Britain for giving the United States so little nuclear intelligence, especially about the plant at Rjukan, and he had almost no faith in what it did get. How could he judge the danger and know how to meet it without the necessary data?

So he scoffed at a letter Wallace A. Akers, an engineer who headed the British Directorate of Tube Alloys, wrote a U.S. scientist on August 18, 1942, stating that "the Germans could not have collected yet enough heavy water to make a working power plant, unless our calculations are very wrong."

They usually were, Groves felt, preferring to forget that the Manhattan Project was founded in large measure on British data, especially the findings of Peierls and Frisch. He thus defied the British even though he apparently feared they might make some ill-conceived move to knock out the Rjukan-Vemork complex without consulting him.

And other U.S. officials, including Secretary of War Henry Stimson, Bush, and Conant, who in the summer of 1942 had been willing, even eager, to compare notes with the British, changed their minds by the fall. For the Manhattan Project had made great strides, and British aid seemed less urgent, except where Norsk Hydro was concerned.

Besides, as Stimson would write to the president on October 29, why should the United States give Britain nuclear secrets that would help it to compete with American industry after the war? Indeed, as Groves would state in his memoirs, he, Bush, and Conant shared the suspicion that Wallace Akers, who not only headed Britain's Tube Alloys program but worked for the Imperial Chemical Industries, "might well be influenced by an undue regard for possible postwar commercial advantages for the British."

Groves, moreover, stressed that the problem of security would grow if scientists from Britain were permitted to work on the Manhattan Project without restriction. Especially since the British insisted that they, not he, must decide who among their scientists should be trusted with the most vital atomic secrets. He had little faith in the security consciousness of anyone but himself, especially that of the British, whom he instinctively distrusted.

Groves's fear would ultimately prove justified, for one scientist sent to the United States from Britain in late 1943 was Klaus Fuchs, a German refugee and secret communist, whose scientific brilliance had earned him a job in England as assistant to Rudolf Peierls. Fuchs would leak every scrap of information he could gather in both Britain and the United States to the Soviet Union.

It was little wonder, therefore, that Stalin was making excellent progress in building a bomb of his own, including research on the use of heavy water in an atomic reactor. As David Holloway would write in *Stalin and the Bomb*, referring to an observation by I. V. Kurchatov, who headed the Soviet atomic project: "The most interesting thing, in Kurchatov's view, was the confirmation that a chain reaction was possible in a mixture of uranium and heavy water."

Kurchatov had learned of this confirmation from reports on experiments, apparently dispatched by Fuchs, that Joliot-Curie's assistants, Halban and Kowarski, had conducted at Cambridge University after having escaped from France.

Groves's security argument, and his others as well, against cooperating closely with Britain made a strong impression on his superiors. And finally, at the end of October 1942, only four months after the Roosevelt-Churchill meeting, Secretary Stimson strode resolutely into the Oval Office and, pointing out to the president that the United States was doing most of the work on atomic energy, suggested that it go "along for the present without sharing anything more than we could help."

Roosevelt tormentedly pondered how such a decision would affect his relationship with Churchill. But then, in December, the British signed a treaty with the Soviet Union to exchange information on new weapons. Would American data be passed on to Josef Stalin? Groves asked—ironically, since Stalin, with Fuchs feeding him intelligence regularly, did not need any under the treaty.

The president now made up his mind: the United States would limit interchange with Britain. It would collaborate on scientific findings, but not on the design, construction, or operation of production plants. The British would even be denied data on heavy water, though Groves was demanding that they give him data on Norway's production.

Britain cried foul. The new American policy, Churchill would write presidential aide Harry Hopkins on February 27, 1943, "entirely destroys [Roosevelt's] . . . original conception" of a "coordinated or even jointly conducted effort between the two countries."

This statement followed a desperate flight by Akers to Washington in early November to plead the British case with Groves, Bush, and Conant. But even as Akers continued to bang his head against Groves's nuclear wall, the general made sure it would not buckle. Indeed, he would build a still higher wall around his project—not always to America's advantage. Aside from intelligence information about Norway's heavy water, Britain had the only large supply of heavy water available in the Free World—that which Halban and Kowarski had spirited out of France. After working for a while at

Cambridge, the two men and their heavy water were sent to Montreal to work on experiments with Canadian scientists, and Halban reported that they had found a way to achieve a chain reaction with heavy water.

American scientists, though skeptical that Halban's formula would work, wanted to test it, since graphite did not work with great efficiency and heavy water was needed as "insurance." But Halban couldn't be called to the United States to demonstrate the experiment because, during the process, he might pick up some American secrets about production methods and plant designs. The British, on the other hand, were suddenly guarded about their secrets, too. The United States would get nothing.

Harold Urey was furious. The American policy of keeping data from Britain, he thought, could jeopardize the nuclear program. In a letter to Conant dated April 2, 1943, he wrote:

> I am appalled at the fact that in the course of two years we have been unable to work with the British closely enough to get such information as can be gotten from the only heavy water available to us and our Allies. . . . [We have failed] to make adequate experimental use of the heavy water in Halban's possession."

But Groves's wall would crumble only in August 1943, when Roosevelt submitted to Churchillian pressure and agreed to a new "full exchange" agreement.

Not surprisingly, Groves, during the period of conflict, would sometimes learn about British plans to deal with Norsk Hydro only after they had been translated into action.

• • •

Leif Tronstad, the Fox, could almost hear the drip of heavy water in his sleep. He had to be informed from day to day on how much of the liquid was trickling out of the Norsk Hydro plant. And the man who was keeping him informed was a Norwegian agent, Lieutenant Odd Starheim, who had fled to Britain by boat in August 1940 and, after being trained there, parachuted into his homeland more than a year later.

Starheim's mission grew in urgency after American scientist Harold Urey visited Britain in November 1941 and agreed that the latest figures in Tronstad's report showed that the Germans had to be building a nuclear reactor. But the Gestapo was on Starheim's trail and he would have to flee to Britain once more to avoid capture.

Starheim, however, could still offer Britain valued service. He would bring with him not only four comrades who were also "wanted" by the Gestapo but someone who could be trained in espionage and secret communications and then whisked back to Norway to replace him as a spy on heavy-water operations.

The man chosen by Starheim was Einar Skinnarland, a blond, deeply tanned twenty-four-year-old native of Rjukan, a champion skier and Resistance fighter who, most importantly, knew some of the technicians in Norsk Hydro. A graduate of the Officers' School for the Royal (Norwegian) Engineering Corps, he fought the Germans near Oslo when they invaded Norway in 1940.

But with the country occupied, Skinnarland went home to Rjukan and, with his brother, Torstein, worked for their father, the superintendent at the nearby Moesvatn Dam, which served Norsk Hydro as a reservoir. He spent much of his time, however, caching away arms and distributing them to farmers working for the Resistance in the surrounding mountains. The Germans captured him, but not realizing who he was, eventually let him go, and he soon made contact with Starheim.

Since Skinnarland was a native of Rjukan and had some radio experience, Starheim asked him to join his group of fugitive agents on what could be a precarious journey to Britain, and remain there for training. Skinnarland immediately agreed. But how would they get to Britain? he asked. The Germans controlled the ports and airports.

They would steal a coastal steamer on the Kristiansand-Bergen run.

The next day, March 15, 1942, Starheim, Skinnarland, and the other four "wanted" men gathered what arms they could, dressed themselves as ordinary passengers, and waited on the pier to board a boat at Flekkefjord. The 600-ton S.S. *Galtesund* finally arrived at about dawn the next day with twenty-one people on board, including the crew. Fortunately, no Germans were among them, as they had missed the boat at a previous port.

The six underground figures boarded the ship, bought their tickets, and posted themselves at strategic points, as planned. With the ship well out to sea, Starheim aimed his pistol at the head of the helmsman, and cried "Put your hands up!" while another man took the captain captive. Starheim then stood at the wheel and, despite the protests of the crew and passengers, headed for Aberdeen, Scotland, instead of Bergen as scheduled.

German-controlled Oslo radio shortly announced that the *Galtesund* was missing, but was thought to be taking shelter from a storm in some isolated fjord.

The ship finally crossed the turbulent waters of the North Sea and, arriving in Aberdeen on March 17, was guided by British aircraft to a trawler, which escorted it safely through a minefield to port. Shortly, Skinnarland learned that he would soon be threading his way through a far more threatening minefield. British intelligence, Tronstad told him, needed someone in Rjukan to gather "all the information we can get" about plans for churning out heavy water. Nothing more was said about why such knowledge was crucial for winning the war.

Skinnarland agreed to the assignment and, after being interrogated in a security detention camp and trained in parachute jumping and radio communications, he was put aboard a plane bound for Norway in the hope he would be home before the Germans noticed he was gone. He was to resume his job on the dam, which would still serve as a cover for his spy activities.

A few hours later, Skinnarland was flying over southern Norway—but off course. The pilot searched in vain for the electronic beacons that Skinnarland's brother, Torstein, was to turn on at the dam to mark the area where Einar would land by parachute.

"Don't you have a better map?" Skinnarland asked the pilot.

"No," came the reply, "and we're running out of fuel. We're heading back."

"Not before I jump!"

And Skinnarland leaped out of the plane, though he was far from the dam and, for all he knew, might find himself in the middle of a German camp. But Skinnarland landed safely and made his way home several miles away, to be emotionally greeted by his parents, four brothers, and three sisters—the only people who knew that he really hadn't been on a "skiing vacation" as he would tell everybody else.

"I was elated to be home," Skinnarland recalled to me fifty years later at his home in Toronto, Canada, where he worked as an engineer after the war. "But I knew the Gestapo would soon be after me again."

Skinnarland cherished those wonderful days when peace had reigned over Norway and he spent his leisure hours roaming the river valleys, sailing the turquoise lakes, skiing and hunting in the hills surrounding Rjukan—reveling in the pure pleasure of living. He loved the hills so much that he didn't mind that they shut out all sunlight from the town for about half the year and turned much of the afternoon into night. Soon, these soaring symbols of his past would be his hideout, where he would be the hunted and his skis would be simply an instrument of survival.

• • •

The day after his return, Skinnarland met with Norsk Hydro's production chief at the man's mountainside home near the plant at the Rjukan suburb of Vemork. Dr. Jomar Brun, a dignified, soft-spoken man, warmly greeted his young visitor and inquired with intense interest about Leif Tronstad, who had helped him plan and build the heavy-water plant.

Brun's career reflected the innovative tradition of Norsk Hydro, which was born in 1905 after a couple of men, an engineer and a scientist, watched a 380-foot waterfall plunge into the gorge of the Maana River below and decided to harness its power to produce fertilizer. Gradually, the fertilizer plant springing up in a mountain wilderness revolutionized the Vestfjord Valley, where 950 families snowballed to 10,000 inhabitants in ten years, and became the site of Norway's first heavy industry. In fact, the granite power station that was built on a shelf of rock below the great Rjukan Foss waterfall in 1911 was the world's largest at the time, its generators churning out 120,000 kilowatts of electric power.

Shortly after Harold Urey discovered heavy water in 1932, Brun and Tronstad realized they could produce the substance as a by-product of fertilizer, and by 1934 much of the power was being channeled into a neighboring electrolysis building they had artfully designed. Urey had demonstrated that the hydrogen given off during the electrolysis of water contains five or six times less heavy hydrogen than the water remaining in a cell. Thus, if 100,000 gallons of water were decomposed in one stage into hydrogen and oxygen until only one gallon was left in the cell, this remaining liquid would contain about 99 percent pure heavy water.

Brun and Tronstad, working on this principle, modified it to save much of the heavy hydrogen that would be given off and wasted in the later stages of concentration. The hydrogen given off was now burned in oxygen to make water, which was fed back into the earlier low-concentration stages. The unburned hydrogen of the first six stages was fed into a synthetic-ammonia plant for the manufacture of fertilizer.

The nine-stage process would yield heavy water with a concentration of about 13 percent, and this water would be funneled into a high-concentration electrolysis plant in which it was concentrated to over 99.5 percent purity. No one dreamed at that time that the end product could serve as an ingredient for a superweapon.

Brun, Skinnarland told me, now eagerly read a letter that he had brought from his old friend Tronstad, with whom he had created what some scientists and engineers regarded as an industrial masterwork.

"Our juice is very important," the Fox wrote, using the code name for heavy water so the Germans, if they intercepted any communications, would not understand references to this substance.

How much heavy water was Norsk Hydro producing? he asked.

What were the Germans using it for, and how fast was it being taken to Germany?

Brun was glad to oblige with all the information at his command, and indeed was playing a precarious double role at the risk of his life. He had convinced his German supervisors that he was seriously trying to roll out more canisters of heavy water, while actually striving to curb production, by sabotage if necessary. He had thus added castor oil to the electrolysis process producing the heavy water, interrupting the system at least temporarily. Other Norwegians, unknown to him, added cod liver oil and the foaming became so intense that Brun, puzzled by the reaction, searched for a way to moderate it before the Germans investigated and learned of his double role.

At least up to midsummer 1942, the Germans had not detected anything, even though the plant had delivered to Germany only 800 kilograms (1,760 pounds) of heavy water, about one-sixth of the five tons Heisenberg had calculated was needed to achieve a chain reaction. Germany's heavy-water experts, including Heisenberg and Bothe, were worried. How could they get more of this vital substance? To debate the issue, they met in Berlin in mid-July and found themselves in bitter discord.

Build another plant in Germany with a new process that had been developed, some demanded.

But the new process would yield only 200 kilograms (440 pounds) of heavy water a year, others argued.

Not if the hydrogen was slightly enriched with deuterium.

And where would they get slightly enriched hydrogen? another asked skeptically.

Finally, the scientists could agree only that "the procurement of heavy water is as urgent as ever." Work would start on a German plant, but meanwhile they would have to rely on Norsk Hydro.

A good thing, they felt, that Dr. Brun was trying so hard to find new ways to boost production.

One of the scientists, Hans Suess, then visited the plant and, with Brun, carried out several experiments seeking a method to speed up the manufacturing process. Suess, a tall, nervous-mannered man, had specialized before the war in heavy water, studying its physical constants. Then two more scientists, Karl Wirtz and Friedrich Berkei, called on Brun and conducted further experiments with him.

In the next three months Brun and Suess would write three joint reports for the German War Office on the steps that would be taken to squeeze more "juice" out of the plant. But as soon as his German colleagues left, Brun would assume his other role and pour castor oil into the works. The water would foam and cause more mysterious delays.

Brun's double role grew especially difficult the more he worked with Suess, for the two men became fast friends. And the Norwegian would even tell London that Suess was really quite harmless and apparently wanted to use the heavy water for research only—claims that did not impress his unsentimental bosses in London. But Brun's personal sentiments did not slow the steady flow of either castor oil or vital information.

Meanwhile, in London, Leif Tronstad grew almost frantic with every report sent by Brun via Skinnarland reflecting German efforts to boost the yield of heavy water. The time had come for action. Could Brun "conceive a plan for transporting a considerable quantity of heavy water from Vemork to Britain?"

Virtually impossible, Brun replied. To have any chance at all, a British plane would have to land on a large frozen lake in the mountains near Vemork.

"If that could be realized," Tronstad wrote, "I might be able, with the aid of Norwegian compatriots, to transfer our juice from the plant to the plane."

Tronstad conferred with Welsh; no, they agreed in frustration, the plan probably could not work.

Toothpaste tubes were then brought from Norway by courier, but not to clean gritted SIS teeth. They were crammed with microphotographs of blueprints, drawings, and vital data, which experts assiduously studied. If British agents couldn't steal the heavy water, they concluded, an attack force would have to destroy it, together with the electrolysis equipment and the nearby power plant feeding it.

Actually, as early as April 1942, Britain's Tube Alloys Technical Committee recommended an assault on Norsk Hydro, "since recent experiments in Cambridge have confirmed that element 94 [plutonium] can be as good as U-235 [uranium] for military purposes, and since it would best be prepared in systems using heavy water."

In any case, it would be impossible to deprive the Germans of uranium, for the uranium mines could not be badly damaged while the uranium already mined could probably never be found. But the heavy-water equipment was concentrated in one place and could be destroyed.

Churchill now sold the idea to the British War Cabinet, and the cabinet asked the Combined Operations Command, representing all the armed forces, to launch such an assault. The details would be kept secret—even from the "ungrateful" United States.

Operation Freshman, the code name for the attack, would succeed. It had to. For who knew how long castor oil could keep Hitler from winning the war?

# 5

## "TO THE LAST MAN"

### *Summer 1942–November 1942*

"GROUSE'S MISSION is of great importance," the British colonel told commandos at the briefing session one day in late summer 1942. "We have to prevent the Germans from getting hold of more heavy water. They are using it for experiments which—if they succeed—may enable them to destroy all of London."

Second Lieutenant Jens Anton Poulsson, a Norwegian officer, was mystified. But imagining London in ruins was enough to fire him up, along with the three other Norwegian commandos who would take part in Operation Grouse, a mission that would send them parachuting into Norway to pave the way for a British attack on Norsk Hydro in three or four months.

The briefing officer was Colonel John S. Wilson, chief of the Norwegian Section of the Special Operations Executive (SOE). Unlike Eric Welsh's SIS, which only gathered intelligence, the SOE conducted sabotage operations and was to "set Europe ablaze," as Churchill summarized its mission when he created it on July 22, 1940. And now, with Combined Operations, SOE would direct the assault in Norway.

Wilson, who had previously served as deputy police commissioner in Calcutta and as director of the Boy Scouts Association in England, was a fascinating amalgamation: he was a religious man, shy and kind, but at the same time ambitious, tough, and, in the view of some, a bit devious, at least in the pursuit of an objective.

And his objective now was to save Britain, and the world, from what could be a German nuclear threat. He worked hand in hand with Tronstad, who had been a Boy Scout himself in Trondheim, the two men sharing the intense patriotism and moral discipline nurtured by the scout movement.

The British hoped to demolish existing stores of heavy water, the electrolysis equipment, and the adjoining power plant, but they couldn't agree on how to do it.

Drop bombs?

No, Tronstad argued passionately. Bombers might hit the liquid-ammonia storage tanks in the deep valley harboring Rjukan and blow up the entire town.

Sabotage the plant?

Impossible, someone replied. The Norwegian guerrillas were not sufficiently trained for it and would probably be killed by the German guards.

Attack with airborne troops?

No, Wilson and Tronstad protested. These troops would be in great danger.

But they would have the firepower to fight their way to the target and then to safety, Combined Operations contended.

How would they get to the target?

By parachute.

No, the planes would have to fly too low, others responded. The Germans would hear them.

What about gliders? They were silent and, unlike parachutes, would not give away the game, and they could easily land on hard, frozen ground, while parachutists might injure themselves. These aircraft would glide to the edge of the lake that fed the turbines at the Vemork plant, and the men would bicycle to the factory, kill the guards, and complete their sabotage mission. They would then split into small groups of two or three and head for the Swedish border.

Both Wilson and Tronstad protested. Norway, they said, was too mountainous, rocky, and swampy for a glider landing, and the commandos would find it almost impossible to withdraw undetected from the target, which was four hundred treacherous, snowy miles from the safety of Sweden. Especially since they were foreigners who didn't know the local language. Also, cloud cover could make it difficult to find the landing site, air currents in the mountains would jeopardize a safe landing, ice would be too fragile to bear the weight of a glider with its men and equipment, and the bicycles would be useless in snow or on ice-coated roads.

Well, then, bomb! someone responded in frustration. Perhaps General Groves was right.

Tronstad again vigorously dissented. But what was the alternative? He decided that, despite the grave danger glider troops would face, they might be the only answer after all.

And everybody agreed—while conceding that a four-man advance team would have to be dropped by parachute, whatever the peril.

Later, Tronstad and Wilson met with Lieutenant Poulsson and Second Lieutenant Knut Haugland, his second-in-command, the leaders of the four-man advance party that would conduct Operation Grouse. Poulsson was a tall, lanky, pipe-smoking man. When I visited him at his home in Kongsberg, Norway, in 1993, I found that his professorial, rather gentle personality did not quite fit the stereotype of the daredevil commando. Yet he was a natural warrior. He joined the army at twenty-one, fulfilling a childhood dream. When the Nazis invaded Norway in 1940, he rushed into battle with his men, though harboring doubts about how he would face death.

"One never knows how one will react under fire for the first time," he would write in his memoirs. But he would add, "The love of my country is a reality; I'm driven by it. It can make weak men brave."

When the Norwegians and supporting British naval forces could no longer resist the German onslaught, Poulsson went underground, refusing to share the defeatist attitude of many other Norwegian fighters.

"The majority of the boys," he would continue in his memoirs, "feel hostile toward Britain; many have lost their hope and believe that the war is lost. It is strange how some cannot handle defeat without losing faith. It is just in times like these that one needs faith more than ever."

The problem was that not all Norwegian fighters were as psycho-logically geared to battle as Poulsson.

"The great majority of Norwegian people," Norwegian his-torian Jacob Worm-Muller would write, "really could not believe that the Germans would ever attack and suppress the Nordic people who desired to live in peace and to carry on their own way of life. . . . We failed to realize, therefore, that this new war vitally concerned us."

Thus, when the Norwegians, with no military traditions, were thrust into war for the first time in 126 years and faced defeat, they were "bewildered and paralyzed," as Worm-Muller would say. They needed time to rid themselves of their despair and confusion.

Nor were they well trained for battle. They would have to learn overnight the science of warfare—strategy and tactics, logistics, the handling of weapons, military discipline. They had certain skills that would help them learn the tactics of war quickly; they were good skiers and mountaineers and were mechanically inclined. They were courageous, rational, and audacious and had an esprit de corps. But these qualities were cancelled out to some degree by the fact that "they had," as British historian William Warbey would write, "a certain squeamishness about taking a man's life, however badly he might behave."

Furthermore, Warbey would say, the Norwegians would have to learn how "to be cunning, secretive, deceitful, two-faced, ruthless toward their friends and comrades as well as toward their enemies. They had to learn the art of lying brazenly, of suspecting all strangers, of concealing their thoughts even from their wives and their mothers."

Poulsson himself, despite his enthusiasm for soldiering, would have to sharpen his knowledge of these requirements, though this would be harder than learning how to parachute or to blow up a building. He was, in any event, determined to join the Norwegian guerrilla force the British were organizing. He sneaked over the border to Sweden, but was unable to find direct transport to Lon-don. So he embarked on a circuitous six-month voyage through Asia, the Middle East, and Africa that finally got him there.

It wasn't only Poulsson's fighting spirit and experience that made him uniquely qualified for his commando mission. A native of Rjukan, he knew the land and the people intimately, even many who worked in Norsk Hydro. In fact, his father, a construction engineer, had helped to build the plant and power station.

Now Poulsson and Haugland listened intently as Tronstad and Wilson briefed them on their mission. The four Norwegians would parachute onto the great marshy Hardanger Plateau, northwest of Rjukan, where they would check the terrain, the roads, and the security risks so that two Horsa gliders, each towed by a Halifax bomber, could safely land there about a month later in Operation Freshman.

The gliders, which would be towed farther than any had ever been towed before, would together be loaded with thirty-four commandos of the British 1st Airborne Division and their weapons, explosives, and other equipment. When they skidded to a halt, the commandos would be greeted by the Grouse men who would lead them along a steep mountain road for about six miles to Norsk Hydro for the attack. Afterward, they would flee to Sweden.

Poulsson was incredulous. How would the British conquer such challenging terrain when they were neither skiers nor mountaineers? But he was a soldier to the core and would do his best to make the mission succeed, especially knowing how great the stakes were.

Since the mission was so important, Tronstad told Poulsson, security must be tighter than ever before. And so he and his men would supposedly be competing for the "Washington Cup."

Poulsson was puzzled. The Washington Cup?

This "coveted prize," said Tronstad, would be awarded to the British or American army engineers who successfully performed the most difficult mission. At least that was the pretense for the intensive special training the men would engage in for Operations Grouse and Freshman. Actually, no Americans would be involved. But the men were to talk up the bogus competition everywhere—in pubs, at soccer games, at parties—and make everyone believe there was such a friendly contest.

Poulsson and the other Norwegians had already sweated for several weeks through a course in commando operations and sabotage at a Scottish base that only the most dedicated and skillful men could endure. They were members of the Linge Company, named after Captain Martin Linge, who had organized the company and was killed in action in Norway in December 1941. Here in this camp—a James Bond kind of training institute—the men learned how to do everything from blowing open steel doors to dropping straight down from balloons in delayed-action parachutes. They became expert in the use of dynamite, TNT, gun-cotton, plastic explosives, fuses, detonators, and booby traps.

Poulsson regretted that, until they had landed in Norway, he was forbidden to reveal the true mission even to the two men on his team who were not at this meeting. For he had complete trust in them, as he had in Haugland, a cool yet intense twenty-five-year-old radioman. Sergeant Claus Helberg, a thoughtful, good-looking soldier, also twenty-five, had been Poulsson's classmate and his closest childhood friend.

And Sergeant Arne Kjelstrup, a short, powerfully built man of twenty-nine, had earned the lieutenant's respect and admiration for his toughness and good humor—traits that had pulled him through the darkest days of the German invasion. He still had fragments of a bullet lodged in his hip. Escaping from a Nazi-captured hospital, he limped around from place to place, firing at enemy columns, before fleeing to Sweden. Like Poulsson, he couldn't find direct transport and finally reached England via the Soviet Union, Iran, South Africa, and the United States.

Toughness and good humor were needed once more when, in September 1942, the four-man team finally soared into the sky on what their leaders thought could be a flight into immortality. But the aircraft couldn't penetrate the dense fog smothering the North Sea and turned back to base. A second try, and this time the plane reached the Norwegian coast, only to puff and chug ominously as one of its four motors failed. Once again, the men barely got back to base, making a forced landing this time.

The group did not find it easy fighting superstition. Was London really in danger of destruction, as Colonel Wilson had said at his briefing? And the full moon, often associated with the onset of madness, did little to calm them. Because the intelligence chiefs feared German detection, they would let the commandos proceed only at night, but under a bright moon that would illuminate the treacherous Norwegian terrain below. And the moon wouldn't be full enough now for a few weeks.

Finally, on October 18, the moon hung in the heavens like a glittering penny. Wearing a snow-white jumpsuit, baggy overalls, leather gloves fitted over a silk pair, and a belt with a flask of precious rum hanging from it, the Grouse men once more boarded an aircraft bound for destiny.

. . .

Soon after the four guerrillas had swept into the cold, gray sky, the telephone rang in the office of Jomar Brun.

Who was calling?

"Mr. Berg," an unfamiliar voice replied.

What did the caller want?

He had a message from the Fox.

Where was the caller now?

In Rjukan.

"I'll see you at my home in an hour," Brun responded, though apparently surprised that Tronstad would try to contact him through anybody but Skinnarland.

An hour later, the visitor arrived at Brun's home in Vemork. His real name, the man said, was Fredrik Bachke, and he was a member of the Resistance. Brun would have to leave for London at once.

Why? Brun asked.

Bachke didn't know, but it was clear that Brun was in danger.

Brun had earlier received hints from Tronstad that he might be called to Britain, but he couldn't understand why the man was in such a hurry. He could not have guessed that Winston Churchill himself, after being briefed by Eric Welsh on the coming attack, had ordered that he be brought to Britain to protect him from arrest following the operation.

"May I take my wife with me?" Brun asked.

"Yes," Bachke replied. "The request was anticipated and permission is granted."

Could he have an extra two days to get ready and prepare a cover story so his parents and relatives would not suffer Nazi reprisals?

Bachke reluctantly agreed. But what a shame, thought Brun, that his wife had just bought a sewing machine. She treasured it, and now she would have to leave it for some German *frau*.

Later, Brun wrote letters to some members of his family and officials at Norsk Hydro "explaining" his absence: he was deeply depressed, he asserted, and was leaving for Sweden to find a new job. And on the eve of departure, the Bruns and Bachke threw themselves a farewell party that abounded with food the Bruns had stored away to ease the hard times they would be facing as the war ravaged their daily lives.

Their baggage loaded with documents, photographs, and variously concentrated jars of heavy water for analysis by British experts, the Bruns left on October 24 for Oslo, where, as instructed, they went to the Holstein suburb train station with a copy of the German newspaper *Fritt Folk* poking out of the engineer's pocket. A man with the same paper in his pocket walked by and, after the two exchanged a password, Brun whispered the name of his hotel.

Hours later, the man showed up there. Tomorrow, he said, the couple would be driven to a secret apartment, followed by a trip to a farmhouse and then a trek across rivers, through swamps, and over mountains to the Swedish border.

After several more days, on November 9, the Bruns were in London. The engineer still didn't know why he and his wife had been put through such an ordeal. What could be so urgent?

• • •

Less than a month earlier, on October 16, Adolf Hitler, enraged by a British commando raid on the Glomfjord hydroelectric plant in northern Norway, issued an infamous order to his top commanders. One of them, Colonel General Nikolaus von Falkenhorst, the commander-in-chief of German forces in Norway, was stunned as he sat at his desk reading the edict, or so he would claim at his court-martial after the war. The order read:

> From now on, all opponents brought to battle by German troops in so-called commando operations in Europe or in Africa, even when it is outwardly a matter of soldiers in uniform or demolition parties with or without weapons, are to be exterminated to the last man in battle or while in flight. In these cases it is immaterial whether they are landed for their operations by ship or airplane or descend by parachute.

Still more ominously, the fuehrer added:

> Even should these individuals, on their being discovered, make as if to surrender, all quarter is to be denied them on principle. . . . If individual members of such commandos working as agents, saboteurs, etc., fall into the hands of the Wehrmacht [Army] by other means—e.g., through the police in any of the countries occupied by us—they are to be handed over to the SD [Gestapo] immediately. It is strictly forbidden to hold them in military custody . . . even as a temporary measure.

According to Falkenhorst, whom Norwegians viewed as a relatively moderate professional soldier, his "first impression was one of rejection." The summary execution of enemy prisoners of war was entirely unprofessional. But what could he do? Ask to be relieved of his command?

"I can only say," he would maintain at his trial, "that I should have liked to do so."

Unfortunately, however, "Hitler refused to dismiss a general just because this general did not approve of one of his orders." Falkenhorst was "in opposition to [the order] in my conscience," the general would say, "but as a soldier, I had to obey."

And he did. On October 26, Falkenhorst issued an order to his forces virtually in the same terms as the Hitler order but adding the passage, "If a man is saved for interrogation, he must not survive for more than twenty-four hours."

After all, he would argue after the war, he gave the captured enemy twenty-four more hours of life, and during that time those close to the fuehrer might be able to persuade him to rescind, or at least modify, the edict. He was, the general would stress, risking his career, if not his life, with this alteration. But he couldn't control the behavior of the Gestapo.

Many Norwegians did believe that Falkenhorst was a man of some conscience, for he comported himself strictly as a military man and did not display the arrogance and brutal pretensions of Reich Commissar Josef Terboven, who, with the assistance of a few Norwegian traitors and opportunists, controlled the reins in the civil sphere. Terboven, a monstrous instrument of oppression, lived in the king's sumptuous summer palace, conducted business in the parliament building, and traveled in an armor-plated Mercedes with an aerial cannon perched on the roof, protected by a bodyguard of thugs to the front and rear.

Terboven needed such protection. The public hated him for interfering in every aspect of daily life, for controlling the press, radio, theater, politics, even social life. He dissolved Rotary Clubs, women's associations, and student societies, and jailed almost anyone suspected of breaking the rules. Popular outrage escalated after Terboven demanded that King Haakon, who was now in Britain, abdicate his throne.

Suddenly, the people awoke from the shock of defeat and there was a "great revival," as one Norwegian writer would say, "a mighty reaction in spirit . . . and it spread like wildfire throughout the country. The common people . . . refused to depose their King and instead rallied around him more strongly than ever before." They despised the "usurper" who now lived in the palace.

By contrast, Falkenhorst was not a lightning rod for public fury. He lived Spartanly in a two-room suite in the Royal Norwegian Automobile Club and traveled in an ordinary touring car with only his adjutant beside him. The general had never been a Nazi party man and didn't appoint a liaison officer to Terboven's staff.

Yet Hitler had chosen Falkenhorst over a number of more senior officers to direct the invasion of Norway in 1940 and, later, to command the occupying forces. The senior officers had opposed Hitler's invasion order, feeling that Germany would be tying up forces unnecessarily in a peripheral state; Falkenhorst, on the other hand, was too junior to dare balk at the order. Hitler would direct the battle himself, and Falkenhorst would be a pliable puppet. This, at least, is what the other senior officers expected. So they were flabbergasted when they noted that Falkenhorst had meddled, however slightly, with Hitler's decree.

It appears that Falkenhorst was, as he claimed, torn between professional code and political coercion. Born in 1886 in Breslau, Silesia, he had been a soldier all his life, like his father. And he looked every inch the haughty Prussian warrior, with his shaven head, heavy brows, and piercing, slightly cynical eyes. In World War I, he began as a company commander and by 1918, four years later, headed the German General Staff in Finland. As an infantry general when World War II began, he commandedan army corps in the invasion of Poland. Then, under the fuehrer's direct command, Falkenhorst was given only a few hours to sub-mit detailed plans for the attack on Norway and was allotted no more than five divisions. But within a month, the fighting was over.

Now, however, with Hitler's order to murder all enemy "commandos," Falkenhorst would face his bitterest test: could a proud professional soldier use Gestapo tactics and remain either proud or professional?

Regardless, Falkenhorst was determined that the raid at Glomfjord would not be repeated, especially at Vemork, where he knew the scientists were making heavy water for a major secret weapon. In early October, he and other high-ranking officers visited the plant to warn the guards to be on the alert for a raid.

You must be ready, he cautioned them. Had commandos not successfully attacked Glomfjord?

Falkenhorst spoke of the attackers almost with admiration—how they burst in firing automatic weapons, hurling grenades, gagging the guards with chloroform. Clearly they had undergone intensive training. And they might next attack the heavy-water plant, perhaps, the general said, posing as tourists with civilian clothes over their uniforms and approaching by city bus.

You must place mines around the plant, he ordered, especially since there weren't enough men to guard every inch of ground.

Falkenhorst then departed. It seemed to him a matter of time until he would have to carry out the fuehrer's psychopathic edict.

# 6

## THE WASHINGTON CUP

*November 1942*

CORPORAL SYD BRITTAIN and his fellow British soldiers were eager to leave on their sabotage mission—a mission so secret that they didn't even know yet what it was. From the rigorous training program they had stumbled through, however, they knew Operation Freshman would be a strong challenge. But most felt they would somehow survive. A commando tended to see himself as nearly immortal, perhaps in order to overcome his fears.

But if the men suppressed thoughts of death, the prospect of being wounded was hard to ignore. Especially since they would be given an injection of morphine and left where they had fallen. Indeed, if anyone strayed from the group for any reason, he had to be abandoned. For as Tronstad pointed out, "whatever happens, someone must arrive at the objective to do the job."

Should someone be captured, he would probably spend the rest of the war behind barbed wire while his more fortunate comrades were out there fighting. But at least he wouldn't be shot—not even if he discarded his British uniform for civilian clothes to evade capture while trying to escape. International law permitted soldiers to disguise themselves, the men were told, as long as they didn't carry weapons or military orders.

Brittain was one of about forty paratroopers of the 261st Field Park Company Royal Engineers who had gathered one day at their camp in Bulford, England, to hear their commander offer them a chance to win special glory. He wanted some volunteers for a job that "has to be done because if we don't do it, the war will be over in six months and we'll be on the losing side."

All but two of the men instantly raised their hands to volunteer. Brittain—slim, wiry, outwardly cool—was especially eager. He was single, so in case the "impossible" happened and he didn't come back, he would not be leaving a wife and offspring behind at his home near Bath, England. At the same time, he had many nieces and nephews, and he "thought them worth fighting for at any risk."

He did not know the purpose of the mission, he would tell me over tea in a coffee shop he frequented in Bath years later. But his superiors had assured the participants that it could determine the outcome of the war.

Brittain was assigned to the "Washington Cup" training program in which the four men of Operation Grouse had taken part before flying off to Norway to clear the way for a full-scale commando attack. The training program was grueling, with endless forced marches without sleep and lessons on how to place charges in a model hydroelectric plant similar to Norsk Hydro. After studying the model with its mock-ups of the heavy-water equipment, Brittain was confident he'd be able to break into the Norwegian plant blind-folded and know exactly where to find every door, window, and machine. And he could hardly wait to prove he could.

Another impatient soldier was Corporal James D. Cairncross, a solidly built man with chiseled features and deep-set, smiling eyes from Hawick, Scotland. Liked by everyone who met him, "Jimmy" savored life and everything it offered. As a carpenter, he enjoyed working with his hands. As a natural athlete, he loved outdoor sports and spent his spare time playing rugby and cricket, climbing moun-tains, and cycling. Every summer he went camping with the Boys' Brigade, a scouting organization. What a wonderful life—before it was interrupted by the war. He joined the paratroopers with his usual verve, and was soon training for Operation Freshman. Cairncross didn't worry much about the potential threat to his own life, but he worried a great deal about the threat to his father's, for the news from home was grim. The senior Cairncross, a cherished role model for his son, was critically ill, and Jimmy hoped to go on leave to visit him immediately after the mission—if it was ever launched.

Delay followed delay as the commanders bickered over every minute detail of the attack plan and were unable at first even to obtain the necessary planes and equipment. Bomber Command had very few Halifax bombers and was reluctant to loan them out for some perilous special operation, however vital. And when the three Halifaxes and two Horsa gliders (one Halifax would not be used) were finally torn from the grasp of the military bureaucrats, one was found to be stripped of operational equipment, while all still had to be fitted out with Rebecca, a new radar homing device.

The weather was also a problem. Since the commandos needed a clear, moonlit night, Operation Freshman would not be launched until the earliest full-moon period, from November 18 to 26.

A few days before the moon bared its full face, Syd Brittain bared his frustration when, during a ten-mile hike with a double pack, he passed some American soldiers atop a hill, probably, he thought, his competitors for the Washington Cup. All were relaxing on the roadside. These chaps were the competition? Some soldiers!

"You're in the wrong army!" Brittain cried to one man who was sitting on the hood of a jeep casually smoking a cigar.

As the Englishman spoke, his eyes moved from the path ahead and he stumbled on a rock and fell to the ground with a sprained ankle. Grimacing in pain, he was helped up by a comrade and carried back to base. Fear seized him. Would he now be removed from the roster of men to leave on Operation Freshman? He couldn't hide the injury from his superiors since a doctor inspected the men's feet daily.

Indeed, that day the doctor examined him and immediately noted the swollen ankle.

"You can't go on the mission," he said.

But he was all right, Brittain insisted. He could keep up with the others.

"I won't have your blood on my hands," the doctor replied. "You can't go!"

Brittain was devastated. He had trained for Operation Freshman assiduously, counting the minutes until it began. How could he stay behind while his buddies went off to battle? Nor did he lose his taste for action when an officer admonished the men: "Never forget that with moderate luck you have a good chance of getting home."

Good chance? Of course he'd get home—if only they'd let him go.

• • •

Actually, the brass were gloomier about the prospects of success than they let on. And more worried than most was Lieutenant Colonel Mark Henniker, who was in charge of training and the attack plan. In several training exercises, he would later write in a report, he "had seen parachutists and glider-borne troops landed miles from the proper place in broad daylight. A flight to Rjukan, across four hundred miles of sea, and over the mountains and valleys of Norway, was incomparably more difficult. . . . I did not believe that any such flight could be done in the dark."

On November 18, the start of the full-moon period, Henniker personally climbed aboard one of two Halifaxes that would fly from Skitten, a satellite airfield of Wick, in Scotland, to Norway in a flight to test the validity of the colonel's fears. Over the North Sea, the plane ran into a cloud bank and "suddenly pitched and tossed like a ship," and soon, Henniker would say in his report, he heard over the intercom some panicky conversation in the cockpit:

"Which cock is it?"

"The one by the main spar. For Christ's sake be quick or we'll have an engine die on us."

"Is it the right-hand or left-hand cock?"

"The right-hand one, just behind the main spar. No, you bloody fool, not that one, the other. And for God's sake, quick!"

"Can't get it to budge, sir."

"Turn the thing the other bloody way. Christ! What happened?"

The aircraft began to shudder, and the navigator was heard to say that when the plane "broke from the base of the clouds in which we were now flying we should either see the Norwegian coastline at once, or we might charge into a mountain almost immediately."

Henniker and the other men shuddered as intensely as the plane. Finally, the pilot announced: "We shall turn for base and I hope to God we get there!"

They did. But the white-faced colonel might have wondered if God would be as generous when the actual operation took place, when the aircraft would have to buck the weather while pulling a jam-packed glider over the sea toward obscure landing areas that even moonlight and Rebecca might not be able to find.

Since a cold front had settled over the west coast of Norway, the unit meteorologist advised that the operation be further postponed. But as the weather, it seemed, would be relatively clear the following evening, November 19, the impatient brass would not wait a minute longer. Operation Freshman would be launched. And two Halifaxes revved up, each connected to a glider that would carry seventeen men, including one officer.

• • •

As Jimmy Cairncross climbed aboard one of the gliders with his comrades at Skitten, he must surely have welcomed the opportunity to show up the Americans. And he could now use the vigorous training he had undergone to strike at an enemy that threatened the wonderful, carefree life he longed to resume.

How great it would be to climb mountains again without a gun slung over his shoulder, to go on leisurely hikes with kids of the Boys' Brigade instead of on forced marches necessary for mere survival. More urgently, however, he had to get back home while he could still share some moments of joy with his father.

But if Jimmy Cairncross was thankful that the mission was finally under way, Syd Brittain had never been more depressed. He stood by his barracks waving good-bye to his comrades, and reflected on all those punishing weeks of preparation for a mission that excluded him—ironically, all because he had sprained his ankle at the last minute while telling off that cigar-smoking Yank.

Brittain, praying for a victorious mission, watched as the first Halifax and Horsa, with Jimmy Cairncross aboard the glider, sailed into the skies at 5:40 P.M., then as the second two aircraft followed a half-hour later.

Why, he bitterly wondered, should he be singled out for such lousy luck?

# 7

## AT LAST A GIRL

### November 1942

**THAT SAME DAY,** in a log cabin nearly buried in the snow of a Rjukan mountainside, the Grouse foursome received a long-awaited radio message: "Girl."

Any German monitoring the airwaves might have thought the message was sent by an obstetrician. And Lieutenant Poulsson delighted in it much as any father might have. Actually, however, the code word *girl* meant that British planes would reach Norway after midnight on November 20, when the two gliders would be released from their towing Halifaxes and sail down to earth.

At last—after a treacherous fifteen-day trek on skis from their own landing site and a two-week, hunger-plagued wait in the snow and sleet near the spot where the gliders, loaded with commandos, were to touch down . . .

Trouble had afflicted the commandos almost from the moment they dropped through a hole in the belly of their plane and para-chuted onto a snow-mantled desert of rock and swamp in south-ern Norway. It began when Sergeant Helberg injured himself after landing rear first on a large stone, and it appeared the swel-ling could turn the hare into a turtle, jeopardizing the whole mission.

Then there was the problem of geography. Where were they? They finally realized they had landed in the glittering white wilds of the Hardanger Plateau near the region of Telemark, a windswept fairyland of waterfalls, lakes, and rivers. The plane was supposed to have dropped them about six miles away, in the Skoland Marshes north of the village of Ugleflott.

The next morning the men began searching for the crates also dropped by parachute from their aircraft—including one with their skis—and spent two days picking them up and dragging them to a stick-marked central collection depot hidden in the snow. Poulsson put on his skis and decided to look for a cabin they could use as temporary headquarters. From there, the men would head over the mountains in the direction of Rjukan to find terrain suitable for a glider landing.

Poulsson and Helberg, who insisted on accompanying his old Rjukan classmate despite his injury, plodded through the thick snowdrifts, searching everywhere for a cabin closer to their objective, but without success. Soon a new snowstorm covered their tracks and, as they started back to join their two comrades waiting with all the equipment, they lost their way.

With darkness descending, they could take their compass bearings only from lake to lake, having to dig into the snow with their ski poles to discern if they were on ice or on land. Finally, after several hours, Helberg stopped and cried out:

"We're here!"

The two men then shouted for the other half of the Grouse team, and, like an echo, a voice bounced back. The exhausted pair had walked some six miles almost blindly and had missed their comrades by only two hundred yards!

But the men were still without shelter, and also without a particularly vital item—paraffin for their two Primus stoves, which had leaked. Without it, they could not risk marching directly across the mountains in the subnormal temperatures. Nor was Lieutenant Haugland, the radio operator, able to contact London and ask for a resupply. Their only choice was to take a much longer, more dangerous, but less frigid route through winding valleys and across thin-iced lakes.

The men packed the minimum equipment they would need and cached the rest in their depot for later retrieval. Then they started on their great march, plodding through snow up to their knees. After several miles, they would lay down the equipment—about sixty-five pounds per man—and return for another load.

They would make three such hellish trips each day, moving sluggishly with wet snow clinging to the underside of their skis. Since the food they carried had to last for at least a month, they ate little along the way—mainly a handful of oatmeal, flour, and a dried powderlike meat loaf called pemmican.

As the men dragged themselves along, wondering how they could trudge on with their burdens for days more, something of a miracle occurred. Poulsson thought he was seeing a mirage when he found a sled half-buried in the snow. "That's my sled!" he cried.

His father had given it to him when he was a child. During the fighting in the Rjukan area in 1940, Norwegian troops had borrowed it. Suddenly, here it was, once more a gift, this time a gift of life. The men could now bring all the equipment with them at once, though it was not easy pulling more than two hundred pounds through the shifting drifts.

Whenever they came upon a lone cabin, they would break in, ransack the pantry, and go to sleep in the warmth of a fire. But as they moved on and their food supply dwindled, one of them would spend a whole day backtracking for miles through unrelenting snowstorms to the last cabin to replenish the supply.

At one point, while Poulsson was crossing a stream, he fell through the ice and almost drowned before a comrade pulled him to safety. A second try proved almost as perilous, and more misfortune followed. The lieutenant's feet nearly froze from the icy water. Another time, he developed a large boil on his hand and had to advance with his arm in a sling, agonizing as he plowed through the heavy snow using only one pole.

Meanwhile, Haugland found that his radio wouldn't work because there wasn't enough acid to fill the batteries. How could they carry out their mission without communicating with Tronstad and Wilson, who might even now think they were dead? How could the gliders land without Grouse's guidance?

Finally, on November 5, after eighteen horrific days, the group, nearly prostrate and half-starved, stumbled into the base area on

Lake Sand near Rjukan and broke into a log cabin, where they would prepare for the glider operation just to the east. Helberg staggered to the dam nearby where Torstein Skinnarland, Einar's brother, worked while serving the underground, and obtained from him a car battery that could be used for the radio.

Haugland, meanwhile, stole two fishing rods from a hut and used them to set up an antenna. And on November 9, as he lay shivering in his sleeping bag, he made contact with London at last.

"Happy landing in spite of boulders everywhere," he excitedly reported. "Snowstorm and fog forced us to go down valleys. Four feet of snow made it impossible with heavy equipment to cross mountains."

In London, Trondstad and Wilson were ecstatic. But then they noted that the sending key was not being tapped in the way Haugland usually sent his messages. Was the operator really Haugland—or a German who might have captured the transmitting station?

The listeners could not know that their man was now pressing the key with a nearly frostbitten finger. How could they make sure it was really he? They decided to ask him a question that no hate-consumed, humorless Nazi would be likely to answer with appropriate abandon: "What did you see walking down the Strand in the early hours of January 1, 1941?"

Haugland was startled. He and his companions were freezing, half-dead from fatigue, and so hungry that when Poulsson once dropped a pot of soup made with meat from a lost lamb they had trapped, the men licked it off the cabin floor and gnawed on the scattered bones. It was better than the dog food they found.

And now London was playing games!

• • •

As suggested by his straitlaced, scholarly demeanor, Haugland was too serious a soldier to play games. Since fall 1940, when underground Norwegian officers asked him to operate a clandestine radio station for contact with Britain, he had been working feverishly day and night to help liberate his country. While continuing his work in a radio factory, he studied radio communication in the underground and was asked to assemble a twenty-watt transmitter and set it up in Rjukan, his native town. Shortly, he brought the transmitter home, where Einar Skinnarland, who was then less experienced in radio work, agreed to help him establish a station.

Haugland then returned to Oslo and waited for a courier from Stockholm who would give him the codes from the British legation there. But just as he arrived, his mother phoned him from Rjukan.

"The police were here looking for you!" she exclaimed.

Someone, Haugland now knew, had informed on him. He moved to a new flat in Oslo, but when he returned to work at the radio factory, two German-supervised Norwegian policemen came to see him.

"Sorry," one of them said, "but you'll have to come with us."

They drove him to his rented room and told him they knew he had taken a transmitter to Rjukan.

"We were there and searched your home and talked with your parents. We couldn't find anything, but we know you took it there."

Haugland feigned outrage. "Are you accusing me of treason?" he demanded to know.

"No," one policeman replied, "but we'd like to look around the room."

After the pair searched the room and found nothing, Haugland asked to be driven to the radio factory. They agreed, promising to return, but as soon as they let him off, he skied to Sweden and headed for the British legation. Soon, he was flown to Britain. As a Rjukan native with expert radio knowledge, he was a logical choice to take part in Operation Grouse.

Always on the go, always evading the Germans or learning how to strike back at them, he had no time to relax, to forget the plight of his country—to play games. Perhaps once, shortly after he arrived in London . . . New Year's Eve . . .

* * *

Suddenly, the riddle from England made sense. What had he seen "walking down the Strand in the early hours of January 1, 1941"? Haugland hammered off a reply: "Three pink elephants."

His London handlers were relieved. The world was still in safe hands.

Within days, the men found a suitable landing area for the gliders. And they assembled the Eureka, a radio direction finder, which
would receive radio waves transmitted from the Rebecca in the
Halifaxes. The planes would then return the signal so the Grouse
commandos could hear them approaching.

On November 17, Haugland brought London further relief with
a heartening weather report: "Lake covered with ice and partly covered with snow. Larger lakes are ice free. Last three nights' sky
absolutely clear with moonlight. Temperature about minus five
degrees Centigrade [twenty-three degrees Fahrenheit]. Strong
wind from north has died down tonight. Beautiful weather."

• • •

Two days later, the icy air finally vibrated with a word that would
justify the weeks of misery.

"Girl."

The next evening, Haugland put on the earphones of the Eureka
radio direction finder and listened for a signal from the expected
planes with their gliders. But the men began to worry as the
weather suddenly changed, with the wind rising and clouds hanging low.

Then the long-awaited sound of motors.

"I hear it!" Haugland cried.

And the men switched on the lights they had brought with
them and blinked identifying signals with a flashlight. In moments,
they were sure, a glider would break through the clouds. The sound
dissipated, but in the next minutes the whirring of motors could be
heard twice more. Then silence. Just before midnight the welcom-
ing party, crestfallen, gave up and returned to the cabin.

The following morning, Haugland flashed a message to London:
Freshman hadn't landed.

What, the men wondered with growing trepidation, had happened to the planes and gliders?

• • •

The gliders were missing?

Lieutenant Colonel Henniker and his technicians in the operations room at Wick Airport felt growing apprehension as they called out signals hour after hour and received no reply. Finally, at about twenty minutes to midnight a faint signal was heard: one Halifax asked for a position. But then silence again for about fifteen minutes, when another message read: "Released glider over sea."

Still another message followed: "Glider in sea."

Henniker was horrified, as were Welsh, Wilson, and Trondstad in London.

■ ■ ■

Meanwhile, Corporal Brittain was constantly waking from his sleep in the barracks, wishing he were on one of those gliders with his comrades. Finally, with the first glow of dawn, he jumped out of bed and looked out a window. There on the airfield he saw one Halifax—one! The plane that had signaled Wick that its glider had plunged into the sea.

Brittain shook off the sluggish remnants of sleep and searched everywhere. No, just one plane. Where was the other one? Both Halifaxes should have returned by now after releasing their gliders over the target. Black thoughts swirled through his mind, and a glance around the barracks deepened the darkness. Empty beds—silence. If they weren't coming back, should he have been spared? Before rushing out to question the men who did return, he prayerfully scanned the orange-tinted sky. Maybe the second plane would still roar through the dawn to a safe homecoming.

■ ■ ■

As Martin Selmer Sandstol, the Norwegian farmer, could attest after climbing Benkafjellet, a mountain near the village of Helleland early that morning in mothlike pursuit of a giant fireball, none of the crew would, in fact, ever return home. Sandstol would learn later that neither would many other men.

Another fireball had lit up a neighboring mountain. The glider towed by the ill-fated Halifax had also crashed after the towing rope snapped.

# 8

## "THIS FILTHY BUSINESS"

### *November 1942*

"ANYBODY HERE?"

Gabriel Nygaard, a farmer in Helleland, was shaken awake as the words echoed through the house, like the baying of a ghost, over the sound of a fierce wind and a torrent of rain. It was 2 A.M. What stranger had entered the house? Nygaard's first thought was that the Gestapo had come to arrest him. But why was the intruder speaking English? Was this a trick? What would happen to him, to his wife and four children?

Nygaard nudged his wife awake and whispered to her to be silent. Then he sprang out of bed, quickly dressed, and, trembling with lamp in hand, edged toward the front door. In the shadowy light he saw two soldiers shivering from the cold, their uniforms torn, soaked, and dirty. Hardly the immaculately dressed, heel-clicking German soldiers he had come to loathe and fear.

"Who are you?" Nygaard asked, suspecting now that they were British soldiers.

In fact, they were, and they needed help, one of the men said. Their glider had crashed in the mountains and many of their comrades were dead or badly wounded. Could he find a doctor? They themselves were injured, though not as seriously as the others.

There was silence as Nygaard stared at the strangers, obviously struggling with himself. He wished he could help them, but many people in Helleland had been arrested simply on suspicion of siding with the Allies. And he knew that the penalty for aiding or sheltering the enemy was death.

No, he couldn't do anything for them, Nygaard finally responded. But the *lensmann*, or sheriff, probably could. The sheriff lived nearby, he said, and he took them outside into the wind and rain and pointed the way to the man's home.

The soldiers thanked Nygaard, who then shrank back into the house, apparently feeling a sense of guilt. For the sheriff, whatever his true sentiment, worked for the Germans. And if he didn't report the crash to them, he would be risking not only his job but his life. Nygaard surely knew he had all but guaranteed the capture of his British guests.

About twenty minutes later, Trond Hovland, son of Sheriff Theodor Hovland and a former policeman himself, was also abruptly awakened by a noise, one that almost every Norwegian dreaded: a midnight knock on the door. The Gestapo? Hadn't his father always obeyed his German masters? Unlike most other sheriffs in the region, he had even arrested all the teachers in his village for refusing to teach Nazi doctrine to their students. The other sheriffs had lost their jobs. Was Theodor Hovland now about to lose his—or perhaps suffer an even worse fate? Trond was furious at his brother, John, who was studying in Oslo. He had warned John not to join that group of students who openly protested German rule.

When Trond opened the door, the two soldiers who had first gone to Gabriel Nygaard's house explained again that their glider had crashed and asked for help.

Trond ushered them into the house, and shortly the sheriff himself joined in questioning the two men while Trond's wife prepared coffee. How many were wounded? How many were killed? The soldiers couldn't be sure—or at least the Hovlands couldn't be. For they understood little English. And they apparently weren't able to reply coherently when the two visitors asked them how they could get to the Swedish border.

Still, the Hovlands managed to express their agreement that help must be sent to the wounded immediately, though, Trond said in stumbling English, it would be difficult to get a doctor. The nearest one lived in a German-run work camp, and he was too ill to come. Another lived in Egersund, about twelve miles to the southwest, but he could be reached by phone only through the central exchange, which was monitored by the Germans.

So, according to Trond, he tried to explain to the Britons that since keeping the crash a secret from the Germans was impossible, it would be best to reveal it to the Germans directly. The wounded would be taken to a hospital while the others would become prisoners of war.

It is not clear whether the soldiers were, in fact, given this advice, understood it if they were, or agreed to it. But the sheriff went to the phone and told the operator, whom he knew, that he wished to inform German headquarters in Slettebo about the crash. The operator, however, hesitated to put him through, saying: "Shouldn't you wait awhile before telling them? Give the soldiers a chance to get away."

But the elder Hovland insisted, and he was soon describing the situation to a German officer and requesting medical help. A force would be sent to the scene immediately, the officer replied, and he hung up.

Hovland felt that, as sheriff, he should show that he had some authority of his own. And so he would interrogate the men himself before the Germans arrived. He thus made another phone call—to Severin Hogstad, a neighbor who had spent many years in the United States and was fairly fluent in English.

"Severin," he nervously said, "please come over right away. Two British soldiers are here and I think they are saboteurs. You must interpret for me."

About five minutes later, Hogstad knocked on the Hovlands' door, about seven hundred yards away.

He had informed the Germans of the crash, the sheriff stammered. It was the only way to get medical help for the survivors.

Hogstad turned pale. It was the "worst moment in my life," he would tell me years later in Helleland. The Germans were on the way to capture these poor boys, and he was helpless to save them from possible death.

"Tell the men that the Germans are coming but that they shouldn't worry," Hovland said. "They should take it easy and not try to run away."

Hogstad reluctantly agreed. Thanks to Hovland, the Germans already knew about the crash and there seemed no way to avoid capture.

"If you try to get away now," Hogstad told the Britons, "the Germans will surely kill you." They simmered with anger, perhaps because they felt that Hogstad was right.

"No one can stop us if we want to run away!" one cried, waving a pistol.

"Then why don't you go?" Hogstad asked.

Without replying directly, one of the soldiers asked how far it was to the Swedish border.

About four hundred miles.

The visitors whispered to each other and, finally, with pained expressions, agreed to stay. Their main concern was for their wounded comrades, they said. They had to see that these men were taken care of.

A phone call was made to a nurse in the German-operated work camp, the wife of the ill doctor, and she agreed to come with a group of young captive laborers to help carry down the wounded. When they arrived at the Hovland farm, one of the Britons led them up the mountain through the wind-driven rain and over slippery rocks that, in the glow of flashlights, poked luminously out of thorny brush.

The soldier lost his way in the darkness, but eventually managed to lead the group to the crash site. There the rescuers found three dead men sewn up in a tarpaulin and three seriously wounded, but were surprised to learn that, like the two men who had come to Hovland's house, the remaining nine were in fairly good condition. These survivors had bandaged the badly wounded, and, strangely enough, were in "excellent spirit and temper," according to one of the rescuers.

When they learned the Germans were coming, the soldiers burned documents and distributed their money, watches, and other valuables, as well as much of their equipment, to the Norwegians before the Germans could confiscate them.

There was still time for the lightly wounded to escape, the rescuers said. But when these Britons learned how limited their chances were of evading the Germans en route to Sweden, they decided, like the two men who had gone for help, not to leave their severely wounded comrades. Better to become prisoners of war. Sooner or later, they felt with a desperate logic, they would return to their loved ones.

Shortly, Trond Hovland arrived with a platoon of German soldiers, and the able Britons helped the Germans and Norwegians carry stretchers with the dead and badly injured down the mountain to the sheriff's house, where a German doctor treated them.

Just before noon, November 20, the dead bodies and stretcher-borne men were piled into an ambulance and the other prisoners into trucks, and the vehicles started off toward German headquarters at Slettebo. One man, noted a Norwegian observer, gave the V-sign from the rear of his truck. A POW camp wouldn't be so bad.

• • •

That morning, in the isolated mountain village of Fylgjesdal (named after the only family that lived there), west of Stavanger, Thorvald Fylgjesdal, a thirty-year-old farmer, was in his room when he heard the cries of his cousin Martine.

"Come down quickly! Some people are outside!"

Fylgjesdal related to me that he rushed downstairs and looked out the window. There, leaning against a tree, were three men in uniform—survivors, he could not know, of the second glider, which like the first, had crashed into a mountain. It had snapped loose from the Halifax that would make its way back to Britain.

"Look," Martine exclaimed, "the Germans have come for us!" And she ran out the back door.

Fylgjesdal, who knew from their uniforms that the men were actually British soldiers, called the woman back, but in vain. Then he strode outside and approached the three strangers.

"Doctor! Doctor!" shouted one with a heavily bandaged leg. "Motorboat! Motorboat!" another cried, making it clear they wanted to reach a nearby fjord in order to escape the Germans.

Then, mainly with sign language, they managed to convey the information that their aircraft had crashed into a mountainside nearby. Some men had died while others lay wounded and urgently needed treatment.

Fylgjesdal, whose thin lips, sad eyes, and large ears gave him an affably pixyish appearance, noted that these three visitors were themselves wounded, though apparently not seriously. He wanted to hear their story and to help them and their comrades get medical attention, but he knew almost no English and didn't have a telephone. The nearest phone was at another farmer's home about five miles away in the village of Hole.

The men then limped along behind Fylgjesdal to a lake close by where there was a rowboat. They crossed the lake and stumbled along for several miles until they finally reached the farm of the neighbor, Jonas Haaheller.

Immediately, Fylgjesdal telephoned a doctor in Forsand, about thirty-five miles away by boat along the fjord, and asked him to come to Hole. He then decided to call Forsand's sheriff to arrange for help in bringing down the wounded from the crash site. This sheriff, a woman, was less fearful of German wrath than Helleland's Sheriff Hovland. She was appointed to the post only after her father, Thorvald Espedal, was dismissed from the job and her brother, Leif, refused to replace him; neither would accept German dictates. Leif's sister, Hjordis, was just as anti-Nazi and stubbornminded but agreed to take the job, feeling that as a woman she would be less threatened if she resisted these dictates.

The sheriff was not home, but Fylgjesdal reached Leif, who immediately cut the phone line to Stavanger so the Germans based there could not eavesdrop.

He should come to the Haaheller farm in Hole with his sister and a doctor without delay, Fylgjesdal urged, or the wounded would die.

A few hours later, in the early afternoon of November 20, Leif Espedal arrived by boat, accompanied by a physician. (Hjordis and two Norwegian police officers would follow later that day.) While the doctor treated the three Britons, they told Leif their story.

The previous day, their glider, towed by a bomber from Scotland, reached the Norwegian coast when the towline snapped in the icy air. The glider crashed into a mountain and seven of the seventeen passengers were killed on impact. The rest were injured, with one man dying of his wounds shortly afterward. The three did what they could for the severely wounded, then left to seek help.

What were the chances of their reaching Sweden or escaping to England across the North Sea?

Almost none, Leif replied.

The three Britons agreed to surrender.

At about 7 P.M., Sheriff Hjordis Espedal arrived by boat with the two police officers. After the soldiers briefed them, the Espedals and one of the police officers followed Fylgjesdal to his farm, leaving the three Britons behind with the other police officer. On arriving at about 9:30 P.M., the sheriff's group found three other wounded British soldiers who had managed to limp down the mountain. Guided by the one who was in the best condition, Leif and the police officer left for the crash site.

When they reached the wreckage—the glider had split in two—they found the front section a twisted heap of metal from which no man escaped alive. Four wounded from the rear section lay sprawled amid the rocks, along with a scattering of food, weapons, and other items, some frozen to the ground in their own blood. By 2 A.M., a number of Norwegians had arrived on the scene with stretchers, and they laboriously carried two of the wounded down the mountain. They were taken to the Sagbakken farm on the bank of a nearby fjord, from where they would sail to Stavanger. The other two wounded remained behind at the crash site to await the arrival of more porters.

Meanwhile, at the Haaheller farm, the police officer who had been left there telephoned German headquarters after much hesitation and reported the crash of the British glider.

Why hadn't he informed headquarters earlier? the German on the line demanded to know. If the British got away, he would suffer the consequences! Two other British aircraft had also crashed in the area. What did these incursions mean? Was this the beginning of an Allied invasion of Norway?

Hours later two boatloads of German soldiers pulled up to the pier in Hole, this time led by a general and a Gestapo officer named Kuhn. The troops, many of them SS men, leaped ashore and surrounded the Haaheller farmhouse where the three British soldiers lay in growing pain. In minutes, the prisoners were being dragged out and prodded to the pier by German bayonets, two of them staggering along while supporting the third, whose leg was in a splint.

When the Britons had been pulled aboard one of the vessels, they were kept on the open deck exposed to the bitter cold. Couldn't they be taken below? a Norwegian policeman suggested to Kuhn.

Let them freeze, Kuhn brusquely replied—though the policeman, aided by a sympathetic German, installed a windshield on the deck.

The boats stopped at Sagbakken to pick up the two wounded Britons who had been carried from the crash scene, and sailed on to Stavanger, where German brass were waiting eagerly to unravel the mystery of the three fallen aircraft.

Meanwhile, some of the SS men, under a Gestapo officer named Hartmann, left Sagbakken for Fylgjesdal's farm to pick up the two Britons still there, and to bring down the two who had been left at the crash site.

When early that evening Hartmann approached the farm with his men, he was enraged to hear the lilting strains of a harmonica. The Germans were being threatened, perhaps by an invasion, and the enemy was being treated to a concert! He stormed into the farmhouse and saw one of the British soldiers playing the instrument, while Sheriff Hjordis Espedal and the second Briton sat listening in a familylike scene.

Hjordis calmed the Gestapo officer, and he ordered her to find people to bring down the two remaining stretcher cases from the mountains. She complied, and in the morning the pair were carried into the farmhouse to join their two comrades.

Hjordis was then ordered to supervise the burial of the eight British corpses at the crash site.

Where were they to be buried? she asked.

In the mountains.

Hjordis vigorously protested that the dead should be given a decent cemetery burial. But to no avail.

The last four wounded Britons were soon aboard a vessel headed for Stavanger. And at least one of them was surely anguished that he would have to sit out the war in a POW camp. Jimmy Cairncross wasn't a man to voluntarily stay out of a battle he felt committed to fight, especially if others might die in his stead.

. . .

Colonel Henniker, in the operations room at Wick, was devastated on receiving the message that one of the gliders had plunged into the sea. He urgently called for an air-sea rescue operation, but there were no ships available, and the two aircraft ready to search the sea had to wait for the weather off the Norwegian coast to clear.

Where exactly had the glider gone down? According to the latest report, about seven miles off that southern coast. But shortly a correction was in order. For a little before 3 A.M., the Halifax that had released the glider landed at Wick—the plane that Sergeant Brittain saw when he awoke in his vacant barracks. The glider, the dispirited pilot reported, had actually gone down over land on the return trip to Scotland. On the flight over Norway he had tried to find the landing area near Rjukan marked out by the Grouse party, but had failed to sight it in two runs; Rebecca, the locating mechanism, didn't work and maps were not clearly drawn.

The aircraft then started back toward Scotland, but unable to rise above a huge cloud because of icing on the wings, it plowed through the mist. The ice-laden rope connecting the plane to the glider then snapped and the glider vanished in the thick haze.

And there was no word at all from the second glider. Henniker finally managed to round up ten planes and sent them out at dawn to search for the three missing aircraft. And all during the day he and his intelligence colleagues, Welsh, Tronstad, and Wilson, sweated out every moment. At about 4 P.M., word came that all the search planes had returned.

Any sightings?

None.

At about this time, Sergeant Brittain glimpsed Colonel Henniker near the operations room, and knew immediately from his troubled expression that Operation Freshman had failed and he might never see his buddies again. If they didn't come back, how could he live with the fact that fate had singled him out to miss the mission?

Brittain, however, was still clinging to a thread of hope that perhaps some of the men had survived. If they had been taken prisoner, the Germans would almost surely treat them according to the Geneva Convention. Hitler was ruthless, of course, but his army was disciplined and professional.

•  •  •

General Falkenhorst's chief of staff was perplexed. How was the army in Stavanger and Egersund to act? he asked the general after informing him that two British aircraft had crashed in those areas and the survivors were in German hands. From their interrogations—and maps that were found at the sites—it was clear that the planes were headed for the heavy-water plant at Rjukan. The aim of the soldiers was obviously sabotage and not reconnaissance.

The general now had to face the difficult but expected moment of decision. He had already told his men that commando prisoners "must not survive more than twenty-four hours," thus backhandedly allowing more time than Hitler's order did. Should he now risk modifying the order still further?

Falkenhorst would claim at his postwar trial that he telephoned General Field Marshal Keitel in Berlin. Was there any flexibility in the fuehrer's order? he delicately asked, apparently failing to mention that he had already modified it slightly.

Keitel gave him "a very general answer and one which in no way changed the fuehrer's order."

Falkenhorst discussed his dilemma with his chief of staff and reached a critical decision. He would again alter Hitler's order to his commanders with these words: "Interrogation and examination" should be conducted "in a legal manner."

This order seemed to contradict Hitler's demand for executions that were illegal under the Geneva Convention. And indeed, the following day, Gestapo Chief Terboven reported to Berlin that Falkenhorst "had issued instructions which ran counter to the fuehrer's order."

He issued this edict, Falkenhorst would claim, "in order thereby to provide a last chance of circumventing the fuehrer's order." He had to risk Hitler's wrath if he were not to completely abandon his soldierly values. But as one German officer would quote him as saying: "Thank God we've nothing more to do with this filthy business."

Whether this quotation is accurate or not, it appears clear that Falkenhorst, feeling he had done what he could, conceded that the fate of the captured Britons was now in the hands of the Gestapo, which he did not control.

Why should he risk sharing that fate?

# 9

## THE METHODS OF MURDER

*November 1942–January 1943*

MAJOR GENERAL Karl Maria von Behren, commander of the Wehrmacht division at Stavanger, was greeted by a startling bit of news when he strode into his office shortly after 9 A.M. on November 20. A British aircraft had crashed in the village of Helleland near Egersund.

Who reported this? Behren asked Colonel Erwin Probst, his chief of staff.

The sheriff at Helleland, Probst replied. Captain Schutbergen, the 3rd Battalion deputy commander at Slettebo, had sent out a search squad to capture any survivors.

How many men were there in the aircraft? How many were wounded or taken prisoner? What was their mission?

Probst could not answer. He had no information yet.

Like General von Falkenhorst, Behren feared this British raid signaled the start of a full-scale invasion. His job was to prepare for one, and he was ready. But whatever the enemy mission, his military conscience, too, might now be sorely tested, for as Probst would remind him, Hitler's order was still in effect.

He should invoke it, Probst advised.

Behren offered no objection, he would admit at his trial after the war, though claiming to be deeply disturbed.

Falkenhorst had sent him a copy of the fuehrer's order, interpreting it to mean that prisoners should be interrogated "in a legal manner." Like the general, Behren, at fifty-two, was an old soldier eager to retire as soon as the war was over. He had had a distinguished military career and had apparently never sullied it with the murder of prisoners. Why sully it now? He was prepared to shoot every commando his men engaged in battle, but would turn over to the Gestapo those who surrendered. Whether the Gestapo dealt with them in a "legal manner" was not the Wehrmacht's business.

. . .

Sergeant Fritz Bornschein watched with curiosity as two army trucks pulled up to the prison in Slettebo and fourteen uniformed enemy soldiers, several of them badly wounded, were pulled or carried into the building, where they were placed in small cells. A cavalryman in charge of the stables in this camp, Bornschein had been strolling to the mess hall for lunch, but together with other soldiers in the camp, stopped at the prison to gawk at the prisoners—the first British they had seen in the war.

The guards were more than willing to keep the cell doors open so the men could satisfy their curiosity. How did so many British soldiers tumble into the German net? Bornschein, a straight-backed youth with dreamy eyes, full lips, and a rather haughty expression, almost envied the prisoners as they stood around in the cells while a doctor tended to the seriously wounded, who were lying on boards. These enemy soldiers, it seemed, would safely sit out the war and probably outlive their captors.

But Bornschein's envy soon dissipated. For during lunch, two Gestapo officers marched into the mess hall and called to attention the hundred and fifty or so men sitting at the tables. One of the officers, apparently *Obersturmbannfuehrer* Wilkens, the Gestapo chief in Stavanger, then addressed them in a commanding voice. He wanted volunteers for an unpleasant but essential task.

Bornschein and his comrades guessed what the task was: to execute the British prisoners. Otherwise, why would the Gestapo be involved? The sergeant had heard that these prisoners had survived a glider crash and that they were probably saboteurs. A case for the

Gestapo—or was it? Weren't the prisoners dressed in military uniform? Shouldn't they be prisoners of war? Bornschein thought so.

About twenty men, almost all privates, raised their hands. Bornschein was not one of them. He had never been a Nazi; in fact, he came from an anti-Nazi family. His father, a blacksmith from a village near Halle in eastern Germany, had belonged to the Social Democratic Party and lost his job as *bürgermeister* when Hitler came to power in 1933. The son was drafted into the army in 1939 and first saw combat in the battle for Norway a year later. He had asked to join a tank unit, but was assigned to the cavalry because of the experience he had working beside his father as a blacksmith. Now, realizing what was about to happen, he could hardly wait to get back to his horses, to be with living beings he could better understand.

Yet Bornschein felt the need to be a witness. Immediately after lunch, at about 2 P.M., he and two like-minded soldiers waited outside the prison and watched while two volunteers escorted a prisoner out. Captain Schutbergen, who stood by the door pointing to the left, barked, "This way!" and the Briton was led down a dirt road that passed through a rocky valley bordered by patches of forest.

As the man trudged along, with one guard in front of him and another behind, each with a rifle slung over his shoulder, Bornschein and his friends followed. If only the Briton suspected his fate, the observers whispered to each other. With only one man to his rear, he could make a dash for the forest just yards away and perhaps escape certain death.

After almost a mile, the party came to a small concrete hut used for storing ammunition, and the guards pushed the prisoner into it. Shortly, eight other German soldiers came from a nearby barracks, pulled the Briton out of the hut, took him to the foot of a small hill, and ordered him to face them. A sergeant in charge of the eight men then motioned to the prisoner to remove his army jacket. The execution squad would feel better if they were shooting a "saboteur" rather than a uniformed soldier.

The Briton now must certainly have known that he was to die.

But, almost mechanically, he obeyed, taking off his jacket slowly, sleeve by sleeve, as if struggling for every moment of life still left to him. There was no blindfold, no last words. The Germans lifted their rifles to their shoulders and at the cry, "Fire!" sprayed the victim with bullets. The sergeant then fired a round into the man's head to make sure he was dead, and ordered his squad to dump the body into a nearby pit.

About five minutes later, a second British soldier was marched to the execution site and suffered the same fate. And then a third and a fourth and finally all fourteen of them, each halted halfway there while the victim in front was being shot so he would not suspect that death awaited him, too. But not all the prisoners succumbed quietly to the inevitable. As one stood at the site, he pulled out a photo from his wallet and, waving it at the squad leader, begged him:

"Please don't shoot! This is my family, my wife and two kids. Have mercy!"

The squad members, clearly moved, started to put down their rifles, but the sergeant refused to look at the photo and ordered his men to get ready, then to fire.

He was especially angered by the refusal of several prisoners to remove their jackets. One of them was the last man shot; the most seriously wounded, he was carried to the blood-soaked hill on a stretcher and placed sitting against the rocky surface. The squad then fired.

After three hours of systematic murder, a truckful of Polish prisoners pulled up and loaded the bodies onto the vehicle, then rushed off to a nearby beach to bury them there.

Fritz Bornschein, who watched the men die, was nauseous. He went to see his Norwegian girlfriend, who would eventually become his wife, and told her: "What a horrifying experience I had today. I saw men being murdered in cold blood. I shall never forget the one trying to show a picture of his family to his executioner. I am ashamed to be in the German army."

The next morning he returned to his beloved horses, but their gentleness and passivity seemed only to accentuate the evil that deceptively lurked in the human character.

• • •

That afternoon between 4 and 4:30, while the British were being gunned down, Colonel Probst dutifully telephoned his superior, General Behren, and gave him a rather skimpy account of what was happening to the survivors of the glider crash in Helleland. The glider had clearly been on a sabotage mission, Probst said, for civilian clothes, Norwegian money, and small-arms ammunition had been found at the crash site. Therefore, he had ordered the 3rd Battalion to take action. But Probst offered no details, telling Behren, in effect, that he really didn't need to know what was happening. Whatever the general might suspect, why burden him with the knowledge that at this very moment his men were criminally violating the military code?

Behren would claim after the war that he didn't question Probst because his subordinate was thoroughly familiar with his views. Actually, before the executions Probst had called a high army official in Oslo, apparently General von Falkenhorst's chief of staff, and asked him what to do with the "saboteurs."

The fuehrer's order must be obeyed, the official replied.

But did he mean Falkenhorst's rather liberal interpretation of the order? Apparently uncertain, Probst consulted with Wilkens, the Gestapo chief, and it seems, tried to turn over the prisoners to him as Behren clearly wished. The two men made a deal: the Gestapo would cooperate with the Wehrmacht, but the Wehrmacht would carry out the executions. Since fourteen prisoners were to be killed, many men were needed to guard and shoot them and supervise their burial. And the Gestapo, a relatively small agency specializing in interrogation and torture, was seen as less suited for this mundane job. Nor was Probst worried about Behren's reaction; the general disliked dealing with matters of conscience and pretty much gave his deputy free rein to work out details.

That night, Behren had a visitor who was less concerned about piquing the general's moral sensitivities: Wilkens. He had interrogated the prisoners, the Gestapo chief said. They were then led out and shot.

Who ordered them shot? Behren asked, as if this atrocity had never occurred to him.

Captain Schutbergen, the deputy commander of the 3rd Battalion.

According to Behren, he was shocked. No one had informed him about the shooting and he was "very frightened." Why, he wanted to know, didn't Wilkens telephone him and request his permission for the 3rd Battalion to act? Then this would not have happened.

Wilkens didn't say so, but that was apparently the point. He had tried to phone Behren, he lamely argued, but was unable to get through to him.

Anyway, said Wilkens, the story had not ended. A second glider had struck a mountain near one of the fjords east of Stavanger shortly after the first one crashed. The general, he suggested, should send a squad to search for any survivors.

Behren, who deeply resented Wilkens's arrogance, agreed, but made it clear that any survivors would be turned over to the Gestapo. The Wehrmacht would not take responsibility for shooting any more prisoners.

Nor was Behren the only German leader infuriated by the haste with which the Britons were dispatched now that he knew the full truth. Whatever his chief of staff had told Colonel Probst, General von Falkenhorst reiterated his order, he would claim at his trial, that the Wehrmacht interrogate commando prisoners in a "legal manner in order thereby to provide a last chance of circumventing the fuehrer's order"—and then give the Gestapo the responsibility for carrying out the order. And Reich Commissioner Terboven and General Wilhelm Rediess, the Gestapo chief for all Norway, felt that the interrogation should have been more intensive, even if this meant delaying the executions.

Rediess, in fact, sent an urgent message to Berlin recounting the crash in Helleland and remarking that "unfortunately the Wehrmacht executed the survivors so clarification [of their mission] is no longer possible." Apparently Wilkens briefly interrogated the Britons before they were led to their death, but failed to find out the nature of their mission.

With the news that a second glider had crashed, however, spirits were revived. If some crew members had survived, the Germans would have a second chance to learn what the British were planning to do. In particular, why was the town of Rjukan circled on that silk map? Was there to be an attack on Norsk Hydro?

When nine men on this second glider were found to be alive, spirits soared even higher. Four would be taken to the Gestapo jail in Stavanger and five to Grini, a concentration camp outside Oslo. This time, none would be killed by the Wehrmacht—or even by the Gestapo—as long as anyone was physically capable of providing information.

■ ■ ■

The prisoners must be shot!

Gestapo chief Wilkens made this clear to Dr. Werner Fritz Seeling, who had just examined the prisoners. He had to report "completion" to his superiors by the next day in compliance with the fuehrer's special order.

Wilkens was in a sour mood, Seeling would later say. Four seriously injured Britons were locked up in the Gestapo prison in Stavanger and were in no condition to talk. Why keep them alive? But Wilkens's own agents defied him, refusing to shoot wounded men. Regardless, the Gestapo chief felt he would get the job done—if only he could finesse Seeling into playing the game.

It seemed he could not, however. Seeling, too, protested. In fact, he would claim, he vigorously argued that the prisoners be taken to a hospital.

They were saboteurs, Wilkens responded, according to the doctor. He "could not do anything except take them to the seashore and shoot them there." It was "regrettable, but there is no other course open."

The Gestapo leader paused for a moment, then muttered, as if prepared to compromise: "Can't you poison them?"

"Astonished" by this suggestion, Seeling would say he replied: "As a doctor, I [have] to help sick and wounded people, not to kill them."

Wilkens replied with a surly smile: "You doctors have put more than one person under the ground before now." Sentimentality, he added, had no place in war and, in any case, "you are only carrying out orders of a higher authority."

It may have been an order to him, Seeling would say he responded, "but not to me as a medical officer. Anybody . . . who knew that I had intentionally poisoned a human being would lose [his] esteem and confidence in me . . . forever."

"Rubbish!" Wilkens supposedly snapped, adding that Seeling held in his hands the more humane methods of killing a man. When the doctor remained silent, he grunted, "Then you will not do it?"

No, he would not, Seeling would claim he finally replied. Nor, he felt, did he have to obey the Gestapo. He was a doctor for the Luftwaffe, the air force, and was responsible only to his superiors in that branch of the service.

Well, then, Wilkens sneered, the prisoners would be shot at once. Seeling "visualized the wounded prisoners in their condition being loaded onto lorries, driven to a beach, having to stand upright with their injured limbs, and being shot. That a man could be shot lying on the ground did not come into my head at that time."

"Try for a moment to imagine the bodily and mental sufferings of these men," the doctor pleaded.

But "in a joking and disdainful voice," Wilkens replied, "You can first give them a blow with a mallet."

Seeling would say he was now convinced, as Wilkens had apparently foreseen, that the prisoners were doomed whether he helped the Gestapo chief kill them or not. He seems to have been equally convinced that even though the Gestapo did not officially control him, he could suddenly vanish in the night.

And Seeling, at thirty-four, was resolved to live out the war. He had a promising career ahead, having earned a medical degree at Leipzig University and served as a highly respected Luftwaffe doctor since 1939. While stationed in Stavanger, he became friendly with Gestapo men who were based near his medical station and treated many of them.

Now Wilkens was trying to exploit this friendship. And the doctor knew how his "friends" often settled scores. Actually, he was rather contemptuous of many of them. Rabble from lower-class families with little education—what did he have in common with them? Still, he had to humor them, to remain in their good graces. It was the prudent thing to do, even if he had to compromise his medical principles a bit for humanitarian purposes.

No, it wasn't necessary to use a mallet. He had a "better way" to ease the suffering of the prisoners, he said.

"What?" Wilkens asked.

"I might give a morphine injection to the wounded [to render them] unconscious. In this way they would know nothing of the frightening and worrying events around them."

Wilkens was delighted by this suggestion. Seeling had fallen into the trap.

An excellent idea, the Gestapo leader said. Now Seeling's conscience "would be allayed, and the prisoners too would benefit by the painlessness."

Seeling would say he then solemnly warned "that the wounded would not be able to stand upright for the executions after they had had morphine injections."

Wilkens laughed. Was Seeling "really so stupid or only trying to give that impression?" he asked. The doctor "only had to give the morphine injections and the rest could be left" to the Gestapo. Seeling took this to mean "that they could, of course, be shot lying down."

But shooting was still a problem for Wilkens, since some of his agents would still not cooperate, and he was reluctant to punish them for refusing to commit an atrocity, or to order others to do so, apparently because such action might cause a scandal in the military—especially after the reaction to the Slettebo murders.

Thus, shortly after Seeling had returned home, Wilkens's deputy called him and said that the captured Britons had "caused too much annoyance." Did Seeling have "any fast-working poison in the hospital or anything else with which [he] could poison them?"

No, he did not, the doctor would say he replied. He only had morphine to render them unconscious.

. . .

That evening, according to Seeling, he fetched two empty bottles labeled "Typhus–Impfstoff" and "Paratyphus–Impfstoff" and funneled into one of them several ampules of morphine with a hypodermic syringe. He then drove to the prison and climbed the stairs to the small cell, where the four prisoners, moaning in pain, lay stripped of their clothing on stretchers resting on the floor. The Gestapo agent escorting him tried to reassure them: they needn't worry, the doctor was just going to inoculate them for typhus. And they were shown the label on a bottle.

Seeling knelt down and injected each of the men in the arm. The two Germans then went downstairs to the prison office to wait for them to lose consciousness. But when they returned after almost an hour, together with more Gestapo agents, they saw that the morphine had had no effect whatsoever. Seeling then injected them with more morphine. Over an hour and a half passed—and still no effect. The victims simply groaned all the louder and one had a fit of coughing. Another shot of morphine and the patients finally fell asleep.

Inject more! the Gestapo man in charge ordered.

Seeling "then realized that they wanted me to poison the wounded men." He desperately tried to think of a way out of the situation," and finally said that he would have to get more morphine. According to the doctor, he went to his clinic and filled a bottle with distilled water, then returned to the prison and injected the men with the harmless liquid, pretending it was a deadly dose of morphine. This was apparently the only way to salve his conscience without provoking the Gestapo to commit another atrocity—on him.

Seeling and his Gestapo companions waited once more for the prisoners to die, but they simply continued to groan. These rattles of agony frayed the nerves of the death watchers, and everyone took turns pressing down on the chests of the wounded with either the open hand or the foot, a trick that seemed to deaden the terrible sounds.

One Gestapo man finally lost patience.

"Let's kill them now!" he cried.

And with a comrade's help, he placed a cord around a prisoner's neck and fastened the other end to a radiator. Then two men lifted the upper part of the victim's body about two feet off the floor while drawing the cord tight until he finally died of strangulation. A Gestapo witness would say at a war-crimes trial of those involved in the horrors that Seeling was one of the men lifting the body, though the doctor would deny this charge and claim he was a horrified bystander, wondering why the Gestapo didn't just shoot the victim.

Another prisoner, according to two witnesses, died when one of the Germans stamped on his throat, crushing his Adam's apple. Each of the witnesses would accuse the other of perpetrating this atrocity. One was a Gestapo driver, Erich Hoffmann, and the other, Dr. Seeling.

A third prisoner died, though the immediate cause was not clear. The prison jailer charged that Seeling had injected air into a vein, an accusation the doctor also denied.

There was still one prisoner alive; he simply refused to die. Gestapo chief Wilkens was furious. The next day, he phoned Seeling and said that the fourth man was to be moved from the prison to Gestapo headquarters.

"Will you come along and see if he is fit to be moved?" he added.

Seeling would insist he thought the man was simply going to be interrogated, though the previous day Wilkens had been eager to kill him instantly, together with his three comrades.

The doctor went to the prison, dressed the man, and helped him into a car they would share with the driver, Hoffmann, and a Gestapo agent, Otto Petersen. As they neared Gestapo head-quarters, Petersen, sitting beside the driver, whispered some words to him. The car pulled up at the building and Seeling, after helping the prisoner out, gently guided him to the door.

Petersen then ordered the doctor to wait in the car, and followed Hoffmann and the prisoner into the building. The Briton was told to descend a stairway leading to the cellar, and as the man hobbled down, Hoffmann, following the order that Petersen had whispered to him in the car, aimed a pistol at the back of the prisoner's head and fired. The victim pitched forward and rolled down the stairs, while Petersen followed to deliver a coup de grâce.

Outside in the car, Seeling heard two shots ring out. He was shaken, he would claim, for he had believed, or wanted to believe, the man was going to be interrogated. Yet he apparently felt a sense of relief, too. Those shots signaled the end of a horror story into which he had been shrewdly drawn by Gestapo chief Wilkens. Now he could go back to the business of saving lives, though there was one more life he would not be able to save—his own. After the war, he and Hoffmann were convicted of murder by a British military court and executed. Petersen would commit suicide before he could be tried.

The four murdered Britons had to be disposed of quickly, leaving no evidence. Their bodies were loaded onto a truck, driven to the quay, transferred to a motor boat, and dumped into the sea.

Jimmy Cairncross, one of the men, would now have to wait in heaven to embrace his dying father.

* * *

Meanwhile, in the Grini concentration camp near Oslo, the five comrades of the four murdered men, only slightly wounded, seemed to have little to moan about. Held in private cells, they were at first threatened with death by a Gestapo interrogator. But then the mood of the captors changed. A personable young man who spoke excellent English visited them and he was most sympathetic.

They had been captured wearing military uniforms, Gestapo agent Wilhelm Esser said, so, of course, they would be treated as prisoners of war and soon be sent to a POW camp in Germany. But meanwhile, he would ask them a few questions. This was routine for all prisoners of war.

True, except that the Germans did not regard these men as prisoners of war—not after maps were found near the crash sites indicating that the soldiers were en route to Rjukan. The British who had crashed at Helleland had all been killed before they could be seriously interrogated, and the four in Stavanger had been too badly wounded to be of much use. Now, only the five at Grini were left, and they had to talk. Was Rjukan their target or not? And if so, why?

Confirmation was absolutely vital, Gestapo headquarters in Oslo told Esser. And he seemed confident, taking pride in his ability to extract information from his prey without resorting to violence or torture, which apparently only stiffened their resistance. Besides, violence could lead to death before answers spilled out.

One by one, Esser confronted the men with "information" they presumably knew. The Germans were aware, he said, that they were headed for Rjukan to attack the heavy-water plant. Could they offer any details?

No, they couldn't, the prisoners said.

But Esser was patient, and over the next few weeks visited them often, asking questions in a warm, friendly manner. Gradually, it seems, they started to trust him and saw the logic in his argument: since German intelligence "knew" their target had been Rjukan, why should they not confirm this established fact—and speed up plans for their transfer to a POW camp?

The prisoners then apparently agreed that Rjukan was indeed the target. It is not clear if they revealed any further details of their mission.

Now, when would they be leaving Grini for the POW camp? they wanted to know. Only when they were transferred out of this Gestapo concentration camp would they feel reasonably secure, however kind and friendly some of their warders might be.

They would be leaving soon was the reply.

After almost two months, in mid-January 1943, the time finally came. They would be leaving, but not for Germany. Another Gestapo agent, Oscar Hans, received an order from headquarters: take the prisoners from Grini to Trandum, a nearby wood, for an important rendezvous.

Hans went with an interpreter to see the prisoners and gave them some good news: a special delegation had come from Berlin and would like to meet with them.

The prisoners must have been exhilarated, for this surely meant the long wait was over and they would shortly be sent to a POW camp in Germany. But for security reasons, Hans said, they would have to be blindfolded. Members of the delegation didn't wish to be identified.

The men understood. Fine. And they were led outside with their eyes covered to a waiting truck. On arriving at Trandum, they were lined up to await the arrival of the delegation. Finally, the command for attention rang out, and the prisoners stiffened their bodies as a mark of respect to the visiting dignitaries.

But only for a moment. The cry, "Fire!" followed, and the bodies crumpled to earth, to be buried in a mass grave that had been dug nearby with ghastly if pragmatic zeal.

Once the prisoners confirmed that their target had been Rjukan, it was time to carry out Hitler's special order. And so the last glider crash survivors had their rendezvous—with death.

# 10

## TRAINING TO DIE

### *November 1942–January 1943*

DESPERATION SWEPT THROUGH the halls of British intelligence when the search planes returned in the afternoon of November 20 without having spotted the three missing aircraft. The worst, it seemed, had happened. All but the crew of one of these aircraft may have been killed before they even reached the target.

General Wilson urgently met with Leif Tronstad. Operation Freshman had clearly failed, they agreed, and the only question was whether any of the men had managed to survive. Regardless, a new mission had to be launched without delay, whatever the cost. But what kind of mission? Should more British soldiers be put at such risk? Hitler himself seemed to answer this question. The following day, the Germans issued a terrifying communiqué:

> On the night of November 19–20th two British bombers, each towing one glider, flew into southern Norway. One bomber and both gliders were forced to land. The sabotage troops they were carrying were put to battle and wiped out to the last man.

Hitler might be bluffing, optimists in the knowledgeable strata of government felt, in order to smoke out a British response that might hint at the victims' objectives. But others, apparently including Churchill, took the fuehrer at his word. The prime minister asked

Lord Louis Mountbatten, chief of combined operations, to look into the question, and Mountbatten, after talking with the military chiefs of staff and other experts, concluded that Hitler was probably telling the truth. The terrible truth. In brutal violation of international law, he was executing enemy soldiers even if they wore military uniforms.

Mountbatten was in a quandary.

How, he asked, could any more British soldiers be sent on raids that spelled certain execution if they were captured, even if they didn't resist? And what if a soldier, in the hope of saving his life, revealed that Rjukan had been his aircraft's destination? The Germans would surely guess that Norsk Hydro was the target and speculate that the Allies were in a race to make an atomic bomb before Germany did.

Wilson and Tronstad agreed. And now there were only two ways left to demolish the heavy-water operation: bombing or sabotage. Tronstad still opposed bombing for fear of killing many civilians, but he favored using a team of Norwegian saboteurs familiar with the terrain. Especially since Dr. Brun had just arrived in London after his harrowing escape from Norway and could furnish minute details about the heavy-water installation.

Wilson approved, but if this plan also failed? Norsk Hydro would have to be bombed, whatever the civilian casualties. Better that a few die for a good cause than millions die for an evil one. Wilson then met with Major General Colin Gubbins, his superior in SOE, to solicit his support, but the general was "shocked" by the plan.

"You can't do that!" he exclaimed. "It's too difficult."

But for lack of a better plan, Gubbins finally agreed. Then both Mountbatten and Churchill backed the idea. And this time, apparently with the prime minister's approval, the Americans were notified that Norwegian commandos would attempt to sabotage Norsk Hydro. For General Groves was growing more impatient, and if he didn't know that the British had an attack plan of their own, he might go ahead and bomb.

Actually, the Americans were highly skeptical of the sabotage idea when they heard about it. Typically, when one agent of the

U.S. Office of Strategic Services (OSS) in London learned of it, he scoffed, according to another agent, "that this was some devious British scheme . . . to cover an ulterior . . . objective." The British didn't even have the common sense, or the courtesy, to consult with the Americans before deciding on the plan. How could it be a good one?

The answer, in part, would lie in the selection of the leader of the commando team.

• • •

Joachim Ronneberg was delighted when his commander at the SOE special training camp in western Scotland informed him that London headquarters had assigned him to lead what would apparently be one of the most important missions of the war. He had been urgently called from the sabotage class he was conducting for fellow Norwegian Resistance fighters and now wouldn't have to return to such unchallenging, rear-line duty. At last a combat role in the struggle to liberate his beloved Norway.

He must report to London headquarters at once, his commander said. With five men he would personally choose, he would return to Norway on a vital mission.

Where in Norway would they be sent? When would they be going? How would they be transported?

"I haven't the faintest idea, it's so secret," the commander replied.

"Before I pick the men," Ronneberg said, "I'd like to know whether we will be attacking the coast by boat or parachuting in from a plane. And are we to make our own way out to Sweden or the coast? Will it be necessary to be good on skis?"

"I can't really say," the commander replied, "but perhaps you should be good skiers."

Intrigued by the extraordinary secrecy, Ronneberg flew to London on December 3 and was soon sitting in Leif Tronstad's office.

"Where are we going?" he asked.

"To Vemork to blow up the heavy-water plant there," Tronstad replied succinctly. "You won't have much time for planning. But fortunately most has been done already. Four of our friends are already in Norway waiting for you. They were sent as a reception committee for the Freshman group, but you are going to take their place."

Ronneberg, who had known nothing about the true mission of Operation Freshman, was shocked on hearing that the operation had failed with such large losses. And he now realized he was being asked to lead his men on what could be a suicide mission.

Why was the mission so important that another terrible risk had to be taken?

Tronstad apparently did not offer any details, but he made it clear that the operation, code-named Gunnerside, could help to prevent an enemy victory.

Ronneberg was more zealous than ever as he contemplated the assignment—even though Tronstad told him that "the Germans know that an attack is being planned, since they found maps of the area and are building up their defenses."

When would his team be going?

"You ought to be ready to go by December 17, when the moon period starts. You have a fortnight to get ready."

Ronneberg would try his best to be ready. After all, the skill and daring of his commando team might determine the outcome of the war. Actually, though he didn't realize it, his burden would be even greater than it might have been only hours earlier. For the day before, December 2, American scientists proved decisively for the first time that an atomic bomb could be built, a finding that would sharply escalate the danger that Hitler might build one first.

• • •

It was the day the atomic pile at the University of Chicago nuclear laboratory would be poked and prodded to reveal whether the neutron was really the key to a bomb. On a balcony ten feet above a squash-court floor, which was slippery with graphite dust, Leo Szilard gazed at the crude reactor with about forty other scientists. Enrico Fermi, in charge of the project, barked orders to subordinates as he stood near the five hundred-ton pile of graphite bricks, stacked in fifty-seven layers, in which tiny cubes of uranium or uranium oxide were embedded. Two shifts of workers had labored sixteen days to build the sixteen-foot-high structure.

Long control rods, plated with the metallic element cadmium, were set up so they could be inserted into holes in the graphite and withdrawn. The graphite, like heavy water, would slow down neutrons emitted by the uranium and the cadmium would absorb them. As the control rods were withdrawn, fewer of the neutrons from the uranium would be absorbed, inducing greater fission. Finally, at some point of withdrawal, fission would produce neutrons faster than the cadmium would absorb them, and a chain reaction would result. If it started going out of control, a three-man "suicide squad" standing on a platform overhead would dump buckets of cadmium solution over the pile, and someone with an ax would cut the rope that would release the safety enclosure.

After a number of control rods were withdrawn, Fermi gave the order to an assistant to withdraw the final one: "Pull it to thirteen feet, George."

And he intently watched the meters that measured the neutron emission inside the pile. Not enough. Another foot. After several hours, at 3:25 P.M., the meters went crazy.

"This is going to do it!" Fermi exclaimed, his fingers working a slide rule to calculate the rate of fission, his eyes darting from dial to dial. Then his intense expression suddenly dissolved into a smile.

"The reaction is self-sustaining," he declared, calmly ushering in the nuclear age.

One scientist pulled the cork out of a bottle of Chianti, and Fermi sent for paper cups. Everyone realized at this ecstatic yet solemn moment that the world would never be the same again. Only Szilard, it seemed, was worried. What direction would the change take? he wondered. He realized that the Allies had to attempt building a bomb if only because the Germans might, but ironically, his fear was magnified now that the experiment made clear that it was in fact possible for them to do so. Once Germany was knocked out of the war two and a half years later, Szilard, who had fought so hard to build the bomb, would fight just as hard to save Japan from its fury, since it posed no nuclear danger.

When the party was over, Szilard and Fermi stayed behind and shook hands.

"This day," Szilard lamented, "will go down as a black day in the history of mankind."

And the day might never end if someone didn't stop Hitler from forging a bomb before time ran out. How much time remained? Hardly had the Chianti been consumed when Eugene Wigner "proved" to his shocked colleagues on a blackboard that the fuehrer could have the weapon by December 1944.

●  ●  ●

Joachim Ronneberg didn't know anything about the atom, but he was determined to stop Hitler from making whatever weapon it was that threatened to spell catastrophe for the Allies. He could not have imagined he would be burdened with such a responsibility when he started on his journey with a more simple goal: to help liberate his small country.

Born in the picturesque fishing port town of Alesund, Ronneberg, before the German occupation, had worked for his father's 125-year-old shipping company, which exported fish and coal and was a cornerstone of the town's economy. He enjoyed his job, though he could hardly wait for the weekend, when he would climb the tallest mountains around and ski through pine-dotted valleys inhabited only by reindeer and a few hermit hunters. He had the ruddy looks and lanky bearing of the sportsman—and commando. His high-cheekboned face with slightly squinting eyes and determined jaw bore a striking resemblance to that of film star Clint Eastwood.

Shortly after the Germans invaded Norway, Ronneberg, twenty-three, arranged for one of his fishermen to take him to the Shetland Islands, then for a flight to London in a British plane. He knew he would be executed if caught, as hundreds of other fugitives were, but what worried him most was what the Germans might do to his parents if he left.

To reduce the danger, Ronneberg gave two letters to a friend for delivery to his parents. One was to be given them immediately, stating that he was "going west." The second letter would be delivered a week after he departed and would say that he had been offered a job building barracks for the Germans in "another place." After a week, his parents could report him missing and, he hoped, escape retaliation. He departed without saying good-bye to them, fearing they would try to talk him out of leaving.

Later, Ronneberg would learn that the Germans had begun arresting the families of all fugitives—and that his father had in fact been imprisoned. But even if he had known about this danger before he left, he would say, he'd have gone.

"I owed it to my country to fight the Nazis at any cost," he told me in Alesund. "My parents would understand."

Once in Britain, Ronneberg volunteered for SOE work and underwent training in various camps. He became so proficient in the ways of the commando and saboteur that he would soon become the chief instructor at the Scottish camp. Now, with his first combat assignment, he returned there to prepare for it. He immediately selected the five men who would share with him the joy—and danger—of the mission.

He chose as his second-in-command Lieutenant Knut Haukelid, a muscular, highly intelligent man from a prominent Norwegian family that included the famous actress Sigrid Gurie, his twin sister. The director of a company that imported American machinery before the war, Haukelid fought against the German invasion, then made a living hunting and fishing until the Resistance sought his services. He radioed information about German activities to Britain and, with his comrades, even plotted to kidnap the Norwegian traitor, Prime Minister Vidkun Quisling, take him to London, and display him in Picadilly Circus for a shilling a look. The plot was thwarted, however, when the Germans arrested Haukelid, though he managed to escape. Eventually, he crossed into Sweden and was flown by the British to England.

The daring Haukelid was happy to join Operation Gunnerside, especially after being scratched from the Grouse mission because he had accidentally shot himself in the foot. But he was less happy to take orders from the man who recruited him, even though respecting his ability. At twenty-nine, he was six years older than Ronneberg and had considerably more military experience. Didn't experience and seniority count for anything? Still, his country came first and he would conquer his pride and suppress his yearning for glory. What was more important than avenging the atrocities of those last days of resistance against the German invasion?

"The Germans set fire to all farms as they advanced," he would later write. "It was a warning to us. Wherever they met resistance everything should be burned. The civilians who refused to leave their homes were shot, and all livestock was burned to death. We swore then that we would never give in—not even if the Germans won the war."

And so he would fight the Germans in whatever role he might be assigned, even under an officer he regarded as junior to him. In the end, history would remember him as a hero of Norway's liberation.

Sergeant Fredrik Kayser, twenty-four, another Gunnerside choice, didn't have to cast aside his pride. He was proud to serve under Ronneberg, though he, too, had considerable military experience. Wishing to fight the communists, he had volunteered for duty with a Norwegian company in Finland when the Soviet Union invaded that country in 1939. He returned to Norway upon the Finnish surrender, only to find himself fighting the Germans until his own homeland surrendered. Then, like Ronneberg, he hitched a ride in a fishing boat to the Shetland Islands, from where the British flew him to London. Kayser was soon training to use explosives in the Scottish SOE camp under Ronneberg, who recognized that his pupil, a deceptively slender, gentle young man, was, in fact, tough and athletic and had the iron will necessary for a "suicide" mission.

Sergeant Hans Storhaug was another man whom Ronneberg fully trusted, being a soldier of uncommonly common sense, an attribute suspended only once when he illegally killed a pheasant and was dragged to military headquarters by an angry gamekeeper, earning the nickname, "the Chicken."

Soft-spoken and somewhat introspective, Sergeant Birger Stromsheim was an extremely courageous soldier who won the respect and confidence of his comrades with the authority not of voice, but of knowledge.

Perhaps the most emotional of the men was Lieutenant Kasper Idland, who was almost fanatically determined to strike a personal blow at the Germans, and didn't even consider the possibility of returning alive. The blow would be so great that he himself could not escape the mortal storm it would generate. Now he was elated that Ronneberg was offering him a chance to strike such a blow, though he worried that he might slow up his comrades, who were far better skiers than he.

Almost immediately, the six commandos of Gunnerside were busy training at a special secret camp, Number 17, where a wooden model of the Norsk Hydro heavy-water plant had been built in a small building, complete with the eighteen high-concentration cells that turned out the substance. Over and over, the men practiced laying charges, handling explosives, fashioning detonators, timing themselves down to the last split-second. They also studied aerial photographs and diagrams of every building, every German military station, almost every square yard of terrain in the area.

What the men didn't know was that Dr. Brun, now code-named Sverre Hagen, had set up and directed this program from behind the scenes. They could not be told, since the Gestapo might force them to reveal his presence in Britain if they were captured, and members of his family left behind in Norway could be punished. Still, the commandos realized that some mysterious expert was behind this training effort, since Leif Tronstad, whose knowledge of Norsk Hydro had been considered unmatched, often had to seek answers to their questions from some unidentified source.

Brun knew all the answers.

Was every steel door to the heavy-water plant locked?

Yes, but they could crawl through a cable duct that led to a basement room adjoining the room with the high-concentration cells.

Should explosives be used to break down a door?

No, the Germans, alerted, would attack before the explosives could be set.

Where could one hide if he was cut off or wounded?

Behind a tool shed outside the gate or in the cable duct leading to the heavy-water room.

Brun knew where the guards stood, when they would be relieved. He knew where charges in the heavy-water room would cause the maximum damage.

Finally, after conferring with Brun, Tronstad, recommended a way to approach and withdraw from the target. The men would land in the mountains, make contact with Grouse, which would henceforth be called "Swallow" (though, unofficially, members would continue to refer to their unit as "Grouse"), and then descend on the north side of the valley near the village of Vaaer. They would then cross the Maana River about halfway between Rjukan and Vemork, climb to the railway track, and follow it to the plant. Avoiding detection by about fifteen guards, they would enter the heavy-water room, set the charges, and withdraw by the same route. Most of them would make their way to Sweden on skis while others would join Einar Skinnarland and set up a new radio station in the mountains.

After the final briefing, the saboteurs were taken to Farm Hall, SOE's Training School Number 6, a heavily bugged station for foreign agents who were going to Europe on secret missions and were waiting for planes. Haukelid would write that "a number of servicewomen kept the house in order, cooked the meals, and gave the boys some social life. . . . But if we asked the Fannies about our comrades who had gone out before us, they became dumb and knew nothing."

Still, shortly before the men were to leave on their historic mission, Tronstad clearly alluded to what happened to some of these comrades when he evoked the memory of those who had vanished in Operation Freshman:

> You should realize that the Germans will not under any circumstances take prisoners. For the sake of those who have gone before, and who are now dead, I ask you to do your best to make the operation a success. You all know how important it is, that what you are doing now will live in Norway's history and be remembered a hundred years from now.

Underlining the price of failure, each man was issued a cyanide pill enclosed in a rubber capsule, which would stick to the roof of the mouth. When bitten, it would bring death within three seconds. Whatever information the Gestapo had managed to squeeze out of its British captives, its torture chamber must not this time echo with the groans of men desperately seeking to suppress the cry, "Rjukan!"

# 11

## REUNION IN PARADISE

*November 1942–February 1943*

SHORTLY AFTER the Freshman disaster, Knut Haugland, the Grouse radio operator, was skiing along a mountain road about twenty miles from Rjukan when he suddenly felt severe stomach cramps and bounded into some roadside bushes to relieve himself. As he squatted down with his pants around his ankles, he heard voices echoing in the cold air and observed through the brush, only a few feet away, a group of green-uniformed men skiing down the road. German soldiers.

They seldom ventured into the mountains. What were they doing here now? Then Haugland realized that they were seeking people who might be connected with Operation Freshman—people like himself! Luckily, he had consumed the soup that Jens Poulsson had cooked the evening before—reindeer ribs, windpipe, brains, eyes, and fat, all splashed with reindeer stomach content and garnished, inadvertently, with reindeer hairs. If that evil brew had not made him sick and forced him to leap into the bushes, the Germans would probably have seen him and killed him on the spot. He had never felt such appreciation for Poulsson's culinary skills.

Not every Norwegian guerrilla was as fortunate. After a false air-raid alarm, the two to three hundred German troops stationed in Rjukan searched every house in that town and neighboring areas and arrested scores of people, including Torstein Skinnarland, a vital Grouse contact who had been supplying Grouse with food and supplies. The Germans apparently did not suspect Torstein himself, but hoped through him to find his elusive brother, Einar, who was still gathering information about heavy-water production and communicating it to London from some hidden mountain hideout. They apparently thought—correctly—that Einar had helped pave the way for Operation Freshman with his messages, but they could never find him.

The Germans were caught with their own pants down by the thwarted attack. General Rediess, the Gestapo chief in Norway, warned Berlin that there were "several indications that the British placed great importance on the destruction of Vemork's heavy-water installations." And General von Falkenhorst and Reich Commissar Terboven personally swept into Norsk Hydro to inspect those installations.

The plant must be better guarded, they demanded. And it was. More soldiers were placed in strategic places, with Germans replacing the less reliable Austrians; many more mines were planted in the area; and floodlights were set up, brightly illuminating the whole complex. Even an insect, it seemed, wouldn't have gone unnoticed.

Meanwhile, Jens Poulsson, forced to boil dangerously exotic soups to keep his men alive, was happy to hear that another group of men, fellow Norwegians this time, would soon be dropped at a new landing area. Since they knew how to ski and to move around the country undetected, he was sure they would stand a far greater chance of surviving than would the British.

"London's radio message about the glider disaster was a hard blow," Poulsson would later write in his diary. "It was sad and bitter, especially as the weather in our part of the country improved during the following days. But we were happy to hear that another attempt would be made in the next moon period."

That would be around Christmas 1942, in about a month. Too long. His men had suffered enough, being stranded for weeks in the wilderness, surviving on the remnants of the food they brought along, chance encounters with reindeer, Iceland moss buried in the snow, and what they could scrounge in hunters' huts they broke into, perhaps some oats, margarine, and sugar. The men lost strength and grew thin, though Claus Helberg and Arne Kjelstrup would suddenly swell with edema, gaining about twenty pounds and getting up about six times a night to urinate.

One day all except Poulsson himself were flat on their backs in a hut they had occupied high in the mountains on a patch of land called Svensbu. Too ill or weak to get out of bed, they could at least keep warm here, for there was a birch forest nearby, which offered ample firewood.

Don't worry, Poulsson told them, he was going out to bag a reindeer.

But how could a man so weak hunt down the elusive reindeer? Poulsson was confident he could, for he had gone reindeer hunting in this region many times before the war. The fog was thick, however, and he was only strong enough to reach the nearest peak. But though he failed that day, he tried again the next, and returned that night, Christmas Eve, smiling in triumph while dragging a reindeer behind him. He had finally shot it after a long, stealthy, frustrating chase in which a herd of the animals kept evading him before he was able to trap one in his sights. With unbounded joy, the men—unbathed, bearded, and sickly—sat down for a holiday feast, grateful to Santa Claus for perhaps sacrificing one of his own.

But the festivities ended early, at about 4 P.M., when darkness descended, for they had no paraffin for their lamp. As usual, they then lay in bed and took turns lecturing on any subject that came to mind so they wouldn't have to think about tomorrow, or some other day soon, when, weak as they were, they would join their Gunnerside comrades in the long-awaited suicide attack on Norsk Hydro. Though the men knew the attack was of critical importance, months of hunger, fatigue, and isolation blurred its implications in the minds of some; instead, survival from minute to minute dominated their consciousness.

Thus, not all were certain how they would react when the time for action came. As Poulsson would later write:

The mountains were big and the difficulties many. The mission was not tempting. There were enough excuses, in case it didn't get carried out. Nobody would ever know about it if we chose to be weak and hide. Deep inside was uncertainty. What really was the purpose of all this? Why should we have to suffer in the mountains? Did we really have a chance to succeed and get away alive? Sometimes I felt like giving up. But I didn't. I never spoke about my doubts.

Certainly not on Christmas Eve.

Actually, the Gunnerside team had been scheduled to land in Norway on Christmas Eve, when the Germans would presumably be less alert, but the operation was postponed because of poor weather. Storm followed storm, and the Grouse men were virtually confined to their hut as blinding blizzards whistled past, threatening, it seemed, to wrench the hut from its foundations before burying it under a mountain of snow.

• • •

**M**eanwhile, in London, British intelligence was not inclined to take unnecessary chances after the Freshman disaster. The moonlight period passed and so it wasn't until January 22 that the Gunnerside team finally climbed into a plane and sped off into a moonlit sky.

The men pondered with some foreboding what was apparently meant to be an encouraging farewell remark by Leif Tronstad: they probably had a fifty-fifty chance of success and a fair one of returning to Britain alive.

A fair chance? Was this a soothing way of saying that, like the Freshman commandos, they were probably doomed?

Despite such trepidation, there was quiet joy in the aircraft as the men headed toward home. Knut Haukelid, one of the men aboard, would write:

The hum of the powerful engines rose and fell, and . . . conversation was almost impossible. For that matter, no one wanted to talk. We sat on our parachutes and packs of equipment or silently jostled for the one tiny peephole that gave us a view over the North Sea. In a little while we should cross the Norwegian coast. . . . A fishing boat flashed her lamp at us as we passed overhead, no doubt recognizing the mysterious aircraft which came and went on moonlit nights. That glimpse of the surf had been like a greeting from the land, and now the boat's lamp imparted a feeling of comradeship with the first Norwegians we had met on our way home.

As was the custom of aircraft entering Norway on secret missions, we flew higher over the coastal belt and descended very rapidly farther inland. Then, so that the German radar stations should not keep track of us, we plunged right down and set our course along the valleys. There was the snow, the forests and the mountains, which we had so sorely missed during our time in England. Never had the country been so beautiful.

As the Gunnerside men were savoring the spectacular aerial view of their homeland, London radioed the Grouse men to prepare for the rendezvous. Thus, they quickly skied to frozen Lake Saure, where their comrades would soon be floating down by parachute. Suddenly, there was a familiar rumble in the distance.

"They give a red light," Poulsson would later report in his broken English, "I get the flare with white light going and point it at the invisible plane, judging its location by the roar of the motor.

" 'They've come at last!' I think.

"But nothing happens. The plane disappears westward and the humming fades. We let the lights burn for fifteen minutes, but the plane has definitely gone. Disappointment."

There was disappointment, too, in the invisible plane, as Haukelid would report:

Our pilot was unable to find the reception committee which was waiting for us down below. We cruised backwards and forwards . . . and had to go right out to the coast to take our bearings afresh. But it was no better the second time, and we could see no light signals. . . . The pilot would not let us jump blind, and we were forced to turn back. It was heartbreaking.

Especially since the team would have to wait almost a month for the next moon. Finally, on February 16, the day came. And this time the men would parachute, whether or not they saw or communicated with Grouse.

. . .

"Do you know where we are?" Joachim Ronneberg asked Knut Haukelid when they had disentangled themselves from their parachutes.

"We may be in China for all I know," Haukelid replied. "I don't know this place."

All any of the men knew was that they had landed on the Hardanger Plateau, the wildest mountain area in northern Europe, a place where reindeer roamed but where no human being would dare reside. Still, Ronneberg thought that, by chance, they may have come down on ice-surfaced Lake Saure, where they were to meet Grouse. But then he noticed branches protruding from the snow, and they were firmly rooted in the ground. Couldn't be a lake.

The pilot of the plane flying them from Britain had obviously dropped them far from their target, and they had no idea where their Grouse comrades were. Would they die of exposure before they found them? The air was frigid, and the wind was so strong that the boxes of equipment dropped with them bumped down the long, low-lying hills after hitting the snow and ice. When Birger Stromsheim ran after one and caught it, he was carried along with it until he and his burden fell into a crevice in the ice. Fortunately, a comrade rescued him.

Finally, one man who had reconnoitered came running back with what seemed to be life-saving news: he had found a cabin nearby. The commandos buried most of their equipment in the snow, using sticks as markers, and trudged to the hut, which belonged to some absentee hunter, breaking in by loosening the door frame with an axe. Exhausted, they changed into the owner's best nightwear and went to sleep in his bed or on the wooden floor.

A few hours later, in the afternoon, Gunnerside set out on the great search for Grouse, with Ronneberg using his compass to calculate where Lake Saure might be. But shortly, a storm howled through the mountains, and the men, blinded in the blizzard, could no longer find their way.

"We've got to go back," Ronneberg groaned.

The men turned around, but the farther they marched the less familiar was the white-blanketed landscape, and Ronneberg began to fear they would freeze to death in this barren wilderness, perhaps miles from their starting point. But then he stumbled into some obstruction that he couldn't even see. It was a wall—the hunter's cabin!

"If we had passed just a few yards to the side, we might never have been seen again," Ronneberg would later tell me.

He chilled at the thought that his mission might have failed because of those few yards. The four commandos, reunited, could only wait now for the extremely violent storm to lose its rage so they could once again continue their search for Grouse.

Finally, after three days, the storm abated, and the team prepared to leave, now armed with a map they found in the cabin. They were, the map showed, in Skrykenvann, about twenty miles from Lake Saure. Having depleted their supply of food, they skied back to the "depot" to retrieve the rest, searching through the heavy snowdrifts as if digging for gold, and, with their rucksacks full, returned to the cabin.

As they were about to leave on their mission on February 22, the group, to their surprise, saw a man skiing toward the cabin while pulling a sled with a dead reindeer tied to it. In alarm, they dashed behind the hut. Was he the owner? They couldn't trust anybody. The man moved with an ease and casual gait that suggested he knew exactly where he was going and was used to going there. As he approached the door, he noticed fresh ski tracks in the snow and apparently suspected that he was not alone. He paused. Suddenly, the commandos grabbed him and he turned pale.

"Seldom have I seen anyone more terrified," Knut Haukelid would say. "And it was hardly surprising, for, in the middle of the Hardanger Plateau, he had been seized by six bearded men in uniform."

The men dragged the stranger inside and searched him. They found a fat wallet packed with three thousand Norwegian kroners and cards showing his name and address: Kristian Kristiansen from the nearby valley town of Uvdal.

"What are you doing in the mountains?" Ronneberg asked.

"I've come to hunt reindeer," Kristiansen replied. "As you can see, I have one on my sled."

He often stayed in this cabin, even though he did not own it. Nobody was there, so why shouldn't he break in?

What would he do with all the meat? someone asked, suspecting he was a poacher.

After considerable prodding, the man admitted that he sold reindeer meat on the black market. These were hard times and he had to make a living.

"Are you a member of the NS [Quisling's Nazi party]?" Ronneberg wanted to know.

Kristiansen's face grew ashen. Who were these men? He didn't seem to recognize the uniform, and they spoke Norwegian like natives. But the only soldiers in Norway were Germans. After hesitating, he replied: "Well, I'm not exactly a member, but that's the party I support."

Was he quite sure? Haukelid asked.

Yes, the man mumbled, he was known to be a supporter of the NS, though he had never joined it.

Kristiansen apparently didn't realize that he might have signed his death warrant. His captors now moved to a corner to decide if he had.

He must be shot, most of them argued, for had he not declared himself an NS man? Ronneberg was one of the skeptical, especially since he, as the leader, would normally be the executioner. Kasper Idland, apparently noting the pain in his eyes, called Ronneberg outside. Convinced that the Gunnerside team could not escape death, Idland felt his comrades must not risk dying in vain because Kristiansen, once freed, might inform on them. Yet was it fair to saddle Ronneberg with the responsibility for the killing when he was at least hopeful of surviving and didn't want this man's blood on his conscience?

"Joachim," Idland said, "I'll shoot him for you."

"That's not the question," Ronneberg lamely replied. "We couldn't do it here, anyway. The owner of the cabin might find the remains. It would be indecent of us."

Idland realized that Ronneberg would not easily agree to the execution. As the two men joined the others, Knut Haukelid said he had a feeling that the poacher "was so frightened that he did not know what he was saying, and that he was professing to be an NS man because he thought we were Germans."

Ronneberg clearly felt relieved by this possibility, and all agreed that Kristiansen should be put to a test. Haukelid asked him: could his neighbors in Uvdal confirm that he had Nazi sympathies?

Kristiansen was taken aback by this question, finally replying: "I've so many enemies down there that they're sure to say I'm not a Nazi, just to make things difficult for me."

"The situation was clear," Haukelid would later say. "The man was afraid, and had not the courage to stand by his opinions."

The commandos then told Kristiansen the truth: they, too, were Norwegians. But it took them some time to finally convince him.

In sudden glee, he cried, according to Haukelid: "Lord, but it's grand to see you men!"

Ronneberg, however, wasn't so sure he could trust his fellow Norwegian. And he had the ammunition to blackmail him. He found a list of black-market patrons in his pocket and he would ask him to sign it. What's more, the poacher revealed to the men where he had hidden his hunting rifle, and the Germans did not permit civilians to own firearms.

If he dared inform on them, Ronneberg warned, the Germans would be handed this incriminating evidence.

But despite a lingering uneasiness, the men now saw how Kristiansen could serve them—as a human compass. Since he knew every nook and cranny of the region, he could help lead them to the Grouse group.

After feasting on chunks of Kristiansen's reindeer meat, the Gunnerside men decided that Kristiansen would pull the sled, now loaded with explosives and supplies, to make sure he wouldn't flee. They then put on their skis and set out into the night. The storm had finally settled into an arctic tranquillity and the moon shone brightly, illuminating the way over hills of cottonlike snow and through pine woods dripping with white crystal.

When the sun finally rose on the morning of February 23, the cotton seemed to dissolve into copper and then into gold. What a splendid Norwegian morning, a perfect day for skiing and hunting reindeer and grouse and enjoying all the beauty and majesty of life in this country. Yes, they had come home—but, ironically, to enjoy this life for perhaps one day. For now they were hunting for a different Grouse—their comrades. And when they found them, all would march together to almost certain death. Meanwhile, they would savor a final flash of ecstasy before leaving this heaven for one they didn't know.

The men stopped off at a hut that Kristiansen said belonged to his brother-in-law and, with the little paraffin they had, cooked a breakfast of oatmeal, powdered eggs, and coffee. Resuming their quest, they were about to traverse a rather steep slope when one man suddenly sighted a tiny dot, like a bug on a wall, edging down the great white valley below.

"There's someone on skis over there," Ronneberg cried, pointing toward the dot, which was swiftly maturing into a human figure.

The men threw themselves behind nearby boulders and peered at the figure. Terror once more seized Kristiansen, and he burrowed his way into the snow trying to hide from a new perceived disaster.

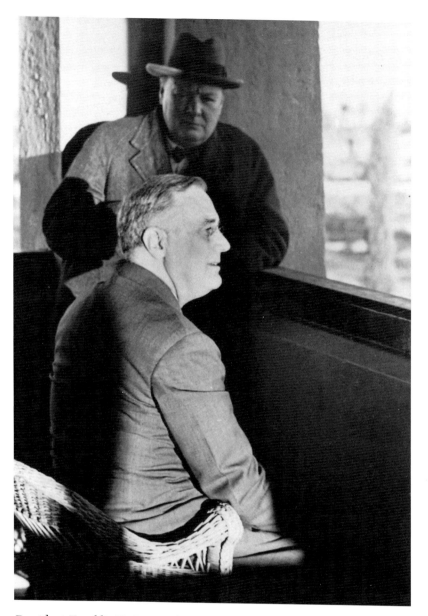

President Franklin D. Roosevelt and Prime Minister Winston Churchill co-operated in building a bomb, but only after a bitter struggle over how much scientific information they would share. (*National Archives*)

Nuclear scientist Leo Szilard, with the help of Albert Einstein, persuaded President Roosevelt to build an atomic bomb before the Germans could. Szilard played a vital role in its construction, but found himself in constant conflict with General Groves over how to run the project. (*Egon Weiss*)

French nuclear scientist Frédéric Joliot-Curie and his assistants helped to smuggle Norway's heavy water into France, then into Britain, before the Germans could get their hands on this precious substance. (*CEA/Jahan, Paris*)

Werner Heisenberg, Germany's greatest nuclear scientist, was running in a dead heat with Allied scientists in the race for an atomic bomb when his heavy-water nuclear reactor exploded. He tried to siphon enough additional heavy water from Norway's Norsk Hydro plant to build another one, but Allied attacks thwarted the effort. (*German Information Office, New York*)

General Nikolaus von Falkenhorst, commander of German forces in Norway (*left*), speaking with Norwegian Nazi leader Vidkun Quisling. Falkenhorst, more a proud militarist than a Nazi, expressed admiration for British and Norwegian commando techniques. (*U.S. Army*)

LEFT: James D. Cairncross, a British commando, was captured by the Germans when his glider crashed into a mountain. His captors poisoned him and three other survivors before throwing their bodies into the sea. (*R. A. de G. Sewell*)

RIGHT: Leif Tronstad, a Norwegian physicist, worked with British intelligence on plans to destroy the heavy-water plant. (*Einar Skinnarland*)

Florence Kurzman, the author's wife, marks the spot on Benkafjellet, a mountain where a British glider crashed, killing its seven passengers, commandos on their way to attack the heavy-water plant. In 1993, pieces of the plane were still visible. (*Dan Kurzman*)

Thorvald Flygjesdal's farm, where British commandos who survived one of the glider crashes were hidden before the Germans captured and murdered them. (*Bjorn Egil Widvik Bjelland*)

IN MEMORY OF
FOUR ROYAL ENGINEERS
1st BRITISH AIRBORNE DIVISION:

1872832 L/CPL. T. L. MASTERS
2110314 CPL. J. D. CAIRNCROSS
2010213 DRV. P. P. FARRELL
1892979 SPR. E. J. SMITH

THEY WERE ON OPERATION FRESHMAN – A MISSION
TO DESTROY THE HEAVY WATER PLANT AT VEMORK.
THEIR GLIDER CRASHED IN FYLGJESDAL 20 NOV. 1942.
AFTER BEING TORTURED TO DEATH BY THE GESTAPO
IN STAVANGER, THEY WERE THROWN IN THE SEA
NEAR KVITSØY — THEY WERE NEVER FOUND.

FOR YOUR TOMORROW – WE GAVE OUR TODAY

ERECTED 8TH OF MAY 1985

Stavanger residents built this monument to four British commandos who were murdered after being captured on their mission. (*Bjorn Egil Widvik Bjelland*)

A view of the heavy-water plant perched on a high cliff in Rjukan-Vemork. (*Kjell Nielsen*)

Norwegian saboteurs who attacked or planned the attack on the heavy-water plant. *Sitting, left to right:* Jens Anton Poulsson, Leif Tronstad, Joachim Ronneberg; *standing, left to right:* Hans Storhaug, Fredrik Kayser, Kasper Idland, Claus Helberg, Birger Stromsheim. (*Claus Helberg*)

Norwegian saboteurs meet in 1993. *Sitting, from left:* Claus Helberg, Birger Stromsheim, Joachim Ronneberg, Fredrik Kayser; *standing, from left:* Hans Storhaug, Rolf Sorlie, Arne Kjelstrup, Knut Lier-Hansen. (*Claus Helberg*)

Arne Kjelstrup (*Arne Kjelstrup*)

Joachim Ronneberg led
Norwegians in a raid on
the heavy-water plant.
(*Arne Kjelstrup*)
Team members included:

Fredrik Kayser
(*Fredrik Kayser*)

Birger Stromsheim
(*Claus Helberg*)

Kasper Idland
(*Claus Helberg*)

Jens Anton Poulsson, who led an advance team of saboteurs. (*Claus Helberg*)

Norwegian radio operators Knut Haugland and Einar Skinnarland kept London headquarters in touch with the saboteurs. (*Knut Haugland and Einar Skinnarland*)

Knut Haukelid, seen here with his twin sister, film star Sigrid Gurie, served as a commando under Joachim Ronneberg and also led an assault on the ferry carrying heavy water destined for Germany. (*Bodil Haukelid*)

The heavy-water plant at Norsk Hydro in November 1943 after the American bombing. (*Claus Helberg*)

That was a German and he was after him, the poacher was sure. Fearing that the prisoner might try to flee even though he was restrained by a leash, Ronneberg removed the man's skis. He then called Haukelid over and asked him to look at the "bug" through binoculars. Was that a German . . . or perhaps a Grouse man?

Haukelid knew the Grouse commandos well, having trained with them over a long period. He lay on the snow and gazed at the figure, who was now only about two hundred yards away. Then he saw a second one about a hundred yards behind the first one.

"There are two of them," Haukelid said.

"Well, do you recognize them?" Ronneberg asked.

Haukelid didn't. The two figures were so heavily clothed and bearded that they were unrecognizable. The Gunnerside men skied up a lower slope and took turns scanning the area through binoculars.

"Go and find out who those men are," Ronneberg said. "If they are strangers, just say you're a reindeer hunter."

Haukelid removed his rucksack, put a pistol in his belt under his camouflage suit, and started toward the hillock where the two men were standing. Ten minutes later, after climbing the slope from their rear, he found himself about fifteen yards behind them. He leaned on his ski poles, breathing in the clear air and marveling for a moment at the great panorama of white emptiness that stretched to a blue infinity. His heart pounded. Were the strangers friends or enemies?

With one hand gripping the pistol under his camouflage suit, Haukelid coughed loudly and the strangers wheeled around, also with pistols in their hands. Haukelid exchanged stares for a moment with two hollow-eyed, yellow-complexioned men with unkempt beards. Suddenly, cries of joy echoed through the valley as Claus Helberg and Arne Kjelstrup embraced Haukelid in a frenzy of emotion.

The heaven up there would find this a tough act to follow.

# 12

## PRELUDE TO GLORY

*February 1943*

"**YOU CAN HAVE THE MEAT** either roasted or boiled, or boiled or roasted, according to your taste and fancy," said Jens Poulsson with mock earnestness between ecstatic puffs on his pipe, which was newly packed with tobacco brought from England.

The Gunnerside men didn't care how their reindeer meat was cooked, as long as eyes, brains, blood, stomach contents, and other unappetizing delicacies were kept off the plate. One would have to be starving to consume them, thought the more finicky newcomers, who now realized how hungry their Grouse companions must have been to throw these indigestible parts into their staple diet.

But no one starved on this night of February 23. The guests had brought with them raisins, chocolate, and other goodies that their hosts had tasted only in their dreams. It was a feast to savor, complete with spirited talk about old friends and colleagues in England, about recent miseries and joys and hopes for the future—though all realized there might not be one.

"Jens put a few wet sticks into the stove," Haukelid would say, describing the warm atmosphere while tempering his description with gusts of adversity. "The stove was hot now, so the wood dried quickly and burned well. A small paraffin lamp threw a faint light on the faces round it. Floor and walls were covered with reindeer skins, but the cold seeped through nevertheless."

The commandos, for all their exhilaration, were exhausted, especially the Gunnerside men, who were not used to skiing long distances in the mountains. And they had covered almost twenty miles that day, reaching the snowbound hut at Svensbu late in the afternoon. They were joyously welcomed by Poulsson and Haugland, who stood outside the door in a large drift of bloodstained snow amid scattered reindeer skins, heads, and horns.

Now all the British-trained Norwegian guerrillas were together—except for Einar Skinnarland, who had been living for several weeks with the Grouse men while on the run from the Germans. He left when he heard that Gunnerside might be coming, for the fewer people who knew who and where he was, the better. He was the secret "safety valve" who would keep transmitting information to London regardless of the fate of his comrades.

Their fate seemed linked to that of Kristian Kristiansen. A Gunnerside man was guarding him in a hut a few miles away so that he would not know where to find his captors. Should they kill him even though he was clearly not a Nazi sympathizer? He might not voluntarily betray the commandos, but what if he was captured and forced to talk? Could they take the risk? Finally, Ronneberg reached a decision, one that did not surprise those who knew him well. He sent one of his men to Kristiansen with a message: "If anything happens to us, your signed statement about your black-market activities will be sent to the Germans. We'll say, in addition, that you helped and guided us. The Germans will then take care of you. Go and shoot more reindeer, earn more money, and keep your mouth shut. Do not return to Uvdal for at least three days."

And Kristiansen was released, his pockets bulging with a hundred Norwegian kroners and a week's food rations, including chocolate, which had long been missing from the candy-store shelves in occupied Norway.

The men went to sleep crowded on a carpet of reindeer skins and woke in the morning trembling from the cold with the realization, more chilling yet, that the party was over. Now it was time to plan for the next one. There would be no chocolate or raisins this time—only blood, if military logic prevailed.

• • •

That morning of February 24, after a breakfast of reindeer meat, oatmeal, and coffee, the men remained at the rough-hewn pine table and perused wrinkled maps and diagrams Ronneberg had spread before them. Nine of these men would attack the heavy-water plant, their leader announced. Since Haugland was the most skilled SOE radioman taking part in the mission, London ordered him to go to Skinnarland's cabin and help keep British intelligence informed of developments.

Ronneberg then announced the roles he and his men would play. He would lead a four-man demolition team including Kayser, Idland, and Stromsheim, while Haukelid would head a five-man covering party embracing Poulsson, Helberg, Kjelstrup, and Storhaug. They were all aware of the terrible obstacles they would have to overcome.

Like a fairy-tale castle fortress, the electrolysis building stood defiantly at the edge of a sheer precipice, seemingly impregnable. The structure was perched on a massive shelf of rock carved out of the nearly vertical side of a 3,000-foot mountain. More than 500 feet below, in a deep gorge, flowed the Maana River, which served as a kind of protective moat, while over 1,000 feet above, water from dams and lakes surged through giant penstocks into turbines that whirled thunderously in the company power plant.

This plant stood just behind the electrolysis building, where water dripped through a gradual concentration process that started on the fifth floor and trickled from cell to cell, floor to floor, to a room in a corner of the basement. Here, the fully concentrated heavy water drained into the cells that the nine commandos would attack. The commandos dropped plans to blow up the power plant as well, feeling a double assault under the nose of the Germans could not succeed.

The question was, how would they get to the "castle," get in, and get away? Ronneberg outlined the attack plan recommended by Leif Tronstad. They would climb down the north side of the Maana River gorge, cross the ice-solid river, climb up the south side to the single-track railway that was used to ship machinery from Rjukan, and follow it around a ledge to the electrolysis building.

It appeared that the river gorge, incredibly, was not guarded, for the Germans obviously didn't believe that anyone could scale the almost perpendicular south wall. And they were probably right, the men agreed. This approach was not feasible.

The other alternatives seemed just as bleak. One was to cross a narrow suspension bridge that spanned the ravine and led almost directly to the building. But since sentries guarded the bridge, the attackers would have to shoot them, and within seconds every German in the vicinity would rush to the scene, assuring a bloody battle. Pure suicide, it seemed to Ronneberg, and with little chance to carry out the sabotage. More than that, Ronneberg stressed, the Germans would grab civilian hostages and shoot them in the morning.

A third alternative was to sweep down an icy flight of stairs that began at the mountain summit and descended along the penstocks feeding the power plant. But this whole area overlooking the shelf complex was heavily mined and protected by machine guns, booby traps, and even an antiaircraft battery. Again, the men would probably be killed before they reached the heavy-water plant.

Until this moment, the saboteurs had not contemplated the pending attack with the microscopic scrutiny required for such a coup. Now the full gravity of their dilemma sank in with devastating effect. Perhaps, they thought, Kasper Idland was right: the chances of emerging from the raid alive were nil.

Before he could make a decision, Ronneberg declared, he would have to know the latest information on German strength and positions. He turned to Claus Helberg. This was the day Helberg was to meet a contact who had promised at an earlier meeting to have this information ready for Gunnerside.

Helberg should leave for his rendezvous immediately, Ronneberg said, and rejoin Gunnerside the next day in Fjosbudalen, a village perched on high ground across the valley from Norsk Hydro. The group would head for the village that morning and stay in a cabin owned by a relative of Poulsson until the attack was launched the following night.

Before Helberg departed, his comrades scribbled questions for his contact on scraps of paper, which were gathered in a pile and sorted out. For underground security reasons, they were not informed who the contact was, but they were confident that Helberg would return with a report that would somehow make the choice of an approach less ominous.

The contact was, in fact, the highly knowledgeable construction engineer at the plant, Rolf Sorlie, a trusted member of the Resistance. The two men would meet at Sorlie's home, which stood dangerously close to a German strongpoint at the lower station of a cable-car lift connecting the mountaintop with the Rjukan valley. But Helberg was undaunted by the danger, in part because he knew this land so well.

The son of a Norsk Hydro civil engineer, he was not only a native of Rjukan but had worked for the Norwegian Mountain Touring Club before the war, helping to build bridges in the mountains, maintaining members' cabins, arranging tours for skiers, and writing tour books. He fought heroically against the Germans when they invaded Norway until he was taken prisoner. After his release, he gathered intelligence for the British and finally was sent to England to join Tronstad's group.

Now Helberg would embark on the most important intelligence mission of his career.

• • •

Ronneberg's group stumbled into the cabin at Fjosbudalen that afternoon after a long, tiring trek and found Helberg already there, his mood far from joyous. He was extremely hungry but had found only an ant-ridden can of syrup in the cupboard. If he was to die, he wanted to die with a full stomach. And judging by Sorlie's assessment of their choices, death did not seem too distant. Whatever the choice, German military power, it seemed, was sufficient to thwart an attack.

Even so, as Helberg wolfed down food the men had brought, he handed his data to them, and they sat down at the dining table to examine every word. Poulsson was heartened somewhat by the information, but one thing puzzled him. Although the Germans probably surmised Allied intentions after crushing Operation Freshman, they had not fully corrected their security system.

"In Rjukan," Poulsson would later say, "there were quite a few Germans. But how they could fail to have a regular guard at the railway gate is incomprehensible."

Ironically, however, the men could hardly exploit this weakness if they couldn't climb up the cliff to the railroad.

On the other hand, the suspension bridge was constantly guarded by two Germans, and if they sensed trouble, they would push an alarm button that would illuminate the whole area and set off a screeching siren calling all soldiers to the scene. On the alert for such an emergency were about thirty men based in a hut near the electrolysis building; eight to twelve of them were scattered around the Norsk Hydro complex at all strategic points—except by the railway gate.

The men groaned. Nothing had really changed since Helberg left on his visit to Sorlie, though they now knew that no one was guarding the railway line. More arguments, more resignation. They would have to cross the bridge, it seemed, regardless of the danger.

But then Ronneberg, who had been shuffling through some aerial photographs, made a startling discovery. In one photo of the almost vertical cliff, he noted that small trees and shrubbery sprouted from it in places. He passed the photo around and said:

"Where trees grow, a man can climb."

His eyes, suddenly alight, focused on Helberg.

"Claus," he said, "how about going out again and checking up on this. Climb down to the river and follow the river bed upstream to a place where you think you can climb to the railway."

Ronneberg handed Helberg a sketch of the approach area based on an aerial photo, and Helberg, swallowing his last mouthful of food, stood up and prepared to leave, but apparently without great enthusiasm.

"I had the feeling that he felt a reconnaissance was a waste of time," Ronneberg would later tell me.

And, in fact, like his colleagues from Rjukan, Helberg still did not believe that the mountainside could be scaled, partly because of an incident that happened shortly before the war. A car driven by two or three boys had skidded off the road near Norsk Hydro and plunged over the precipice into the river below. The youths were killed and their bodies were recovered by several men who had to use ropes just to climb down into the gorge.

How, then, could his commando group climb up, especially with rucksacks of explosives and supplies on their backs? A waste of time, yes.

Still, it occurred to him, nobody had ever tried the feat before. So how could he know for sure that it was impossible? And since failure seemed almost certain if the men attacked over the bridge, why not waste a little time checking out the only possible alternative?

At 9 o'clock the following morning, February 25, with the weather fortunately "mild and clear," Helberg slipped on his skis and set off on his exploratory mission. He headed southward, then eastward, avoiding any small villages where he might be seen and reported to the Germans.

When Helberg reached the road leading to Rjukan, he followed it until it curved like a hairpin downward toward a small village. Deciding to skirt the village, he removed his skis and, carrying them, clambered down through the snow-gowned brush to a lower section of the road that overlooked the gorge cradling the Maana River. He then put his skis on again and slid slowly along, searching for a place where he could turn off once more and continue descending toward the bottom of the gorge.

Helberg was hopeful that he could find a path down this side of the gorge, especially since it was embroidered with ample shrubbery that could break a potentially fatal fall. It was the wall of rock on the other side of the river that seemed so formidable.

And his optimism was not misplaced, for as he skied along the Rjukan road, he suddenly spotted a possible route that twisted downward through the juniper bushes to the river. The commandos could climb down from here, cross the river, and then attempt to scale the opposite cliff to the railroad ledge. Helberg removed his skis once more and plodded upward from the Rjukan road to a narrow, parallel road, seldom used, about forty yards away. The men, he figured, could leave their skis here, launch the attack, then return for the skis while fleeing to safety.

Helberg traipsed down to the main road again and followed the newly found path toward the river. He slid over icy rock faces, stumbled into knee-deep snow, tripped over branches of birch, and jumped onto precarious ledges before finally dropping to the frozen riverbed. Day, it seemed, had almost turned into night. Except for a strip of morning sky, light had been blocked out by the walls of stone that enclosed this desolate, eerily silent corridor of deliverance—or death.

Helberg cautiously moved along the ice-laden river toward Rjukan and happily found another path leading up to the main road that seemed easier to negotiate than the one he had taken down. And a short distance away, on the other side of the river, he found what he dared not believe existed: a "somewhat passable way up the factory side." Also, as Ronneberg's photograph had shown, small trees and bushes poked out of ancient cracks in the wall that would give the men at least some support as they climbed from ledge to ledge. There was no need for him to risk the climb now, Helberg felt. But he and the others should do it that night, he thought, even in the blackness of night, with each one carrying sixty-five pounds of explosives and equipment.

The men, it seemed, would stand a better chance of climbing this wall than of crossing the suspension bridge. He hadn't run into one German or detonated a mine. Thank God, he mused, that the enemy thought, as he had, that the cliff could not be scaled and thus was not guarding this approach.

Even as he exulted in his find, Helberg did not try to rationalize his own "blindness."

"Local people," he would later write, "often do not know their own area all that well, when you boil it right down."

• • •

The Gunnerside men were elated when Helberg returned to their cabin with the news. They might make it to the railroad track after all, and then break into the heavy-water plant without having to wage a suicidal battle. Ronneberg warmly congratulated Helberg, but there was still a blur in the blueprint: the escape route.

They should leave the same way they came, Helberg urged. Down into the gorge, then up the other side, all the way to the secondary road running parallel with the Rjukan road, where they would pick up their skis and fade into the mountains.

Ronneberg, backed by Haukelid, was wary of this plan. The getaway would take too long, he argued. And when the alarm sounded, Germans in the area, as well as those from Rjukan, would close in like hunters after wild game and trap them in the gorge. Every minute counted, and the quickest way out would be over the suspension bridge.

Helberg and his Rjukan comrades strongly objected to a bridge retreat, as they had to a bridge approach. In both cases, the guards there, they argued, would have to be killed, and this would not only alert the other Germans but, they repeated, would probably trigger savage reprisals against civilians. If this were the only alternative, they would agree to it anyway. There was now, however, another choice. And so they could not, as Rjukan natives, support a plan that might spell doom for some of their friends, neighbors, and relatives.

But they must be realistic, Ronneberg persisted. Even if they managed in withdrawing to clamber down to the river and struggle up the other side of the gorge to the secondary road, they would be too drained to tramp over snow-draped mountains all the way to Sweden. The Germans would easily catch up with them.

Helberg thought he might have the answer. When the men reached the secondary road and put on their skis, they would head not into the mountains but down to the main road. They would ski in the direction of Rjukan to the lower platform of the cable-car lift. There they would turn into the narrow road Helberg had followed on his way to meet Rolf Sorlie, skiing beneath the lift and zigzagging over hard snow to the peak.

And what if the Germans on duty at the upper platform spotted them? Ronneberg asked. They could block their path.

That peril was not as great as the one they would face if they tried to shoot their way across the suspension bridge, Helberg replied.

"I felt," Ronneberg would later say, "that the attack might be our last action and that the unit would be stronger if a majority was happy because they contributed to its planning."

So Ronneberg consulted with each man separately and found that the majority favored the Helberg plan.

"Okay," he agreed, "we'll withdraw as Claus has suggested."

They would leave the cabin at 8 P.M. and reach the heavy-water plant about 12:30 A.M. Any questions?

There were many, even though the men already knew most of the answers. They had to confirm everything. There could be no slipups.

What if they couldn't open the plant's steel doors or get through the cable duct of the heavy-water plant?

They would blow open one of the doors and, while the covering team held off a German attack, the demolition team would enter and destroy the heavy-water cells.

But what if the demolition team was killed before it could finish its job?

It would take about seven minutes to do the job, and if there was fighting, anyone who survived would have to do it.

Ronneberg didn't have to tell his men what they must do if they were captured or wounded too severely to escape. The fate of the commandos of Operation Freshman was etched in their minds.

With a few hours to wait, the men put on British army uniforms that Gunnerside had brought from England, hoping that an attack by "British soldiers" would reduce the chances of the Germans killing Norwegian civilians in retaliation for the attack. As they stuffed their rucksacks with equipment, medicine, and food, Idland took Ronneberg aside and said: "When we retreat across the gorge, don't mind me. You and the others rush to Sweden as fast as you can."

"What do you mean?"

"I don't want to delay you."

"Nonsense, you won't."

"I should have told you I wasn't a good skier before we left England," Idland replied. "But I didn't because I felt our journey would end in Vemork and that I would be able to keep up with the rest of you to that point. I didn't think anybody would get away alive. But then when I realized I should tell you, it was too late, for we were about to leave for Norway. So I kept my mouth shut."

Ronneberg was moved by this "confession." "You've kept up with us up to now," he said. "And you will all the way to Sweden. Now go pack up."

He was glad to have Idland on his team, a man eager to fight even though certain he would die. Then a frightening thought: was Idland simply being realistic, perhaps prophetic, in believing their journey would end in Vemork?

With a few hours still to go, the men were packing their equipment and cleaning their guns when suddenly there was a knock on the door.

A German raid? Was their vital mission to end before it began?

While Poulsson walked slowly to the door, pistol in hand, the others hid in a back room of the cabin, ready to burst out shooting. Poulsson pulled the door open and, seeing a young man, grabbed him by the throat and dragged him inside. Jabbing the caller in the stomach with the barrel of his pistol, Poulsson cried:

"Who are you?"

The man stared at him, his face a mask of fear and puzzlement.

"You know me," the caller finally said. "We were in the same class in school."

Poulsson's eyes narrowed searchingly as he tried to recall.

"Koria Tangstad!"

Images of an age long past cascaded through Poulsson's mind, an age when he and his classmates could ski across this wonderland and go hunting without feeling hunted. An age of joy and freedom in which the only enemy was the early darkness that sent them home before their youthful energy was fully expended.

"What are you doing here?" Poulsson asked Tangstad.

He was spending the weekend at his family's cabin about sixty yards away, the man explained. His fiancée and another couple were to meet him there later. The cabin was snowed in and he had come to this neighboring hut to ask if he could borrow a shovel.

Poulsson had "completely forgotten that even though there was a war on, it was natural for Rjukan people to visit their cabins on the weekend"—and this was Saturday. He wanted to embrace the visitor and talk about old times, their classmates, their teachers, their loves, and their laughs. But there was not even a smile now. How could he trust anyone at this point, even a childhood friend?

The other commandos emerged from hiding, and Helberg, too, recognized Tangstad from his school days. Poulsson handed the man a shovel and spoke to him in a clearly threatening tone: "Return to your cabin and stay there with your friends until morning."

Tangstad left, guessing that his neighbors must be working in the underground. But why were they wearing British uniforms?

"What should we do now?" Poulsson would later say of this moment. "Act normal and hope that they wouldn't reflect on the fact that there were people in the cabin next door? Intern them until the job was done? Talk to them and give them the best possible cover story?"

As the commandos were about to leave for the attack on this night of February 27, 1943, Ronneberg went to talk with their worrisome neighbors. How they reacted would determine their fate. He shortly returned with a report that eased the tension.

"They are all good Norwegians," Ronneberg said with a smile.

Poulsson and Helberg were especially relieved. It somehow seemed fitting that they should return to their early years in what could be their last hours. And they wanted nothing to tarnish the magic of this ephemeral journey.

# 13

## ASSAULTING THE CASTLE

### *February 1943*

"**THE HUM OF THE MACHINERY** came up to us through the ravine," Knut Haukelid would write. "We understood how the Germans could allow themselves to keep so small a guard there. The colossus lay like a medieval castle, built in the most inaccessible place, protected by precipices and rivers."

As the nine commandos slid down the steep mountainside after leaving their cabin, their skis almost invisible under the soft snow, their newly donned British army uniforms hidden under white camouflage suits, they suddenly glimpsed the "castle" glowing faintly in the moonlight. This vision in the distance sent tremors through some of the men. Their objective was no longer a photo or an "X" target on the map, but a seemingly unassailable concrete fortress. The map was now the territory.

The tremors vanished quickly, however, for the men were too busy maneuvering around bushes and trees in the shadowy snow to worry long about what might happen when they finally confronted destiny. Indeed, a fierce wind threatened to send them flying into a dark oblivion prematurely. Moreover, the wind blew in relatively warm gusts, turning the snow and ice into slush. Would the river still be a solid ice bridge across the gorge? Terrible weather, but at least it would keep others from venturing out and informing on them.

Claus Helberg was perhaps the most confident commando, for,

as a scout for the speeding file of skiers, he merely traced the route he had taken when he had earlier surveyed this approach to the heavy-water plant. He guided himself by following the trembling telephone lines luminous with snowflakes that flew off like sparks with every blast of wind. He knew almost every tree, bush, and bump along the way, and what he didn't know his sixth sense somehow did.

But the going was tougher this time, for the blizzard-fed snows were too heavy now to permit skiing in places. The men thus had to plod through snowbanks up to their waists, with their skis balanced on shoulders already sagging under the weight of 65-pound rucksacks. As they approached the Rjukan road, they put on their skis again and began sliding down the slippery grade, when suddenly they saw with a twinge of terror two buses, lights blazing, grinding ahead just beneath them. Night-shift workers from Rjukan headed for the heavy-water plant! The commandos dug their poles into the snow and edged their skis, desperately trying to brake themselves.

"It was only by a hair's breadth that a large part of the sabotage group missed landing on the roof of one of the buses," Haukelid would later say.

When the buses had passed, the men gathered in a little shanty along the road to catch their breath, and the cold air grew misty from their sighs of relief. How close they—and their mission—had come to a bungled end.

The commandos skied cautiously along the icy Rjukan road, then followed Helberg to the parallel secondary road. Here, along the roadside, they dug a shallow snow depot where they hid their skis and poles, excess equipment, and white camouflage suits, which they would retrieve after the operation—if they managed to get away. From here on, they would act as "British soldiers."

Weighted down now with pistols, tommy guns, grenades, knives, ammunition, and explosive charges, the saboteurs, with Helberg leading, returned to the main road and began climbing down toward the river, sliding part of the way over smooth, snow-covered rock. When they reached the bottom of the gorge, the sound of splashing water reinforced their fears that the warm air had melted the river ice. Would they have to swim with all their equipment across a freezing river?

It appeared so when the men had all descended to the edge of the river. The ice was breaking up and the water ran high above it. Helberg led the others along the narrow bank, searching for an ice bridge. He finally found one, but would it support their weight? About three inches of water already flowed over it.

"I'll test it out," Helberg said, knowing he could drown in the attempt.

While his comrades tensely watched, he dipped one foot into the water until it reached the ice, then gradually pressed down with both feet. He gingerly treaded on the ice, barely able to balance himself on the slippery surface. Finally, he reached the opposite bank. The ice had held. He now motioned to the others to follow, and each of them staggered across even as the ice began to crumble under them. One more crisis solved.

They had no time to dwell on how to maneuver a return river crossing if the ice continued to melt, for facing them was the greatest obstacle of all. Stretching almost straight into the sky was the wall of rock they had never imagined could be scaled. They could not even see the railroad ledge that rimmed the wall about 150 yards into the black infinity. Would they really be able to conquer this cliff—or was this, in fact, the end of the long, treacherous road they had traveled since landing in Norway?

Helberg guided his comrades to the narrow path he had found earlier, with shrubbery sprouting from it in places. They would have to move from ledge to ledge, bush to bush, finding foot- and finger-holds as they climbed. The men were silent, contemplating the enormous challenge. This was more than a wall; it was a test. A test not only of their sinews but of their souls. Would they have the inner strength, the superhuman will, to scale the wall inch by inch even if sapped of physical strength? This question, it seems, burned most brightly in the minds of the Grouse men, who had still not fully recovered from their long ordeal in the mountains. And to the fear of falling was added the fear of being detected and killed before they could complete their mission.

But they were driven men, driven less by the desire to personally survive—most did not believe they would—than by the momentous implications of failure. They had to succeed.

And so Ronneberg gave the order to climb.

Finding footholds in the bare rock rising from the river bank, the commandos lifted themselves gradually by fingers that poked into cracks and held on to narrow ledges. About a third of the way up, Kasper Idland dangled from a ledge by the fingers of one hand as he drew the other hand over the rock face, feeling for another niche. As the clinging fingers were about to give out, he swung like a monkey toward some shrubbery a short distance away, releasing his hold with one hand while grabbing the greenery with the other. A moment later, a gust of wind swept by him, a moment too late to claim the first victim of Gunnerside.

While some men did not dare look down as they edged upward, others did, peering with a strange compulsion into a black canyon dripping melted snow that rained below with the rhythmic echo of a Latin dance. But their eyes abruptly fixed on the wall, searching for crevices, cracks, any clump of reeds within grasp. At the same time, each one felt pressured to move faster by the fear that he was holding up his buddies.

Gradually, minds went nearly blank and bodies became robotlike machines, wound up by an irrepressible, almost subconscious will untainted by fear or anxiety. Inch by agonizing inch, the saboteurs, their hearts pounding from the strain, rose toward the heaven of the railway ledge, and finally near-paralyzed fingers locked onto its outer edge. One by one, the men, with a final lurch, crawled to horizontal ground, then helped to drag those behind across the threshold. Exhausted, they collapsed beside the track for several minutes, gasping for breath, silent, mesmerized, it seemed, by the lullaby of the plant turbines whining in the distance over the intermittent roar of an angry westerly wind. Finally, they looked around. How many had made it? All nine.

The commandos were elated; they were still alive. But for how long? As they had hoped, there were no Germans around, but they could close in at any moment. Ronneberg glanced at his watch. A few minutes after eleven. He ordered his men to start moving in single file along the track toward the plant, with Knut Haukelid leading the five-men covering group so it could clear a mine-free path for Ronneberg's demolition party and protect it from gunfire. Whoever had to die, the heavy-water tanks must be destroyed.

After marching for half an hour in the moonless night, the men halted in front of a small, snow-covered transformer shed about five hundred yards from the gate leading to the plant. Now they could see the suspension bridge and watch the guard change at midnight. At 12:30 A.M., when the new guards would be relaxed at their posts, the commandos would make a final dash toward the electrolysis building. Meanwhile, they sat down behind the shed to shield themselves from the wind, munched on food they removed from their pockets, and listened to Ronneberg go over each man's role in the most intricate detail.

"Do you understand your orders?" he asked them one by one.

And whatever they replied, he repeated them. One mistake, he feared, would foil their mission. Never had he felt his burden weighing on him so crushingly. They had miraculously come this far, but how many miracles did God owe a man?

The others shared Ronneberg's tension, but also his resolve. And the loud hum of machinery in the background drowned out their chitchat about nostalgic incidents in their past—classroom pranks, training camp foulups, romantic encounters—though they said little about their future, which could vanish in hardly more than an hour. If death was almost inevitable, it was somehow comforting to face it together after exchanging cherished memories of the joys of life.

Finally, it was midnight, and reality intruded on the memories. Two guards marched from their barracks nearby to the suspension bridge and relieved those on duty there. One half-hour more. It seemed stranger now than ever. Out of all the billions of people in the world, it was left to them—nine simple Norwegians—to possibly determine the outcome of the war.

In one half-hour.

. . .

At exactly 12:30 A.M. the men re-formed, with Knut Haukelid's covering group in front, followed by Ronneberg and the demolition party. The column halted at a tool shed about one hundred yards from the gate to the plant. Ronneberg walked up to Haukelid and issued his final order before the attack.

"Knut," he said, "you and Kjelstrup advance alone and break the lock on the railroad gate, while the others cover you."

And as the two men started forward, Ronneberg simply said: "Good luck."

They would need it, they knew, especially if the Germans had laid mines near the gate to protect the plant. The commandos held their breath as the two advance men edged their way along the railroad track. They reached the gate . . . intact. Kjelstrup, drawing on his plumbing experience, now took a pair of shears from his pocket and cut through a link in the padlocked iron chain.

The way was now open, as Haukelid would later say, "to one of the most important military objectives in Europe."

All five members of the cover group now rushed through the gate into the yard and lay prone in preassigned positions. Helberg covered the gate; Kjelstrup, the penstocks; Storhaug, the suspension bridge. Haukelid and Poulsson took cover behind a crate about twenty yards from the guard barracks, the most likely source of danger. If the alarm went off, they would fire at the off-duty guard force with their tommy guns and pistols, and toss grenades.

Meanwhile, the demolition team of Ronneberg, Kayser, Stromsheim, and Idland stealthily moved along the inside of the fence and cut the chain on a second gate that would serve as an alternative escape route. They then headed for a steel door of the electrolysis building leading to the basement, where the highly concentrated heavy-water–filled metal cells stood upright like tin soldiers. Ronneberg tried the door handle.

"Damn it! Locked!" he mumbled.

Explosives could blow the door open, but that would alert the Germans, who, amazingly, were not guarding or patrolling this area. And even if he and his men accomplished their mission under gunfire and managed to escape alive, Germans would surely be killed or wounded, triggering, as they had always feared, reprisals against the civilian population.

Ronneberg ordered Stromsheim and Idland to rush up a nearby stairway to the first floor. Maybe they could enter through the door there and get to the basement. Meanwhile, Ronneberg and Kayser dashed around the building in a frantic search for the cable tunnel that Tronstad had described in a pre-mission briefing. Suddenly, they came to a window, blacked out except for pinpoints of light escaping through it in thin beams. Ronneberg peered through one of them, and his heart nearly stopped. There, in a room several feet below the window, his eyes were transfixed on two rows of cells and an elderly civilian sitting at a desk between them. The high-concentration heavy-water cells! And nearby the canisters into which they would be emptied for shipment to Germany—unless the contents could be spilled down the drain of history.

In his excitement, Ronneberg wanted to break through the window to set his charges. But the Germans might hear the noise of glass shattering or the old man screaming. Where was that duct? Ronneberg and Kayser raced along the wall until they saw a ladder that led to a narrow opening just below the first floor.

"This must be the tunnel," Ronneberg uttered in relief.

They looked around, hoping to see their two comrades who had gone to check the door on the first floor, but no one emerged from the black night.

"As every minute was valuable and as there was no sign of the others," Ronneberg would later write in a report, "we decided to carry out the demolition alone."

Removing a flashlight from his pocket, he leaped up the ladder and slid into the opening headfirst, followed by Kayser.

The two men inched forward through the stuffy tunnel, which

was so narrow they couldn't look behind them. It was especially cumbersome crawling over a tangle of rusty pipes and snake-like cables. The journey seemed endless. What if they ran into an obstacle they couldn't get past? How would they crawl back when they could barely move forward? This duct might be their coffin.

When the pair had crept through almost the full thirty yards of tunnel, Ronneberg suddenly heard just behind him a loud clang that resounded through the cavelike passageway. Kayser's pistol had slipped out of his holster and landed on a pipe. Both men froze until the echo faded into a faint rumble barely audible over the perpetual hum of machines grinding out the raw material of death.

Kayser carefully retrieved the pistol and, hopeful that the guard inside the high-concentration room had not heard the clang, the two men continued their snail-like advance. Finally, the bright beam of Ronneberg's flashlight blended with a dull glow at the end of the tunnel. And in minutes, they crawled out onto a ladder inside a basement room adjoining the heavy-water chamber. After climbing down, they strode with pistols drawn to a set of double doors that led to the chamber.

Ignoring a sign on one of them warning in German and Norwegian, "No Admittance Except on Business," Ronneberg cautiously turned the doorknob and, to his surprise, found the door unlocked. He opened it just enough to peek inside at the watchman, who was still seated at a desk—his back to the door.

Kayser burst in first waving his pistol and cried: "Put your hands up! If you resist, I'll shoot you!"

The watchman turned around in his chair, then stood up, trembling, with hands raised. He gaped in shock at the intruders, as if at an apparition. While Ronneberg locked the double doors from the inside with the Yale lock hanging from one of them, Kayser, rushing forward, aimed his pistol at the man's head and pointed to the British army insignia on his sleeve.

"We're British soldiers," he announced in Norwegian, so the man, clearly a compatriot, would be sure to understand. The hope was that the watchman would tell the Germans that the saboteurs were British commandos. "We've come to destroy these cells because the Germans are trying to make a high explosive with them. Just be quiet and cooperate and we won't hurt you."

The watchman, less frightened now, nodded that he would.

Meanwhile, Ronneberg put on rubber gloves to protect himself against an electric shock and went to work placing the charges on the eighteen heavy-water cells. He did it with ease, since he had practiced in Britain with perfect replicas of these steel-jacketed, four-foot-two-inch-long cylinders.

As he moved from cell to cell wrapping a twelve-inch charge around each one, the guard, Gustave Johansen, observed his every move admiringly. He was finally convinced they were British soldiers, or at least worked for the British. And he did not seem at all disturbed by their incredible intrusion. At one point, he warned Ronneberg about the dangers of the electrolysis process.

"Be careful," he said. "Lye might leak through your gloves."

When Ronneberg had placed charges on about half the cells, a sudden crash of glass broke the tense silence. Kayser aimed his pistol at the window, which now framed a partly shattered pane, fearing the worst. With success only minutes away, was it up to him to save this vital mission?

• • •

Meanwhile, in the yard, the covering party waited to hear the explosion that would be the signal to withdraw from the plant area.

"The time seemed long to us who stood waiting outside," Haukelid would later write.

He felt fortunate, however, for he at least had a companion hiding with him behind two storage tanks. And they could talk, even reminisce on old times because of the noise from the plant, though the silhouette of the German guardhouse loomed only twenty yards away. His three other comrades were isolated and silent out there at strategic points.

"What was it like for the Chicken, Claus, and Arne, who were quite alone?" Haukelid would recall musing. He would report:

We waited and waited. We knew that the blowing-up party was inside to carry out its part of the task, but we did not know how things were going. Jens had a tommy gun and a pistol. If the Germans gave the alarm, or showed any sign of realizing what was going on, he would start pumping lead into the [guardhouse]. I had a pistol and five or six hand grenades. The intention was to throw them in among the Germans through the doors and windows.

To ease the tension, Haukelid and Poulsson entertained the idea with the forced humor of men balanced on the abyss.

"You must remember to call out '*Heil* Hitler' when you open the door and throw the bombs," Poulsson suggested with a smile.

Haukelid was "reminded of something which had happened" during the German invasion of Norway. In one village, "we had surrounded a section of Germans in a wooden house. There were dead Germans hanging out of the window, and dead Germans lying inside before we had finished shooting the house to pieces."

The horror of the images this thought evoked apparently made him doubt for a fleeting, irrational moment that he had a duty to slaughter other human beings for some higher cause.

Poulsson glanced at his watch. The demolition team had been gone for about twenty minutes. "The time passed extremely slowly," he would later say, "and we started to wonder whether something had gone wrong."

■ ■ ■

**A**ctually, nothing had—so far. And Ronneberg and Kayser knew it when they saw a familiar face suddenly pop into view at the window partly obscured by jagged triangles of glass: Birger Stromsheim!

Kayser lowered his pistol and resumed pointing it at Johansen, taking no chances on where his loyalty lay. Ronneberg interrupted his work and ran to the window to remove the broken glass and help Stromsheim climb through it. Idland was with Stromsheim, but Ronneberg ordered him to remain outside on watch. The two new arrivals had been unable to find the cable duct, so they decided to enter through the window, gambling that the Germans would not hear the noise of shattering glass.

"Damn it!" Ronneberg cried, as he grabbed his hand.

He had cut it on the glass, which tore through his glove, and the blood was flowing freely. He had been through so much without suffering a scratch. And now, at this crucial moment, he had to worry about stopping the blood, which soaked his glove and would make it more difficult to place the charges. Fortunately Stromsheim was also trained to do the work and took over some of the load.

"Take care not to short-circuit," Johansen said. "If you do, there may be an explosion."

"Explosion!" Kayser exclaimed. "That's just what there's going to be!"

And his two comrades worked frantically to make sure there would be. Finally, when all the charges were in place, Stromsheim checked them over twice while Ronneberg, wiping away the blood from his cut every few seconds, coupled the eighteen fuses so he would have to ignite only nine of them. He would ignite two-minute as well as half-minute fuses, just in case the shorter ones did not work. Nothing could be left to chance.

As Ronneberg was finishing his work, Johansen, who had been ordered to rush to the second floor as soon as the fuses were lit, suddenly cried out: "I can't find my glasses. Please help me find them. I can hardly see without them!"

Ronneberg stared at him incredulously. This was a life-and-death moment, not only for his team but perhaps for the Allies. A German guard could appear at any second and sound the alarm. Yet with Stromsheim busy and Kayser in the next room opening the steel door to the yard with a key he had taken from Johansen, the watchman expected Ronneberg to drop the fuses and look for his glasses! Was he mad?

But the saboteur saw before him an elderly gentleman, no doubt a good Norwegian, who was probably working there to keep his family from starving. And how could he work without his glasses, which were virtually irreplaceable in the austerity of German-occupied Norway? The man could have been his father.

"It was a good thing to realize that even in war we're human beings," Ronneberg would philosophize when I interviewed him years later.

"Where the hell did you put them?" he asked Johansen.

And he dropped his fuses and went to search for the man's glasses. After scanning the room, he found a glasses case in a corner. Picking it up, he handed it to Johansen, who thanked him profusely. But hardly had Ronneberg returned to his work when the watchman called to him again.

"My glasses are not in the case," he said in a broken voice.

Ronneberg paused for a moment. Could he afford to lose any more time? No—but he took the time. Again he quickly glanced in every corner, then riffled through reams of paper piled on the man's desk. Finally, he found the glasses, hidden between the pages of a book.

Again Johansen expressed his deep gratitude. But Ronneberg had no time for amenities. He left some British army insignias in the room to convince the Germans that British soldiers had been there, and was about to light a match to ignite the longer fuses when Stromsheim, who was working near a stairway, rushed to Ronneberg and whispered: "Someone is coming down the stairs!"

Ronneberg froze. It was probably a German guard. His good deed could end in catastrophe. He and Stromsheim drew their pistols and Kayser covered Johansen with his gun to make sure he would not betray them. As footsteps grew louder, hearts pumped faster. A shadow finally appeared against the staircase wall. Guns took aim. And then the shadow suddenly became a man: the Norwegian night foreman, Gunnar Engebretsen.

The foreman gazed at the three trespassers in shock. How in hell, he seemed to be asking himself, had they gotten in here? How had they eluded the guards? But the saboteurs didn't wait to satisfy his curiosity. While Stromsheim and Kayser covered the two civilians, Ronneberg lit a match and ignited the two-minute fuses. Then, as he lit the thirty-second ones, he cried:

"Let's go!"

Kayser shouted to the two workers, who were standing by the

stairway: "Run to the second floor as fast as you can or you'll be blown to bits!"

Ronneberg added: "And keep your mouth open or your eardrums will burst."

Then Ronneberg, Kayser, and Stromsheim dashed through the steel door, slamming it shut behind them, and into the yard, where they met Idland. Hardly twenty yards from the building, they heard an explosion, muffled by the competing sounds of machinery rhythmically grinding away in the yard. Half a ton of heavy water had suddenly "evaporated."

• • •

"**A**t last there was an explosion," Haukelid would later report, "but an astonishingly small, insignificant one. Was this what we had come over a thousand miles to do? Certainly the windows were broken, and a glimmer of light spread out into the night, but it was not particularly impressive."

Poulsson would agree: "There was a bang. A distant, faint blast. We looked at each other. This couldn't possibly be the real thing."

But then they concluded that perhaps it was. For the heavy-water apparatus was, after all, situated in the insulated basement of the electrolysis plant.

The Germans apparently didn't think the "faint blast" was the real thing either, for, according to Haukelid, none reacted for several minutes. But then, from behind the two storage tanks where he and Poulsson were hiding, they saw the door of the guardhouse open. An unarmed German stepped out with flashlight in hand and sauntered to the electrolysis building about fifty yards away and tried the steel door. It was locked. He then strolled back to the guardhouse, and the two commandos groaned in relief.

But in a moment, the German reappeared, and this time he moved toward the two storage drums. Haukelid grabbed a hand grenade and held it ready to be thrown with his left middle finger in the safety-pin ring. Poulsson aimed his tommy gun at the approaching soldier.

As he gradually advanced, the German swung his flashlight from side to side along the ground.

"I had a very strong urge to shoot," Poulsson would say.

And he asked Haukelid: "Shall I fire?"

"No," Haukelid whispered. "He doesn't know what has happened. Leave him as long as possible."

He would later explain: "Our task was to blow things up, and not to shoot one German more or less."

Poulsson lowered his weapon, but raised it again when the man directed his beam on the ground just behind them. If he lowered the beam to the foreground, he might be able to see the two commandos, who sat curled up behind the tanks trying to conceal themselves. Poulsson's finger began tugging on the trigger.

But at that moment, the German swung the flashlight around and returned to the guardhouse, closing the door behind him. All kinds of noises spewed out from the electrolysis building and the power plant behind it. Nothing special on this night, he apparently felt. Perhaps the snow had exploded a land mine.

Haukelid and Poulsson waited a few minutes to give Ronneberg's party time to escape from the electrolysis building, if they hadn't already left it, and then ran to the yard gate. There they heard a familiar voice. Arne Kjelstrup, another member of the covering party, called out the password.

"Piccadilly."

The answer should have been "Leicester Square," but Haukelid and Poulsson assumed Kjelstrup knew who they were and didn't bother to reply.

"Piccadilly," Kjelstrup repeated.

His two comrades, after miraculously surviving up to now, were in no mood for "chicken-shit" formality at this point. But they were in the mood for a little fun. They coined a new "password."

"Shut up, you fucking bastard!"

About three hundred yards from the gate, they found the others waiting for them. The nine men, all in perfect shape except for the cut on Ronneberg's hand, embraced and joked and slapped each other on the back.

Now they had only to retreat the way they came, hoping the Germans wouldn't trap them in the gorge, and then scramble across four hundred miles of German-controlled territory—over towering mountains and through deep slush melting in the relatively warm air all the way to Sweden.

# 14

## THE HEAVENS CELEBRATE

*February–March 1943*

"**WHEN WE WERE DOWN** in the bottom of the valley, we heard the air-raid sirens sound," Knut Haukelid would write. "This was the Germans' signal for general mobilization in the Rjukan area. They had at last collected their wits and found out what had happened."

Haukelid and the other saboteurs had "hopped and slid" down to the Maana River. Though it had swept over its banks, the men then managed to hopscotch their way across once more, jumping from one chunk of almost invisible ice to another. The blast of the sirens, however, was a ringing reminder that their lives were still in peril. Once the Germans turned on their powerful illumination system, they could easily trap them in the gorge.

What the saboteurs didn't know was that the German guards couldn't find the switch until it was too late. And the saboteurs' blood pressure collectively soared when, as Haukelid would report, they saw "beams of flashlights moving about. The German guards had discovered the line of our retreat." They merely had to follow the trail of blood that dripped from Ronneberg's injured hand.

In desperation, the saboteurs clambered up the opposite side of the gorge toward the main road, virtually leaping from foothold to foothold, grabbing on to mere weeds rooted in the rocky soil, hoisting themselves with an energy flowing from pure will. Now that they had triumphed in their suicide mission, they were no longer resigned to probable death; they were obsessed with staying alive. They wanted to fight again, to love again, to one day tell their grandchildren bedtime stories of how they helped to save the world. They couldn't die now.

Staggering to the main road, the men hid behind brush along the roadside as several cars packed with German officers and Norwegian plant executives zipped past. When, one by one, they finally dashed across the road, the last man had to dive into a ditch to avoid the glare of a speeding car's headlights.

The saboteurs struggled through the snow-clad woods stretching above the main road until they reached the secondary one, where they had hidden their skis, coveralls, and excess equipment. They put on the white coveralls over their British uniforms, which they would continue to wear to conceal their Norwegian identity.

The men felt safer when they gazed down at the main road, which looked like a luminous string of beads as military vehicles, transporting troops from Rjukan proper, clogged the route. The soldiers swarmed toward the plant rather than fan out in the eerily dark, forbidding mountains encircling the plant in search of foes who might be waiting to ambush them.

The saboteurs now reversed direction and headed toward Rjukan along the secondary road, despite the danger that they might come face to face with a German force there.

"The German cars went toward Vemork on the road right below us," Helberg would recall. "Nobody must have thought that we would go toward Rjukan."

The commandos would turn off onto the road that zigzagged under the cable-car lift and led upward to the Hardanger Plateau and finally back to their base cabin in Svensbu, where Gunnerside had joined Grouse to plot the sabotage venture.

With Helberg leading the way, the men began the long trek, still savoring the sight of a never-ending line of vehicles moving past them below as they skied along in retreat. The more Germans who were whisked to Vemork, the fewer there would be to hunt them in the mountains. The men veered onto the road leading to the lower cable-car platform at a height of eighteen hundred feet, and were soon plodding up the steep, slippery path toward the plateau.

Already sagging under a backbreaking load of equipment, they now had to carry their skis as well, though they were still utterly drained from scaling the cliffs that were supposed to protect the heavy-water plant. As the snow grew deeper and softer, they mindlessly trudged upward, slipping, falling, crawling. Three hours later, at about 5 A.M., they stumbled onto a ridge, and there spread before them was the plateau.

"We felt great satisfaction," Helberg would say, "when we sat and looked at Vemork and thought of the commotion we had caused."

• • •

The commotion erupted minutes after the explosion, when Gunnar Engebretsen, the watchman who had stumbled into the high-concentration room at the wrong time, answered the telephone and heard an excited voice. Alf H. Larsen, Jomar Brun's replacement as chief engineer of Norsk Hydro, had heard the blast while shuffling a deck of cards at a neighbor's bridge party and wanted answers.

What happened?

Some British soldiers blew up the plant!

Could the man be drunk? Larsen wondered.

But in a moment, he was on the phone to Bjarne Nilssen, Norsk Hydro's regional director. Nilssen was stunned. The Germans would surely crack heads, and his might be the first. To convince them of his loyalty, he alerted the German garrison in Rjukan, then ran to his wood-burning car and sped to the plant past the saboteurs, who were peering from behind the roadside brush.

Shortly, several black official cars screeched to a halt in front of the plant and SS General Rediess and Reich Commissar Terboven stepped out of one of them, and, surrounded by soldiers and Gestapo men, they surveyed the scene. In the darkness, they could not see much, but probably enough to make them suspect that someone was playing a joke on them. How could any foe penetrate this isolated fortress protected by guns, mines, and sheer cliffs?

But when they entered the heavy-water plant with Nilssen

and Larsen, they knew this was no joke. All eighteen cells were shattered and a half-ton of the treasured liquid soaked the floors and crumbling walls. How long would it take to repair the damage, install new equipment, and make up for the loss? Months? Years? What would this mean for the German war effort—and for their careers? These are surely questions that must have haunted them.

In fear and rage, the brass grilled the two watchmen who had been in the heavy-water room before the explosion, but all they could say was that three British soldiers had broken in and set the charges. Soon afterward, Rediess reported to SS leaders in Berlin:

> On the night of 27th–28th February 1943, about 1:15 A.M., an installation of importance to the war economy was destroyed at the Vemork factory near Rjukan by the detonation of explosive charges. The attack was carried out by three armed men wearing grey-green uniforms. They gained entrance to the factory by cutting a chain in the gate, and passed both German sentries and Norwegian watchmen undetected. From the effects they left behind, it can be assumed that they came from Britain.

The sabotage, he speculated, "was a combined British Intelligence and Norwegian Resistance operation. Security police investigations are still proceeding into the matter."

Terboven was impatient. Why wait for investigations? He arrested ten prominent civilian leaders in Rjukan and wanted to shoot them. But General von Falkenhorst arrived before he could act and, after inspecting the damage, seemed more impressed than enraged by the sabotage.

"The English bandits," he marveled, "performed the finest coup I have seen in this war."

And he concluded, or wished to conclude, that the "bandits" were military men, not civilians. Hadn't they worn British uniforms and left behind British insignia? So there was no need to shoot any hostages.

Release the ten leaders, he ordered.

Falkenhorst reserved his fury for the guards. When they had been lined up before him, he ordered them to take off their sheepskin coats. And they must never again turn their tunic collars up and pull their caps down over their faces, no matter how cold the weather.

"You look like a bunch of Santa Clauses!" the general roared. "You can't see or hear saboteurs with all those clothes on. Besides, you're up against the most dangerous men the enemy has. They're men who use pistol, poison, and knife, the one as easily as the other. They're specially trained to kill silently and quickly."

Yet there were no men watching the high-concentration plant and the railway gate, he barked to the guard commandant. From now on, he ordered, those places must be guarded twenty-four hours a day.

"When you are ordered to guard a chest of gold, which this heavy-water installation actually is for us," Falkenhorst went on, "you shall sit on the golden chest. You shall not walk around it with your Santa Claus costumes."

The commandant, a sergeant-major, nervously sputtered out all the steps taken to thwart an attack since the British gliders crashed in the mountains. The men had laid mines, strung barbed wire, planted machine guns on the roof, and installed floodlights that could light up "the entire area at the turn of a single switch."

"Turn those lights on!" Falkenhorst commanded.

"Yes, sir!" the sergeant-major said.

And he left to carry out the order. Falkenhorst waited—and waited. But the commandant didn't return and the lights didn't go on. The general glanced at his watch. No wonder the man was late. He was one of the Austrians whom he had failed to replace. Couldn't trust them. Finally losing patience, the general climbed into his car and sped off.

The next day, the sergeant-major asked a Norwegian engineer where the switch was. No one had told him. He was soon shipped to the Russian front.

Other leaders now learned faster. They doubled the guard,

searched houses, made arrests, laid new minefields, set up road-blocks, allowed only freight on the railroad, and cut civilian telephone service.

What if the enemy attacked by air? Artificial trees soon camouflaged the penstocks, and smoke-screen gear graced the mountain.

Nor was the ordinary citizen ignored. The local radio proclaimed a partial state of emergency and an 11 P.M. curfew, while posters plastered on almost every wall warned the populace:

> On February 28, unknown persons destroyed important apparatus in the Vemork Hydro plant. In the event of similar sabotage actions, the sharpest measures will be taken against the civilian population.

• • •

Once he reached the ridge that led into the great valley, Claus Helberg decided to leave his comrades and ski back part of the way toward the cabin in Fjosbudalen, the launching pad for their attack. He had left his civilian clothes there and the pockets were bulging with identity cards and other telltale documents that the Germans must not get their hands on.

"I'll meet you guys in Svensbu later today," Helberg told his comrades.

He and Poulsson were then to head together for Oslo, but if they didn't meet in Svensbu, he suggested they meet several days later, on March 8, in the capital—at the Majorstua Cafe. While his comrades feared he was risking capture by returning to a place so close to the plant, they knew his intimacy with every inch of the land and his mastery on skis made him an extremely elusive target. Yet their hearts were heavy as they watched him fade into the loneliness of what could still be a deadly night.

They then trekked on to the northwest across the mountains to Lake Langesjaa and found a hut where they would stay for the night. Shortly, a storm swept across the peaks, which, Ronneberg would report, became "one mass of driving snow." The men tried to buck the storm the next morning, but the gale had only grown fiercer, turning the snow on the ground into a blizzard of dirt-encrusted ice pebbles.

"In order to breathe," Haukelid would report, "we had to keep our hands over our mouths. The ice-needles tore our faces till our cheeks felt like open wounds."

Gunnerside had started in a storm, and now it was ending in one. The heavens had tested them the first time, some liked to feel, and were hailing them now. As the men reluctantly struggled back to the cabin, they thanked the Lord for having held back the storm while they were inching up that almost vertical cliff a few hours earlier.

In the afternoon of March 1, the heavens ended their celebration, and in the calmer weather the saboteurs finally reached Svensbu that night. They did not find Helberg there, nor did he appear the next day. Had the storm held him up? It was the most comforting explanation. They dared not voice their fear that perhaps the Germans had captured or killed him.

The men recalled the great joy they had felt when they found themselves reunited in this cabin where the Grouse commandos had stayed for months waiting for the Gunnerside comrades to arrive. Drawing on their cherished memories, they could almost smell the delicious reindeer meat and hear the animated voices chatting about happier times on that unforgettable Christmas Eve. But the revelry had hidden a terrible tension. It would surely be their last Christmas Eve.

Now the tension was gone, and there was hope they would survive the war. They might once more enjoy the beautiful life that had made childhood and adolescence such a delight amid these very mountains, lakes, and forests of pine. There might be more Christmas Eves after all.

Yes, the operation had gone perfectly. But Helberg's absence dimmed the joy. The sharing of adversity and danger under the most merciless conditions had drawn all the men into a close-knit family. And now one of them was missing.

After anxiously waiting until the morning of the third day for Helberg to arrive, his comrades had to move on, for with the weather improving, the Germans, who normally could not spare men for duty in the wilderness, might be combing the mountains for prey. Also, Ronneberg was to leave a message for London in a stone hut farther north, informing intelligence how the operation had gone. Knut Haugland or Einar Skinnarland would pick it up and radio the news from their own hidden hut. The message read:

HIGH-CONCENTRATION INSTALLATION AT VEMORK
COMPLETELY DESTROYED ON NIGHT OF 27TH-28TH STOP
GUNNERSIDE HAS GONE TO SWEDEN STOP GREETINGS

And shortly, on March 4, the group reached the cabin and Ronneberg dropped the message into a designated coffee can. The men then skied on to another hut near Lake Skryken, where the Gunnerside men had buried supplies shortly after parachuting onto the plateau two weeks earlier. Here the men were to separate and divide up the food and equipment to be carried in their rucksacks for their long and rough respective journeys. Ronneberg, Kayser, Stromsheim, Storhaug, and Idland, wearing British uniforms, would ski the four hundred miles to Sweden, an incredibly challenging trek across frozen wastes, down trackless valleys, and along stormy mountain trails.

The other three men, Haukelid, Kjelstrup, and Poulsson, would travel in civilian clothes, since they would remain in Norway in the Resistance, at least for a while. Haukelid and Kjelstrup would head southwest, where they would try to organize new underground units.

And Poulsson would set off for Oslo, where he would devise new schemes with Resistance leaders, and then thread his way to London via Sweden. Helberg was to be at his side, but he was still missing, and so Poulsson would be alone. He was devastated. What had happened to his old schoolmate? If Helberg hadn't found the route to the heavy-water fortress, all of them might be dead. Now he may have been the only one to die. Even the thought that Gunnerside had succeeded in its mission could not soothe the pain of this irony.

"When everything was packed," Haukelid would later write, "we said farewell to the others. 'Give our best regards to Colonel Wilson and Tronstad. Tell them that we shall manage whatever happens. Send us a wire on your arrival in England, and have a good trip back.' We shook hands all around."

. . .

Poulsson, the first to leave, headed south toward Oslo and speedily glided across hills and through valleys, a lone white figure who blended into the great white wilderness. But in one valley he could no longer ski through the thick, soft snow, and so he had to plod ahead by foot, carrying his skis on his shoulders. He planned to crawl into his sleeping bag after he reached a forest some distance away, but doubted if his weary body could make it.

Suddenly, Poulsson saw lights. There, along a country road in the village of Uvdal, was an inn. After all the weeks of hell in the mountains, he envisioned himself sprawled between clean white sheets on a mattress of soft down. But could he take the chance?

"The temptation was too great," he would later say. "Eight days had passed since the operation at Vemork and everything seemed quiet and peaceful. After a long debate with myself, I ended up asking for a room for the night and some supper."

The innkeeper was curious. "You're on holiday?" the woman asked.

Poulsson nodded, and was soon feasting in the dining room on food he had dreamed about—fish, fresh vegetables, cheese, and other delicacies. He then went upstairs to his room and soaked in a hot tub. Grime peeled off like a second skin. He even felt lighter as the steaming water gently washed out every dirt-clogged pore. Paradise!

But it didn't last long. He had hardly stepped out of the tub when he heard loud talking on the floor below and then heavy footsteps on the stairs. Pulling his trousers on, he put his pistol in his right-hand pocket and sat half-dressed on the edge of the bed. Suddenly, there was a knock on the door.

"Come in," Poulsson called out.

And two men entered.

"I am the district police superintendent," one of them said. "And this is my assistant. Could we see your identity card?"

Poulsson pulled out his card, which identified him as "Jens Dale," and the visitors studied it for a moment.

"Why are you here?" Poulsson was asked.

"I'm on holiday. I skied here from Geilo."

The assistant walked over to the sleeping bag in a corner.

"A nice sleeping bag," he said. "Suitable for sleeping outdoors."

Poulsson held his breath. Would the man notice the English label on the inside? He didn't. Then he moved over to the rucksack in the middle of the floor. And another nerve-wracking moment. The rucksack was open and it was bulging with British-labeled food rations, maps, cigarettes, and cartridges.

"I was still on the edge of the bed with my hands in my pockets and a sweaty hand around the pistol," Poulsson would later say. "I'd already decided that if they looked into the rucksack or showed any suspicion toward me, I would have to shoot and set off into the woods as soon as possible."

But to Poulsson's relief, the men did not peer into the rucksack.

"Why are you interested in me?" the saboteur asked innocently.

"Well," the superintendent replied, "something happened up at Vemork and everyone coming down from the mountains is being controlled."

Finally, the men walked toward the door.

"Excuse us for disturbing you," the superintendent said. "Good-bye."

For a second, Poulsson would say, he was tempted to shoot both men, since it was too risky to let them go.

"But they might be good people," he would explain, "so I dropped the idea. Instead I wished the superintendent a good hunt and said I hoped they would succeed in their search for these bandits, whatever they had done."

"Oh, I don't exactly feel like meeting any of them; they're probably armed," the man responded with a knowing look that seemed to suggest suspicion but a lack of interest in pursuing the matter.

When the men had left, Poulsson pondered what to do.

"Should I set off immediately or pretend as if nothing had happened? If I left, I would prove that I had something to hide, and a big search would be organized."

Poulsson stared at the fluffy mattress on the bed. He compromised.

"In the end," he would say, "I got completely dressed with boots and outdoor wear, packed my rucksack, had the pistol in my hand, crawled underneath the blanket, and fell asleep immediately."

•  •  •

The next morning, Poulsson resumed the trek to Oslo, leaving Uvdal about the time that Kristian Kristiansen, the poacher held captive by Gunnerside before the attack on Norsk Hydro, returned to his home dragging a sled piled high with reindeer meat. Soon afterward, Kristiansen, a kind-hearted man, removed from his pocket some of the chocolate bars that his captors had given him and handed them out to children in the neighborhood.

Eyes popped. Chocolate in occupied Norway? The children were surprised. Their parents were shocked. And as word spread of the "chocolate man," the Gestapo was exhilarated. The chocolate was English—just like the commandos who had blown up the heavy-water plant. Shortly, Gestapo agents pulled up to Kristiansen's home and rummaged through his possessions, uncovering black-market reindeer meat and forbidden rifles. But they were more interested in chocolate.

Where, they asked the terrorized hunter, had he obtained the chocolate?

From British soldiers he had met in the mountains, he replied.

After squeezing out of Kristiansen every snippet he could remember about their weapons, dress, conversation, and facial features, the interrogators gave a full account to General Rediess. And within hours, Rediess, followed by General von Falkenhorst and Reich Commissar Terboven, rushed to Uvdal and, with the Norwegian's testimony in hand, mapped out a plan to round up every Briton and Resistance member hiding in the Hardanger Plateau.

• • •

**M**eanwhile, Knut Haukelid and Arne Kjelstrup skied westward through the mountains that led to Skarbu, where Knut Haugland and Einar Skinnarland were operating a radio transmitter. On reaching their hut, they found Haugland angrier than the storm they had weathered for two days. He had searched in vain for the stone hut where Gunnerside was to leave a message about the results of the sabotage.

"I looked everywhere, but I couldn't find the place," he groaned. "How did it go?"

"Don't worry, Knut, keep calm," Haukelid said, leaning back in his chair with his feet resting on the table.

After a theatrical pause, he went on: "It all went according to plan. Help me draft a telegram to London."

"There was jubilation in the hut," Haukelid would say. "Arne and I swallowed the last remains of our coffee, and we sat down and coded."

And that evening, three days after the sabotage, a message finally went off to London with the momentous news that the heavy-water installation had been destroyed. But though ignorant of the Uvdal dragnet plan, the men surmised that Gunnerside's ordeal was not over.

"Now you can bet the Germans are in a fury," Haukelid said. "And you can be sure that they'll search every corner of the mountains."

• • •

**M**eanwhile, the five Gunnerside men led by Joachim Ronneberg edged their way forward through the snowdrifts toward the Swedish border, catching their breath only when they slid down into valleys or crawled into their sleeping bags at night. Fearing they might encounter a German detachment at any moment, they moved as swiftly as possible, though no faster than the one poor skier in the group, Kasper Idland. His comrades would not leave him behind.

Actually, no people at all could be seen whizzing through the desolation, since the usual skiers and hunters, potential informers, feared arrest themselves. And if a Norwegian skier did suddenly loom into view, he quickly vanished over some hill, apparently convinced that the commandos, all wearing white snow suits over their British uniforms, were German soldiers seeking victims. Since cabins were abandoned, the Gunnerside men, expert at breaking locks, could be sure as they streaked along that they would have lodging for the night, usually with breakfast they found in the pantry.

Still, the trek over four hundred miles of rough, sometimes storm-swept terrain was enervating as the team advanced day by day, steering entirely by compass in a land without landmarks, never certain that a moving dot in the distance was not a point man for a German patrol. And in fact, though the big German sweep had not begun yet, it seemed miraculous that no patrol had stumbled upon these moving targets.

Finally, on the fourteenth day, March 18, the great snowy forests leading to the frontier stretched before them like a garden of giant white mushrooms. Ronneberg would later write in a report: "It was dreadful broken and stony country . . . with no visibility."

But if the saboteurs could see nothing, neither could German soldiers guarding the Swedish border area. And after having led one of the most daring clandestine exploits of the war, Ronneberg would report with typical understatement:

"At 2015 hours we crossed the Swedish frontier to the great satisfaction of us all."

# 15

## FLIGHT OF THE GLADIATOR

### *March 1943*

IN OSLO, Jens Poulsson felt strangely out of place amid the jostling throngs that strolled past largely empty shops, morose, silent, unaware that they might have been saved by nine men who had performed an incredible feat. After living so many months in a frozen wilderness, sick, unbathed, feeding on scraps, and with almost no hope of survival, the sights, sounds, and smells of the city with its veneer of civility came as a shock.

An infinite white world had given way to a maze of dark buildings, shadowy cobblestone streets, and crowded boulevards virtually devoid of vehicles, since there was gasoline only for the Germans and the Norwegian Nazis. The ringing clang of the trolley had replaced the whistling rage of a mountain wind.

Norwegians rubbed elbows with the enemy along the avenues, at the movies, in the cafes—German soldiers whom, until now, he would have shot on sight. They looked well-fed, unlike the bony civilians with their crumpled ration cards, having taken for themselves most of the food available in the skimpily stocked shops—eggs, chocolate, rice, fat, vegetables, coffee, tea, meat, and all the best fish. Even the bread left for the people, a mixture of flour and cellulose, was barely edible. And for lack of coal, there was no paper for wrapping the items that could be bought.

Poulsson, on the evening of March 8, entered the Majorstua Cafe and gazed around. Just possibly his dear friend, Claus Helberg, had survived after all, though he had failed to show up in Svensbu after leaving his comrades on the ridge overlooking the Hardanger Plateau. They agreed to meet at this cafe on this day if they got to Oslo as planned.

Poulsson's eyes flitted from table to table, and finally came to rest on a man sitting alone in a corner. It was Helberg. In a moment, the two men embraced and, after ordering ersatz coffee and cake, immersed themselves in conversation.

Why didn't Helberg meet the others in Svensbu? Poulsson asked.

He had tried to get there through the storm, Helberg replied, but his map had been swept away by a gust of wind, and when calm skies finally prevailed and he could orient himself, it was too late to make the rendezvous with his comrades. And so he skied to the nearest railroad station and jumped aboard the train to Oslo.

Did he run into any Germans in the mountains? Poulsson inquired.

Not one. Everything was normal. The Germans were apparently tight-lipped about the sabotage operation.

Helberg, they decided, could safely return to the mountains to gather equipment the commandos had left behind in various huts and hide them. Both would eventually ski on to Sweden and from there take a British plane to England, where they would meet again.

As the two men parted, Poulsson said: "Take care of yourself, Claus, and good luck."

. . .

Unknown to Helberg, the big German sweep began just about the time that he boarded a train for Uvdal, from where he would ski to the cabin the Gunnerside men had occupied at Lake Skryken on the Hardanger Plateau. Some ten thousand Germans were fanning out across the plateau in all directions and searching every hut, following every track, questioning every civilian.

Helberg reached the cabin without incident, but when he opened the door he found the place a "pigsty" and in utter disarray, with chairs and tables overturned and mattresses ripped open. Only the Germans would have done this, he realized. He ran to the door and was petrified on seeing five Germans only several hundred yards away skiing toward the cabin. Apparently they had seen him. He quickly put his skis back on and headed westward into the sun so that its rays would make him a more difficult target.

The crack of pistol fire split the icy air, and Helberg thought he was doomed. But a grim silence followed as the Germans, failing to hit their quarry, concentrated on the chase. Helberg was a top-flight skier and he had always loved competition, but now he was racing for his life. With his adrenaline flowing, he pushed himself forward, up hills and down, through valleys and around bends, glancing back every few minutes to see if his pursuers were gaining on him. He realized that they, too, were expert skiers and could not be shaken; they kept pace about forty yards behind him.

Finally, after about an hour, exhaustion took its toll; three of the Germans dropped out, followed by a fourth some twenty minutes later. Now there was only one left. And the race of death dragged on. When the German would start to draw near Helberg, the commando would reach into his gut for some new strength and regain lost ground. They would never take him alive; he still had a death pill in his pocket.

To the two men, it seems, the race somehow became more than a contest between faceless enemies. Helberg and his adversary, like ancient gladiators, had developed a fierce competitive relationship, with each blindly striving for a personal triumph over a grudgingly respected foe. War had become a deadly game.

"One German kept my speed," Helberg would say. "Fortunately, he also just had a pistol. Thus, the chances were equal, and the best shooter would win."

Actually, it seems, neither man wanted to kill the other. The German, at times, drew within shooting distance but didn't fire after that first volley, apparently preferring to capture his prey. And Helberg, though realizing that "the chances were equal," did not attempt to turn and fire at his pursuer. Perhaps he would fall out like the others. But the man didn't, even after two hours of merciless physical exertion.

Gradually, the German edged closer to the weary Norwegian,

and when he advanced to within thirty yards of him, called out in German: "Hands up!"

Helberg ignored the order, but when the German had come within twenty yards, he knew it was time for the showdown. At least he could die knowing he may have helped to win the war against Hitler.

He drew to a sudden halt, wheeled around, and reached under his jacket for his Colt .32 pistol. At that moment, the German fired his Luger, one shot after the other. Even as the bullets whizzed by him, Helberg fired his Colt. Then an eerie silence as each man waited for the other to collapse. But neither did, for not a single bullet struck home. The German had pulled the trigger with the sun in his eyes; Helberg had reacted while in shock from the enemy's rapid fire.

But both men knew who had won the duel. The German had fired all six bullets in his magazine, and Helberg had fired only four. He had two left. The German turned around and began skiing away with a new, panic-generated energy. Helberg instinctively followed for a while, almost enjoying the role of the hare chasing the hound. He fired twice at the fleeing German, who suddenly stopped and slumped over his ski poles. But the Norwegian wasn't sure whether the bullets struck the man. He hoped they hadn't.

"If I knew I hit him in the back," Helberg would tell me in his Oslo home, "I would regret it all my life, even though he was the enemy and tried to kill me."

Turning around again, the commando continued skiing westward into the gathering night. But in his fatigue, he hardly noticed where his path led. It led off a cliff. Down, down, he plunged, and now his luck had finally run out. Or so he thought until he hit a snowdrift about a hundred and twenty feet below and realized he was still alive. When he tried to move, however, he groaned in pain. His left shoulder had been hurt and his left arm twisted, obviously broken. But at least his legs were all right. He would have to find a doctor.

Pulling himself to his feet, he skied southward, able to use one pole, to a farm some distance away where a friend from the Resistance lived, arriving there only after hiding in brush along the way to avoid German patrols crisscrossing the area. At the farm, he could stay only long enough to eat, since the Germans were conducting a house-to-house search in the area.

Finally, after having covered 120 miles in thirty-six hours, Helberg reached Rauland, the largest town in the district—only to find he had entered the viper's nest.

"Rauland was standing on end," he would say. "I could not have chosen a worse haven. There were about three hundred German troops there. The weather turned mild, and it was impossible for me to consider moving on."

The snow, he knew, would soon turn to slush and skiing would be difficult. So, despite the risk, he moved in with a merchant he knew, but had to sleep on the kitchen floor since the Germans had requisitioned the other rooms in the house! Before falling asleep, he decided that the wisest course to take in a viper's nest was to dazzle the viper before it could spit venom.

Thus, the next morning he went to a German field hospital in town and asked a sergeant if he could see a doctor. He had broken his arm.

How had he broken it?

"I had reported as a local scout for the Germans in their search for the Vemork saboteurs and broken my arm in their service," Helberg replied with an innocent frown.

The sympathetic sergeant immediately took him to a doctor, who examined his arm and shoulder—while the patient nervously kept his eye on his jacket, which he had hung on a hook nearby. One pocket sagged. If the Germans found his Colt . . .

After treating Helberg's injuries, the doctor called for an ambulance, which would take him to Dalen, farther south, from where he would sail to Oslo. In Dalen, Helberg bid *"auf Wiedersehen"* to the ambulance personnel and they "parted as good friends."

"The Germans," he would later reminisce, "must have thought that I was quite a likable fellow."

Since the boat to Oslo was not to leave until the following morning, Helberg, needing a good night's sleep, checked into the Bandak Tourist Hotel near the port and was about to retire when he heard loud voices downstairs. He immediately recalled the story Jens Poulsson told him about his narrow escape at the hotel in Uvdal. Why hadn't he resisted the temptation to live for one night like a human being? But there was no time for regrets. He had to hide his pistol, just in case the room was searched. He tied a length of cord around it and hung it out the window.

There was the inevitable knock on the door and a couple of officers entered.

"Identity card."

It was in order.

What was the problem? Helberg asked.

Most of the rooms were being requisitioned by SS General Rediess and Reich Commissar Terboven and their staffs. No one could leave the hotel. But since Helberg was injured, he could keep his room for the night.

Could all this be true? Helberg asked himself. In the last hours, he had been shot at and had broken his arm, and now he was sharing a hotel with the two most powerful and brutal Nazis in Norway! Somehow he had to escape before they learned his true identity. But before he did, he would make sure, as he had before the attack at Vemork, that he would die on a full stomach.

He went downstairs to the dining room and ordered a fish dinner topped off by huge strawberries and, astonishingly, real coffee. One of the finest meals in memory, thanks, no doubt, to the presence of the two German leaders. But the taste turned slightly bitter when these leaders marched in with their parties and sat down at two large tables near his own. If only he could kill them on the spot.

And the desire grew when a waiter, on their orders, asked an attractive young woman sitting at another table to join them for a glass of wine. The woman declined at first, but was finally persuaded to go.

When her hosts, clearly enjoying the company of so pretty a companion, inquired about her family, she was blunt: Her father was in England. He was a colonel in the Royal Norwegian Army.

"And I'm proud of it," she added.

The Germans frowned. Her father would be back in Norway fighting for the king.

Still, his daughter could prove her loyalty to the occupier. Would she go upstairs with them?

When she disdainfully refused, their smiles vanished.

"Go back to your table!" one of them ordered.

And the next morning belligerence bore revenge, as Helberg would learn when he was rudely awakened by a call from the corridor.

"Downstairs, everybody, immediately!"

Helberg jumped out of bed, dressed, and pulled in the pistol hanging from the window, thrusting it into his belt under his ski jacket. A German soldier then pushed open the door and escorted him downstairs to the lobby, where soldiers were gathering the civilian guests.

All of them would travel by bus to the Grini concentration camp in Oslo for questioning and possible internment, a German told them. They had displayed an "impertinent attitude" toward the German leaders. Anyway, why were they vacationing at a time like this? They should be working for the Third Reich.

A large bus then stopped in front of the hotel, and the arrested guests were ordered to line up and board the vehicle one by one.

Helberg made sure he was last in line so he would get a seat right by the exit door. But a German, thinking he moved too slowly, kicked him in the rear, and he went sprawling on the stairs leading to the street. As he fell, he heard a metallic banging on the stairs. His pistol had fallen out of his belt and, bouncing down step by step, landed on the ground between the shiny boots of a German guard.

For a stunned, horrifying moment, Helberg stared at the gun, then at the guard as he, too, gazed down at the weapon—with, it seemed to Helberg, the exhilarated look of a venomous killer suddenly anointed executioner. Almost a comic end to the miracle of Gunnerside!

"Well, it's not loaded," Helberg said meekly, his demeanor reflecting an utter disdain of violence.

Since no officers were present, the soldiers now surrounding the saboteur were perplexed. Should they hold him until an officer arrived? Or should they keep him together with the other guests?

The guards finally decided that orders were orders. They had been told to send these people to Grini, and Helberg was one of them. The officials in Grini would know how to deal with him. And so a soldier pushed him into the bus, though it was already crowded.

"Sit on the floor!" the soldier ordered, shoving him toward the back of the vehicle.

And Helberg sat down in the aisle, though determined to somehow work his way to the front near the door before the bus reached Oslo. At least he found himself sitting next to someone he had wanted to meet—the pretty young woman who had dared to defy the Nazi chiefs at dinner the night before.

The two were soon engaged in conversation, and Helberg, though not at all sure he would survive the next few hours, was comforted by this sudden friendship with so remarkable a girl, whose name, he learned, was Ase Hassel. They talked about the joys of Norway before the war, their common love of winter sports, and other benign topics. But even while Helberg thrust himself into the nostalgia of a life long past, part of his mind was plotting his escape.

It wouldn't be easy. Two motorcyclists, each with a companion in a side cabin, convoyed the bus, one in front, the other in the rear. And a guard sat next to the driver facing the passengers. His eyes soon reflected jealousy as he noted Helberg winning the attention of the attractive Ase. After three or four hours, he felt compelled to join in the conversation.

"Many of my friends have been sent to the Russian front," the guard shouted over the drone of the bus engine, staring at Helberg ominously. "Why don't you volunteer to be sent there? It would be better than Grini."

"I'll think about it," Helberg replied, hoping to humor him.

"Ya, ya," the guard responded sarcastically, and, turning to Ase, he smiled and tried to converse in a friendly way with her.

But when she ignored him and resumed talking with Helberg, a scowl replaced the smile. Why should this prisoner enjoy the attention of that pretty young woman while he, a soldier of the Reich, was humiliated before all these people? He stood up, and as he started walking toward the couple, Ase, sensing that Helberg had deliberately planned a confrontation, whispered:

"You mustn't try to run away."

Just then, the guard halted before Helberg and said: "Get up and take my seat. I'll sit here."

Exactly as Helberg had hoped; now he had a seat by the door. And with little time to spare. Darkness had descended and the bus was nearing Oslo. He knew it would soon be driving up a steep hill and be forced to slow down. Fortunately, at that point, woods stretched away from the right side of the road. That was the time to move. Meanwhile, he noted that Ase, apparently understanding his intention, seemed to be deliberately engaging the guard in conversation to divert his attention.

After about nine hours on the road, the moment finally came. And once more Helberg wondered if he was about to die. He glanced at Ase one last time, clinging to her image as if to life itself. He would see her again, he seemed to say with his eyes. Then, as the bus groaned and coughed up the hill, he grabbed the door handle, swung open the door, and leaped into the night.

Landing on his injured arm and shoulder, Helberg suppressed a cry of pain as he struggled to his feet and staggered ahead into the bushes while voices shouted, rifles crackled, and grenades exploded. His life was still charmed; the bullets and shrapnel whistled harmlessly past him.

As he hid behind a spruce tree, the guards, searching for him, ran toward a nearby house just as a panicky old man, his pants still around his knees, stumbled out of an outhouse. He was struck by shrapnel, but managed to make it into the house. Only after the soldiers confronted him and his hysterical wife in their bedroom did they realized they had the wrong man.

When the guards finally gave up the search and went off in the bus, Helberg returned to the road and, still in pain, hobbled to the nearest town looking for a hospital where he could get treatment for his reinjured arm and shoulder. He entered a building he thought was a hospital, especially when he saw people in white smocks.

"What hospital is this?" he asked a man in the corridor.

"A mental hospital," the man replied.

After all his hairbreadth escapes, Helberg felt strangely at home. He even joined the patients in a Saturday night celebration, imbibing very bad homemade liquor. Then, his pain dulled, he was taken to a doctor, who sent him to a general hospital. Soon, he took a train to Oslo, then another part way to Sweden. He skied to the Swedish border undetected by the Germans, and from there flew to Britain.

Poulsson, his other comrades, and the intelligence chiefs were incredulous when Helberg suddenly reappeared. He was not surprised they had thought he was dead. Several times he had thought so, too.

Gunnerside had now culminated in triumph without a single casualty. On reading the details of this mission, Churchill wrote across the front page of the report: "What is being done for these brave men in the way of decorations?" Their chests were soon glittering with medals awarded by the British and Norwegian governments.

# 16

## THE ANGELS ARE WAITING

### *March–November 1943*

THE EXPLOSION IN NORSK HYDRO did not make a deafening noise, but it furiously reverberated two weeks later in Washington. General Groves could hardly contain himself when he read the translation of an article in the March 14 issue of a Swedish newspaper, *Svenska Dagbladet*, reporting the attack. The British had not only failed to consult with him before the operation took place but they didn't bother to inform him promptly about the results. His rage was tempered only by relief that the sabotage attempt had apparently succeeded. The news report read:

> The sabotage of the Norsk Hydro plant at Rjukan a couple of weeks ago, according to information now available, was one of the most important and successful undertakings the Allied saboteurs have carried out as yet during this war. All the apparatus, machines and foundation for the production of heavy water were blown up by the saboteurs, who were dressed in British uniforms, and they managed to escape unscathed and find a safe refuge.

Despite this good news, Groves was shocked by the background presented in the article: "Heavy water has for some years come into extensive use in scientific investigations, especially in attempts to break down the atom. . . . Many scientists have pinned their hopes of producing the 'secret weapon' upon heavy water, namely an explosive of hitherto unheard-of-violence."

The general would write in his memoirs that while "the first reports on this action were most encouraging," these same reports "caused me some headaches when they went on to speculate at considerable length about the importance of heavy water." The basic secrets of the atomic bomb had been discussed in the press, and the Allied effort to build one was now public knowledge.

Especially galling was the fact that he had to learn about the attack from the press. Over two weeks had apparently passed since the action and he hadn't received word from Britain that the event had even occurred. Groves knew that London was planning a commando raid, for Wallace Akers, the engineer who headed the British Directorate of Tube Alloys, had told him so. But Akers did not say when it would take place. The British, he fumed, wanted to know all of America's secrets but were keeping their own from America.

In his frustration, Groves went to General Marshall and apparently convinced him that the government should buy the facts if necessary. On March 20, Leif Tronstad wrote in his diary in clear reference to Gunnerside: "The juice story still of highest big policy importance. USA has offered 1 mill USD [United States dollars] for information."

The British, however, seem to have ignored the offer. For Groves was unable to obtain data from them for the next few weeks, and had to continue rummaging through newspapers to learn more about Gunnerside and what nuclear information was being leaked to the public. A *New York Times* report from London, dated April 3, left him especially rattled:

> "Heavy water," derived by an electro-chemical process from ordinary water, with hidden atomic power that can be used for the deadly purposes of war, apparently has become a source of anxiety for those Allied leaders who plan attacks against enemy targets. . . . While it is not believed here that the Germans . . . have developed some fantastic method of hurling the shattering force of split atoms at Britain, it is

known that heavy water, when added to other chemicals, gives a powerfully destructive force.

This article fed the curiosity of other publications, which bombarded Harold Urey, the discoverer of heavy water, with questions about the explosive potential of the substance. Apparently after consulting Groves, Urey replied to these queries: "I am quite sure that [heavy water] cannot be used as a deadly explosive of any kind. I think the best thing that can be done with such stories is to ignore them."

Urey was technically correct; heavy water could not be used as an explosive. It could only facilitate an explosion.

Groves, meanwhile, urged Marshall to confront Britain and, apparently with or without a monetary bribe, insist that it immediately furnish details of the reported raid and agree to an air attack on Rjukan if the raid had failed to knock out the plant permanently. Thus, on April 3, the day the *New York Times* received its report from London, Marshall sent a memorandum to Field Marshal Sir John Dill, Britain's military representative in Washington, politely making these demands:

> The latest information is that there has been no interruption in the production at this plant. Mr. Akers . . . informed one of my officers on January 26 that the British were planning a commando raid on the plant. . . . [But] no information has been received to the effect that this raid has actually been made. . . . A commando raid does not appear feasible. . . . It is felt that although the procurement of a quantity of the heavy water would have its advantages, the delay incidental to the staging of the commando raid, which might not succeed, makes it desirable to bomb this target at the earliest opportunity.

And Marshall suggested that Dill cable Sir Charles Portal, chief of the Royal Air Force, recommending that the plant "be set up as a first priority bombing objective."

That same day, Dill, also apparently ignorant of Gunnerside, cabled Portal asking about the raid Akers had mentioned in January. "AS NOTHING HAS BEEN HEARD OF THIS RAID," he wired, "AND AS

IN FACT A RAID MAY BE IMPOSSIBLE, MARSHALL, AS ADVISED, FEELS STRONGLY, REPEAT STRONGLY, THAT THE INSTALLATION SHOULD BECOME BOMBING TARGET OF FIRST PRIORITY."

Portal replied three days later, on April 6:

> SOE STATE THAT AFTER ONE UNSUCCESSFUL ATTEMPT THEY
> SUCCEEDED ABOUT A MONTH AGO IN DESTROYING THE
> PLANT WHICH THEY NOW CONSIDER TO BE INEFFECTIVE
> FOR AT LEAST TWO YEARS. . . . ALTHOUGH QUESTION OF
> BOMBING THE PLANT DOES NOT NOW ARISE, IT HAD IN FACT
> BEEN CONSIDERED EARLIER BUT IDEA WAS NOT PURSUED
> OWING TO TACTICAL AND OTHER DIFFICULTIES.

The reference to "one unsuccessful attempt," it seems, was the first indication to the Americans that Operation Freshman had even taken place. Indeed, Robert R. Furman, Groves's intelligence officer, indicated to me that his boss was ignorant of the operation until then. The revelation no doubt escalated the outrage of Groves and Marshall over British secrecy. Were the two countries allies in this war or not? This was the same question the British had been asking up to now.

Nor did Groves believe that the plant would be "ineffective" for two years. The British, he felt, were always exaggerating their successes. And, in fact, one day after Dill received the cable from Portal, the RAF chief cabled a correction:

> AS A RESULT OF INFORMATION I HAVE RECEIVED SINCE
> DESPATCHING . . . STATEMENT THAT SOE CONSIDER THE
> PLAN QUOTE TO BE INEFFECTIVE FOR AT LEAST TWO
> YEARS UNQUOTE SHOULD BE ALTERED TO READ QUOTE
> WILL NOT BE FULLY EFFECTIVE FOR MORE THAN 12
> MONTHS UNQUOTE

Groves disputed even this "correction"; Norsk Hydro, he felt, would be delivering heavy water to Germany again within three months. And he challenged British experts James Chadwick and Michael Perrin when they told him that summer at a meeting of Anglo-American officials that, according to their information, the

Germans probably couldn't build an atomic bomb before the end of the war. The general reportedly grunted:

"You might be right, but I don't believe it."

And the danger posed by Norsk Hydro grew in Groves's eyes when that spring he heard that the Germans might use an atomic reactor not simply to build a bomb but to manufacture radioactive material for use as a kind of poison gas. In May, he asked Conant to investigate the question, and on July 1, Conant reported: "It now seems extremely probable that it will be possible to produce by means of a self-sustaining pile large quantities of radioactive materials with varying half-lives of the order of magnitude of twenty days."

If one week's output of such materials were distributed over two square miles, Conant wrote, it would be necessary to evacuate the area, and a large proportion of the population would be "incapacitated." But he added: "If any attack is made by the Germans using radioactive poisons, it seems extremely likely that it will occur not in the United States but in Great Britain."

Groves may have felt some slight relief, but the British, who received a copy of Conant's memo, surely could not have. And jitters over the new perceived danger on both sides of the Atlantic only seemed to add to the tension between the two countries.

In any case, Groves's skepticism about the accuracy of British information proved well founded, at least regarding the pace of repair at the heavy-water plant. On July 8, little more than five months after Operation Gunnerside, Einar Skinnarland radioed London from his hideout on the Hardanger Plateau that the Germans had repaired the heavy-water apparatus in April and that the plant was expected "to reach full production . . . again from August 15."

On August 3, Skinnarland revealed that "partial production of the 99.5% heavy-water concentrate started in June" and that "the output has now reached 4.5 kilos (about 10 pounds) per day," though six days later he reported that "the daily production at times had been reduced to 1.5 kilos (about 3 pounds) as a result of adding oil to the distillation vats." Plant engineers and workers, bitterly disappointed that the heroic Gunnerside operation had only a limited effect, had resumed corrupting the heavy water with castor oil.

THE ANGELS ARE WAITING • 187

Despite such sabotage, Groves, after learning of these reports, felt he had the evidence he needed to convince Marshall that Rjukan should be bombed with or without British support. He met with General Strong and Vannevar Bush, and on August 13 Strong sent a memorandum to Marshall stating:

> Dr. Bush and General Groves consider it of highest importance that the heavy-water plant with adjoining power plant and penstock at Rjukan, . . . which have been restored to operation be totally destroyed. The destruction of the power facilities as well as the actual manufacturing facilities is desired as this is the only immediately available source of the power [DC] necessary for producing heavy water in any quantity. I concur.

So did Marshall. But not everyone did. General Ira C. Eaker, commander of the 8th Air Force based in Britain, whose units would drop the bombs, objected. Bush, who broached the subject to the general but apparently did not reveal the true reason for such an attack, "received the very distinct impression that . . . Eaker, and particularly the RAF, were not disposed to regard these targets as of any high importance."

But the British were still the main problem. They were even more opposed to a bombing than General Eaker, with Tronstad warning them that hundreds of civilians would be killed. Perhaps unnecessarily, too, since London felt that Germany would probably not be able to build a bomb before the war ended anyway.

Under tremendous pressure from Washington, however, the Combined Chiefs of Staff gradually bowed to the inevitable. Supported by Prime Minister Churchill, they would finally argue, or rationalize, that "the Germans [have] strengthened their security to the point where it would be impossible to carry out" any new sabotage operation. And since the United States was determined to bomb even without British support, there seemed to be no point in resisting the pressure.

Now, Eaker, in view of his reluctance, was given "specific

direction on the highest level for immediate action." At the highest level, of course, was President Roosevelt, who agreed with Groves that the heavy-water plant had to be demolished in order to end the German atomic threat once and for all.

And on October 22, Eaker, referring to Norsk Hydro, ordered his officers: "When the weather favors attacks in Norway, the target . . . should be destroyed."

. . .

The predawn fog blanketed the U.S. airfield that sprawled at the heart of Thorpe Abbotts, merging the dim runway lights into a hazy glow as shadowy figures prepared to swoop into the heavens to meet the enemy, and perhaps the angels up there waiting to welcome a select few.

The roar of motors revving up awakened the citizens of Thorpe Abbotts earlier than usual on this morning of November 15, for the B-17s of the 100th Bombardment Group based in this farm village, about ninety miles northeast of London, would be flying a longer route than they normally did. They would head not south toward Germany this time but north toward Norway.

The airfield was a simmering cauldron of activity. Tankers drained tons of high-octane gasoline into aircraft tanks; mechanics made last-minute checks on equipment that could be strained to the breaking point on this long trip; pilots hammered home final instructions to their nervous crews, punctuated occasionally by the mooing of a Durham cow grazing in nearby pastureland.

Munching on a crumpet from a breakfast wagon making the rounds as he stood by the 100th Group's lead plane, Second Lieutenant Owen Roane, the pilot, skeptically scrutinized the new group commander, who would be sitting next to him in the co-pilot's seat. Roane now met Major John M. Bennett, Jr., for the first time.

The lieutenant knew the attack on that hydroelectric plant in southern Norway would be a high-priority mission, for at a briefing held at about 4 A.M. crew members were told that they would be bombing not an ordinary plant but a place where a new "high explosive" was being developed. An explosive, Roane guessed, that might be able to blow up a whole city block. But while his plane would be the first to bombard this vital target, Bennett would presumably bombard him with orders.

It didn't make sense to Roane. He might be only a second lieutenant, but he had already flown on twenty-three missions and was considered one of the best pilots not only in the 100th Group but in the 3rd Division, indeed in the 8th Air Force. And this major had been on only three previous missions.

Bennett had recently been assigned to the 100th and already was reputed as a hard-nosed disciplinarian. In short, he was a threat to Roane, who sometimes mixed his expertise with a little horseplay. Actually, muleplay. Once, while in North Africa, he returned to base with an unusual mascot in tow—a baby ass. To many airmen in the 8th Air Force, it was a fitting group symbol.

The 100th was a jinxed group of motley men. Commanding officers never stayed with it long. One was relieved of his command. Another became ill. Still another was wounded. And two others were soon promoted out of the group. Meanwhile, it seemed, the men acted virtually on their own. They seldom flew in proper formation during combat missions, and one time the Germans shot down a plane on a practice mission while the gunners slept in the radio compartment. It was said that other groups were delighted when the 100th joined them on a mission, for the Germans focused their fire mainly on its scattered aircraft. The group suffered so many casualties that it became known as the Bloody 100th.

Bennett was a handsome, serious-minded thirty-six-year-old officer as tough as he was green. He had come to the group to turn a bunch of talented but dangerously maverick airmen into a smoothly operating killing machine. And Roane was one of those mavericks. Thus, other than sharing a Texan heritage, the two men had almost nothing in common.

Roane, a gregarious, good-natured man of twenty-one with squinting, humorous eyes that exuded a country wisdom, was born in Valley View, north of Dallas, the son of a poor tenant farmer who grew cotton and wheat and raised cattle for seventy-five cents a day plus room and board. Young Owen thus grew up herding cattle, earning his nickname, "Cowboy." Joining the Army Air Corps in 1939, when he was only seventeen, he soon became a flying sergeant and eventually a lieutenant piloting B-17 bombers.

Cowboy never hesitated to streak into a storm of flak, even as he watched many of his comrades plummet to their death. On one occasion when his own plane was set on fire, he tried shutting off the fuel and using a fire extinguisher, but to no avail. So he went into a steep dive, hoping to blow the flames out. However, to make enemy fighters on his tail think his plane was plunging to earth, he spiraled down in a spin. And when he finally rolled out of the plunge, the flames were out and he made it back to base, in wonderment that he was still alive.

Bennett, a native of San Antonio who was driven by the need to excel, followed a different route to the Bloody 100th. He was also a cattleman, but he owned the cattle. Indeed, his family owned one of the biggest ranches in Texas, as well as one of its biggest banks. After graduating from Andover and Princeton, he earned a commercial pilot's license and passed the flight test for the National Guard. He was ordered to duty as a second lieutenant in November 1940, and eventually joined the 100th as a crew pilot before moving up to squadron and group commander.

On taking over as commanding officer, Bennett wasted no time trying to turn the Bloody 100th into a disciplined, less sanguine organization. To make his point, he chose as his first "victim" Major Harry H. Crosby, a self-described "straight-arrow," who didn't drink, gamble, or hustle women in and out of his quarters. Crosby was taking a shower one morning when he suddenly heard Bennett's voice blare forth from a loudspeaker for the whole base to hear: "Major Crosby will run, not walk, to Group Operations."

Crosby was taken aback. As an officer with an impeccable disciplinary record, he wasn't used to being talked to like that. He dressed, jumped into a jeep, and "tore its wheels off" getting to Group Operations.

"Sir," he greeted Bennett with barely contained indignation, "I was in the shower. I came here as soon as I could. You owe me an apology."

"Major," Bennett said with a cold smile, "come into my office."

And they entered a room with a glass front where they were visible to a crowd of personnel, who could not hear a word but could see Crosby standing rigidly at attention while Bennett talked.

"Maybe you came fast enough," Bennett said with a deliberately stern expression. "I think you are one of the most respected of the original 100th, but I have been appointed commanding officer. I want everyone on this base to know that even with you I mean business."

Bennett, still with a false scowl, then asked Crosby about his pregnant wife and the impending birth of his son.

The spectators walked away, convinced this commander was an iron-fisted brute. How could he chew out Crosby of all people?

Such tactics would soon pay off. The 100th would gradually develop into a disciplined group that followed orders, obeyed the rules, and suffered fewer casualties while chalking up more combat successes.

But on the morning of November 16, 1943, Cowboy Roane had little reason to doubt that Bennett would be holding him on a short leash. And, in fact, he would never learn to fully appreciate Bennett's wizardry in shaking the chaotic 100th into a top-rate fighting force. For there was, he felt, something to be said for a little bit of chaos. War was war and though the interests of the individual had to give way to those of the group, he conceded, the commander had no right to verbally bully his men, as Bennett sometimes did.

Actually, it appears, Bennett was hurt when his victims reacted with anger, though he would seldom give even a hint that a sensitive, caring nature might be hidden under his macho armor. Why didn't they understand, he wondered, that he was simply trying to save their lives?

"As leader of a group I am constantly inspired by the soldiers under me," Bennett would write his father from England. "Their heroic acts are always a challenge. I frequently asked myself what the men expect of me. Living up to what I think they expect and deserve is a driving force which is ever present."

As the 100th prepared to set off for Rjukan, Cowboy was particularly eager to operate as he saw fit, since he could sense from the briefing that this would be a historic mission. The scene would cling to memory: the dramatic way the briefing officer slowly pulled back the curtain that covered the map of Europe, gradually tracing the route and finally revealing the target—a hydroelectric complex in Norway. Bombs were to wipe out an electrolysis plant, a power plant, and an electrochemical works.

Three hundred and eighty-eight B-17s and B-24s of the 8th Air Force based across southern England would attack in three divisions. The 3rd Division with 160 B-17s, including the 100th Group, would bomb the primary target at Rjukan. Thirty-nine B-17s of the 2nd Division and 189 B-24s of the 1st Division would make diversionary raids on secondary targets near Oslo.

The greatest peril came not from the few German fighter planes in the area but from the six 1,000-pound high-explosive bombs and the full overload of gasoline that each bomber would carry. Each would have a gross weight of about 65,000 pounds, 15,000 pounds overweight.

"Even in broad daylight with perfect weather," Bennett would write his father, "I would be nervous with this load."

• • •

When twenty-one aircraft of the Bloody 100th finally swept into the sky at 6:25 A.M., Major Bennett had good reason to be nervous. For the airmen had to climb their shaky way through a quilt of clouds so dense that they could not fly in formation, but had to grind blindly upward on their own. And even if they managed to thrust into the clear, would they be able to find each other and assemble for the trip to Norway?

Owen Roane's plane finally struggled through three thousand feet of swirling moisture into a black moonlit infinity, and the crew was thankful for, but not surprised by, their pilot's maneuvers. For who could pilot a plane better than Cowboy? Bennett, who was usually stingy with compliments, would later concede: "The success of our take-off and climb through the overcast was due to no skill of my own, but to Lt. . . . Roane, my pilot."

But success meant loneliness, for no other plane was in sight. Roane thus flew in circles waiting for his comrades, and suddenly another aircraft broke into the clear, then another and another. Finally, eighteen aircraft. Three wandered aimlessly in the maze of clouds.

With Bennett barking instructions over the radio, the planes assembled in the darkness with difficulty, and so many now filled the air that a collision seemed more than possible. In fact, the group soon grew to twenty-one planes again. Three B-24s, unable to find their own group, had tagged on to the 100th. Lost planes were returning to base or scurrying around in search of their comrades. Utter confusion marked the start of the mission.

Bennett, responsible for all the planes in the 100th Group, could only hope that when they reached their target the confusion would dissipate into order. He had to show his men on this first combat flight with them that he was a deft commander if he was to win the respect needed to mold a disciplined group. More important, this was a special mission that, he understood, could seriously damage the war effort if it failed.

Bennett was acutely aware that his men would be bombing installations in a friendly country, and would probably be taking the lives of people already suffering under the Germans. Fortunately, orders called for the force to drop its bombs between 11:30 and 11:45 A.M., when the workers would be at lunch, mainly in their well-protected basements.

Still, how many would die if this initial chaos spread all the way to Norway, where the skies were more tempestuous than they were over Britain?

# 17

## THE COFFINS ARE FULL

### *November 1943*

AT ABOUT THIS TIME, Birger Boilestad awoke in his home in Vemork, happily contemplating the days ahead. His fiancée, Julia, had come from Oslo two days earlier and would stay with his family for a week. The couple had met in Oslo in 1941, when both worked for a machine-tool company there, but Boilestad, twenty-one, soon returned to his native Rjukan. Though the Germans had wanted him to work for them in northern Norway, they finally agreed that he could serve Germany best at Norsk Hydro.

Now he and Julia were together again and relishing every moment of her visit. They went skiing, visited Birger's friends, and, over dinner at home, spoke about happy prewar days with his parents and brother, who warmly approved of Julia, a pretty young woman with a shy, gentle manner.

The wedding day? All agreed it should be delayed until the war ended and their finances improved, when there was more to eat than the skimpy rations they were now being served. Nor would it make sense for Julia to leave her relatively well-paying job in Oslo at a time like this.

Besides, Boilestad secretly worked for the Resistance and, being in grave danger, did not wish to leave Julia a widow. While employed by the German-controlled machine-tool company in Oslo, he had sabotaged its products, and now in the Norsk Hydro machine shop in Rjukan he made sure that malfunctioning machinery continued to malfunction. The danger had grown since the commandos raided the heavy-water plant months earlier, for the Germans were well prepared for another attack, perhaps this time from the air. They had set up more antiaircraft guns, as well as smoke pots to cloud the area so the enemy couldn't pinpoint targets. At the same time, Norsk Hydro had built a large bomb shelter in Vemork's residential area, not far from the Boilestad home, a four-family house provided by the company. But the shelter was simply a ground-level enclosure of concrete and stones.

"To stay in that bomb shelter would be like staying in a garage," Birger's bother had told him. "It's the last place I'd run to if the air-raid alarm sounded."

But no one at Norsk Hydro thought the Allies would really bomb a Norwegian factory and risk the workers' lives, even if the Germans were running the place. The Norwegian leaders in Britain would never permit such a thing. Still, Boilestad felt, where could his family hide if bombs did start falling?

Norsk Hydro was the lifeblood of the Boilestad family. Birger's brother worked in the electrolysis plant and his father in the power plant just behind it; they walked to work. Birger rode to his job in Rjukan on the firm's train. On the morning of November 16, he rushed to catch the next train, afraid he would be late for work. After a quick breakfast, he bade good-bye to his father and brother, kissed his fiancée—his mother had gone out of town to visit her brother on his birthday—and departed.

He would count the hours until he returned home to Julia.

• • •

While Birger Boilestad left home for work, Dagfinn Frantsen, another Norsk Hydro employee, left work for home. He had just finished the night shift in the electrolysis building and was eager to get some sleep. In a sense, Frantsen had two full-time jobs. He worked in the compressor room but spent much of his time hiding arms in a "crawl space" under the basement floor next to the high-concentration room that the Gunnerside saboteurs had so masterfully penetrated.

Frantsen, twenty-seven, belonged to the Resistance, and when he wasn't sleeping during the day, he was giving the Germans severe headaches. He thus arranged for a fellow member to come each day with a horse and wagon to deliver food supplies to the electrolysis building and the neighboring power plant. Actually, the crates that were unloaded contained more than herring and smoked salmon. Packed underneath the delicacies were guns, which British planes had dropped in the mountains of Rjukan for retrieval by the Resistance. Plant employees would use the weapons to prevent the Germans from destroying Norsk Hydro after the Allies landed in Norway.

Like Birger Boilestad, Dagfinn Frantsen was a devoted child of the company. His father had served it as a machinist all his life, and he and his brother planned to do the same. Dagfinn left his job only once—in 1940 when the Germans invaded Norway. He went off to war and fought them until Norway was forced to surrender. After being interned for several weeks, he returned to work, vowing to continue the battle secretly.

Besides caching away weapons, he filled artillery shells with explosives that would blow up German cannons in the area when fired, and stole batteries from factory tractors to be used by radiomen hiding in the mountains, like Knut Haugland and Einar Skinnarland. After the Gunnerside raid, he was put to work reconstructing the high-concentration room and did his best to slow up progress, though he was under the watchful eye of German experts.

When Frantsen arrived home on the morning of November 16, his wife, Liv, whom he had only recently married, served him breakfast and then left to visit her in-laws on the other side of the gorge.

"Give them my love," Frantsen said. "And take Truls with you."

He had given her a puppy, Truls, and he didn't want the animal barking. Utterly exhausted, he hoped that nothing would disturb his sleep.

. . .

"This was really a beautiful sight," Major Bennett would later write of the journey over the North Sea, "sun on the right, fleecy clouds below, blue sky above, and bombers in every direction."

It was easy to let such heavenly splendor erase from his mind the deadly purpose of those silvery, birdlike bombers. But not for long. The clouds finally dispersed under them, and there was Norway in the distance. Bennett glanced at his watch—11 A.M. The planes were more than half an hour early.

The major found himself caught in an agonizing dilemma. If the planes attacked now, many Norwegians working in the target buildings would surely be killed. But if the aircraft simply circled the target zone until lunch hour, they would not only be risking the lives of his men but would be jeopardizing what was apparently one of the most crucial missions of the war. For the Germans would be poised with their guns, fighters, and smoke pots that would conceal the target area.

Cowboy Roane was happy, and a bit surprised, that Bennett had given him pretty much of a free hand up to now, but he was glad to leave to him the Solomonic decision whether to "go on in." Bennett weighed his options. This was war, wasn't it? One had to sacrifice many lives in order to save many more. Yet could he wipe his soul clean of humanity as long as there was an alternative, however risky?

"Make a large circle over the North Sea," Bennett ordered Roane.

In minutes, the decision bred misfortune. Two German boats patrolling the coast fired their antiaircraft guns at the circling planes and one piece of flak struck home. The damaged plane pulled out of the formation with a motor smoking and dropped its bombs into the sea. It then feathered its number three propeller and limped off toward Scotland.

Bennett was dismayed. That morning he had asked the pilot of that aircraft, Lieutenant Pete Biddick, to go on the mission even though he had not been scheduled for it.

"It'll probably be a milk run," he said, not wishing to order him to go.

And Biddick had immediately agreed. Now he cried over the radio: "Milk run! Shit!"

But his plane made it back to base—barely.

Shortly, another aircraft was hit and started to smoke, and Bennett "counted ten parachutes blossoming out below" while the plane continued flying by itself, performing "some of the fanciest bomber acrobatics that one could possibly imagine." The German patrol boats raced toward the men as they splashed into the water. Their fate is still unknown.

Finally, the time for the attack on Norsk Hydro came and Cowboy Roane steered his plane northeast toward the target area. But to his dismay, he couldn't see it, for it was shrouded by a blanket of clouds. What would they do now? Were they to drop bombs blindly and perhaps kill hundreds of civilians?

Roane, as resourceful as ever, thought he might have the answer. He was sure he could fly under the billowy cover by heading due north and then curving eastward and down over the target. His bombardier, Captain Bob Peel, would not only have a clear shot at the target but would drop the first bombs—an honor the crew would relish.

Actually, two other 3rd Division groups were to lead the way, but they had already flown over the target without releasing their bombs because they couldn't see through the clouds and were now circling a second time. Why should the 100th follow them around again?

And so Roane, with a nod from Bennett, turned north then east under the cloud, only to be enveloped by a blinding blend of smoke from the ground and mist from the condensation trails left behind by planes that had followed this path earlier. Nevertheless, the navigator, Joe Paine, skillfully directed the plane "straight into the target," in Bennett's words, and at 11:43:30, just one minute and thirty seconds off schedule, Bob Peel dropped his six 1,000-pound bombs through the haze on the electrolysis and power plants.

. . .

In the next twenty minutes, 161 other planes released their deadly loads on the various buildings and structures in the Norsk Hydro complex. They included some unexpected support. Because of stormy skies near Oslo, twenty-nine B-24s had been unable to drop their bombs on their diversionary target and had veered toward Rjukan to help out the 3rd Division.

The B-24 formations were a hodgepodge of several groups, the remnants emerging from the clouds shortly after takeoff in Britain. Major Kenneth G. Jewell piloted one of only two B-24s of the 44th Group that reached blue skies. As the two planes flew together over the sea, they picked up four B-24s from the 93rd Division.

"The planes kept switching positions," Jewell would later recall. "No one seemed to be in charge."

Finally, Jewell decided that someone had to take over control. But how could he discuss this with the other pilots, who, for security reasons, had been ordered not to reveal their movements and intentions over the radio? The answer: pig latin. In this perversion of English, Jewell proposed that he take over command.

"Soon, all the planes were talking freely in this crazy talk," he would later laugh, and they all formed on him.

Since dense clouds floated over their primary target near Oslo, the six planes swerved toward Rjukan and were about to bomb the power plant and the penstock pipes that fed it when they saw people running, apparently survivors of earlier bomb strikes. Circling until the area was clear, Jewell finally gave the order to bomb—in pig latin.

■ ■ ■

Not every B-24 missile was meant to annihilate; one, at least, was meant to simply humiliate. Robert Wright, a radio operator for a 93rd Group crew, had a stomach problem, and the doctor had given him a laxative that morning. It began to work when his plane reached Norway. Near the target, he removed his soiled long johns, wrapped them into a knot, and dropped them out of the bomb bay, crying: "And this is for you, Kraut!"

No one could say if this missile contributed in some small measure to the smoke and grime swirling up from the scorched earth below.

▪ ⸱ ▪

The bombs dropped by the B-24s of the 392nd Group were more conventional and no doubt caused heavier damage, but to the wrong targets. The 392nd never did emerge from chaos after piercing the mists that smothered its base at Wendling in northeast England. Major Lawrence Gilbert, the group leader, had led his plane into a seemingly infinite cloudbank—12,000 feet, 15,000 feet, 17,000 feet . . . finally clear, at 18,000 feet. And Gilbert found himself alone even after circling several times over the North Sea.

He flew on toward Norway and was relieved to sight another plane, and then a second. Now there were three. Then, thirty minutes later, a cluster of thirteen planes flashed under the sun. Gilbert's aircraft and its companions tacked on to the 93rd Group—whose bombardier, Robert Wright, dropped a homemade bomb—but were clearly unwelcome. The gun turrets of the 93rd swung around toward the three intruders, which were seen as "threatening our integrity," as one airman in the group would later explain. "We wanted to bomb as a unit."

Gilbert's trio of planes broke off, headed toward its objective near Oslo, but because of the blustery weather turned toward Rjukan, its secondary target, where they were to hit the electrolysis and power plants. The bombardier would later report:

> I was finally able to see a group of buildings that looked like a target. The buildings did not look like the picture that we were briefed on, but we were briefed that those pictures were prewar pictures. . . . Landmarks around the target were covered with snow and it was very hard to pick any of the briefed surrounding landmarks.

But finally the bombardier cried out: "I think I've got it."
"Yeah, I think that's it," the navigator agreed.
Gilbert knelt on the catwalk and watched the bombs plummet. Those buildings didn't look like the target to him, but he wasn't

going to second-guess his navigator and bombardier. He called to another pilot:

"How does it look to you?"

"Great."

"On returning to the base," the bombardier would report after checking his maps, "we found that I had bombed another target and not the secondary. The target that we bombed was two and one-half miles east of the briefed target."

He had virtually destroyed the nitrate plant, which sprawled only about 300 yards from Rjukan proper. If the missiles had been released seconds later, hundreds of civilians in the town might have died.

• • •

**N**ot again!

Kjell Nielsen, a Norsk Hydro engineer, could not believe his luck. Just four months earlier, in July, he had been working at a company metallurgical plant in Heroya, south of Oslo, when American planes destroyed it, killing many civilians. Although he was a leading member of the Resistance, he had not seen the need for that bombing and accused the Americans of attacking simply "in order to train their pilots."

Nielsen had since been transferred to Vemork and was now working in the electrolysis plant there. Suddenly, at 11:33 A.M., the same familiar siren with its terrifying message screamed in his ears. He had walked into another "useless" air raid. A few bombs couldn't hold up production here for more than a few weeks or months, but they could kill a lot of innocent civilians.

With other plant personnel, Nielsen rushed down to the basement, which served as an air-raid shelter. And within seconds, the telephone in the shelter rang. Nielsen picked it up and heard the excited voice of the operator cry:

"I can see fifteen, maybe twenty planes approaching!"

Several moments later, she called again: "I can see more than fifty!"

Just then, the building shook with a great explosion. And Nielsen suddenly realized that in the rush to escape danger all personnel had neglected to put on their helmets. Would they be killed by falling concrete? More blasts followed, sprinkling a white rain on the refugees, and during each lull several men would scamper to the other floors or to the power plant nearby to rescue any wounded. Soon, three badly injured men were carried in.

Someone then cried out: "My God, what's happened to my family?"

Einar Moe sputtered to Nielsen, his neighbor, that his wife and three children must have run to the above-ground cement shelter in the residential area. But how could the structure withstand a bomb strike?

Nielsen tried to reassure the man: The likelihood of a bomb hitting a small target like that was negligible. He shouldn't worry.

But Nielsen knew there was good reason to worry. After arriving in Vemork, he told me in his present home outside Oslo, he had warned Chief Engineer Larsen about the flimsiness of the shelter.

"You're inviting death here," he had said.

"Don't you accuse Norsk Hydro of negligence!" Larsen indignantly replied.

As soon as the bombs stopped falling, Nielsen would go out and learn if, God forbid, his warning was prophetic.

• • •

When the alarm sounded, Birger Boilestad was on his lunch hour in Rjukan, though he was skipping lunch. He was too busy browsing in a gift shop. What should he buy his fiancée? The shelves, as in all the shops, were largely empty because of wartime shortages, but he couldn't return home empty-handed. He paused on hearing the siren.

"Don't worry," another customer said. "It's probably just a test."

Boilestad sensed that this was the "real thing," but he wouldn't permit himself to think so. His loved ones would be in a vulnerable position if Vemork was bombed and he had to believe they were safe. But he nevertheless returned to his small plant to find that the other workers had gathered in the basement of a nearby building.

Joining them, he soon learned that this was no test exercise. Bombs exploded in the distance, and when he peeked out the door he saw with dread smoke rising leisurely over his factory and an adjoining building just down the street.

Even before the bombing stopped, Boilestad, a former fireman, rushed out with others and, after attaching a hose to a hydrant, tried to put the fire out, but in vain. The water pressure was too low to quench the flames, which partly demolished the factory and burned the neighboring building to the ground. Then someone shouted:

"They've destroyed Vemork!"

In panic, Boilestad ran to the railway terminal to catch the train to Vemork and jumped into a car jammed with workers being sent to help save the remnants of the village. When the train pulled into the plant terminal, he dashed toward his home and saw that there was little left of it. He desperately searched through the ruins, but found no bodies or trace of life. His family and the others in the building, he surmised, must have taken refuge in the bomb shelter nearby, even though his brother had said this was a death trap.

He rushed to the shelter—but it wasn't there. All he saw was a deep hole. But scattered around it were bloody clumps of flesh, "pieces of people." There was a leg, a torso with the stomach split open, a head without features.

As he gazed around in numbing horror, his eyes finally focused on the remains of two people he could identify by their clothing— his fiancée and his brother. He fell to his knees and wept. This wasn't true. It was a nightmare, and he would soon wake up. He closed his eyes as if to expunge the scene from his mind. But when he opened them, nothing had changed. Why, he asked himself, had God let Julia visit him at this time? He was at least grateful that his mother was out of town, and that his father was at work, though he didn't know yet if he had survived attacks on his plant. (He had.)

Other people had begun to congregate, and more cries of agony vibrated through the chilly air. One of the mourners was Einar Moe, who could not be consoled by his neighbor Kjell Nielsen. He was convinced that his wife and three children were among the scattered pieces of flesh, though he would later learn that, while his wife was indeed a victim, his children had been visiting friends in Rjukan and were safe. Others weeping hysterically were the parents of newlyweds. None of the sixteen people in the shelter—eleven women, two children, and three men—survived a direct hit by a bomb.

About sixty children had escaped from that death chamber just in time. They had been in a nearby school when the air-raid alarm sounded, and their teacher had led them to the shelter. But when the drone of planes sounded almost overhead, the teacher looked out and cried:

"They're right over us! Run to your homes!"

The pupils piled out and scattered. Most of them hid in their cellars as the bombs dropped.

But the other refugees had not run. And now, in a tormented daze, Birger Boilestad struggled to his feet and helped to gather up the pieces of flesh and place them in coffins, the recognizable ones in individual boxes and the others in a common one. He buried his brother in a grave of his own, but Julia would sleep in a grave with many others.

Who was at fault for this tragedy? Boilestad placed the blame on those who owned the factory and "cared only about making weapons and money and war."

•  •  •

Dagfinn Frantsen, who had hoped to get a full day's sleep after working the night shift in the electrolysis plant, was awakened after only four hours, but not by the family dog this time. The air-raid siren continued whining even as he leaped out of bed and put on his trousers. He ran outside and saw what looked like scores of fleeting silver crosses skimming the glary-white mountaintops and "covering the entire sky."

Seconds later, the first bombs virtually tore off the two upper floors of the electrolysis building. Frantsen dashed into his cellar and huddled in a corner as explosions shook the ground under him. There was a pause, and then still more blasts, one so near that the house was lifted several inches off its foundation. When it crashed down again, Frantsen found himself buried under a pile of table-cloths, chairs, and other household items. The house was in ruins, though its owner managed to escape injury.

But what about his wife, Liv, who was visiting his parents across the gorge? He had to find her.

Frantsen stumbled outside toward the suspension bridge that crossed the ravine, but saw to his despair that it was hanging down the side of the mountain. The only way left to reach his par-ents' home, it seemed, was to take the train to Rjukan, cross the river there, and find transportation back along the opposite bank of the river. And that could take hours. He moved to the edge of the gorge and gazed across it at his parents' house. It was a total wreck.

The saboteurs, Frantsen suddenly remembered, had climbed up the nearly vertical wall. Perhaps he could climb down. And he didn't care now whether he died in the attempt. As he looked for a path he could take into the canyon, he passed near the black hole where the air-raid shelter had been, and stared with disbelief at the remains of his aunt and the newly married girl, whom he knew from school. Lying face down in the snow, the bride was still neatly dressed, but below her skirt there were no legs.

Though more anxious than ever about the fate of his family, Frantsen felt compelled to stop at the electrolysis building to aid any wounded he might find there. The bombs, he observed, had destroyed the upper two floors of the structure, wrecked much of the neighboring power plant, and demolished the penstock pipelines leading to it. He groped his way through the thick dust bil-lowing in the electrolysis building to the high-concentration heavy-water room in the basement, where many employees were huddled. This room, the most important target of all, was intact and the cells were still full of the priceless liquid.

Though damage to the building was extensive, production, it seemed to Frantsen, could probably resume within three months. But he wasn't interested in heavy water at this terrible moment, and seeing that he could be of little help here, he rushed to find his wife and parents. He began climbing down the steep mountainside, clutching bushes and moving from foothold to perilous foothold. Finally reaching the river, he climbed up the opposite, less challenging side of the gorge, and there, nearby, were the ruins of his parents' house.

Frantsen found his father rummaging through the wreckage, dazed, it seemed, almost to the point of madness. He was looking, the father said, for his wool cap. He was cold. The son found a silk stocking and put it around his father's head.

"Where are Mother and Liv?" Frantsen asked.

His mother had taken refuge in the cellar with him and was unhurt, the father replied. She was now visiting a neighbor to console her. The neighbor was the mother of Frantsen's newly wed schoolmate.

And Liv?

The father paused, and the son feared the worst. But the elder man then mumbled that Liv had been walking the dog just before the raid, when it ran off and Liv chased him to her sister's house nearby. She was safe.

The son was elated. The dog he had bought for his wife was a gift from God: it may have saved her life. He would never again complain about its bark.

The problem was that, like his parents, he no longer had a home to return to. Why, he wondered, had the Allies wreaked such destruction on poor workers like himself, who were risking their lives to help them? Just to stop production of some new kind of water for three months?

• • •

The airmen who dropped the bombs had never heard of heavy water, and were told only that Norsk Hydro produced the ingredients of a new, powerful explosive. But they knew from the secrecy and urgency of their mission that this was no ordinary mission. Thus, the question of who dropped the first bombs was viewed through a prism of historical significance, triggering a verbal attack on John Bennett and Cowboy Roane almost as explosive as their bomb attack on Norsk Hydro.

"You went in early, missed the target, and screwed it up so no one else could see it," a colonel in the 95th Group charged at a heated critique of the mission when the planes had returned to base.

The 100th Group was supposed to have followed the 95th Group over the target, but had struck first after the 95th had passed over it without attacking because of the heavy clouds crowning the area and circled around waiting for them to lift. Bennett and Roane were now being accused of disobeying orders by dropping the first bombs—which supposedly missed the target anyway—while leaving a condensation trail that helped to shroud the target even after the clouds lifted. A clear case, in sum, of insubordination and greed for glory.

The two 100th leaders vigorously denied the charge, and were backed by the group photo interpreter, who countered: "But sir, the 100th Group, according to our interpretation, dropped eighty-five percent of its bombs in the target circle."

"Captain," the 95th colonel replied, "sit down and shut up. If we need anything from you, we'll call on you."

The colonel never called on the captain, nor did he ever take action against the accused pair. The two reveled in their victory and congratulated each other. Roane's suspicions that Bennett would seek to trample him underfoot subsided, especially after the major recommended him for the Silver Star, if in vain, and praised him to his flyers as a man to emulate.

But then Cowboy suddenly became a man to deprecate, owing to a health problem. He contracted hepatitis and was ordered by the doctor to maintain a certain diet at specific times. One day he left an assignment temporarily in order to eat according to the prescribed schedule. When he returned, Bennett demanded: "Where the hell have you been?"

Roane explained his medical problem, but Bennett was unsympathetic. "I couldn't care less about your stomach," he barked. "We're over here to fight a war!"

"Major," Cowboy replied, "this stomach will be part of me all my life. And, God willing, you won't be part of it much longer."

John Bennett walked away, but apparently without bitterness. "Cowboy Roane is a top pilot," he would later write. "He might have even helped to prevent an Allied defeat. An excellent role model. A skilled, quick-thinking leader despite a streak of independence he has now managed to suppress. Someone who could instill discipline in the others by stimulating pride in duty and group."

But no one's stomach, especially that of an "exemplary" airman like Cowboy Roane, could be permitted to impede efforts to whip the men into a group that would no longer be labeled the Bloody 100th. A group that could hit a target and return to base without suffering many casualties—or killing many civilians.

# 18

## AN AGONIZING DECISION

*November 1943–February 1944*

"**VEMORK COMPLETELY DESTROYED** except for basement in electrolysis plant."

From his snowbound cabin high in the mountains overlooking Rjukan, Einar Skinnarland, now working alone with a waterwheel-powered radio after Knut Haugland was ordered to Oslo, transmitted this somewhat exaggerated message to London on November 30. The American bombs, he added, had killed twenty-two people—eight men and fourteen women and children.

The British and Americans knew the air attack had essentially failed even though Norsk Hydro had been severely damaged. This was clear from reports submitted by both Skinnarland and the U.S. 8th Air Force. Though 174 aircraft dropped 828 1,000-pound and 500-pound bombs, only two of them, it seems, hit the electrolysis plant, and the heavy-water apparatus was untouched. Yet its demise was the point of the raid, which was considered so important that it was undertaken despite the risk of civilian slaughter.

The British were chagrined but not unduly alarmed, since Hitler, according to their intelligence, probably could not build an atomic weapon before the war ended anyway. General Groves was far more pessimistic about German atomic progress. Air raids, he still believed, had to smash the heavy-water works or the Germans might well produce the bomb before his own scientists did.

The Norwegian leaders, who violently opposed the bombing,

were enraged by the results of the American assault—and not simply because the world was still in danger. Twenty-two civilians had been killed "unnecessarily." The Norwegian government-in-exile, supported by Leif Tronstad, strongly protested to the British and Americans that the raid "was carried out without any advance notice being given to the Norwegian government . . . and seems out of all proportion to the objective sought." And the protest added: "If the aim of this bombing was to stop the production . . . of heavy water, better results could have been achieved by specialized methods of attack than by overall bombing."

The Germans, ironically, were more impressed by the bombing than the Allied leaders were. Once more, General von Falkenhorst and other top German leaders visited Vemork and inspected the ruins. Fortunately, they observed, the bombs did not reach the high-concentration heavy-water cells. But one physicist, Friedrich Berkei, reported to Berlin that the damage to the rest of the plant was so extensive that it would be impossible to produce any more heavy water here. Besides, there might be more air attacks. And how could suspected sabotage by the Norwegian workers be stopped? Falkenhorst and his Gestapo colleagues grimly agreed; they could not afford any further embarrassments.

In any event, three days after the raid, Berlin announced that a heavy-water plant would be erected in Germany. Also, a Montecatini electrolytic plant in Italy, using a different process and having only half the capacity of the Vemork plant, would be converted to heavy-water production. Meanwhile, all the heavy water and plant facilities in Vemork would be shipped across the Baltic Sea to Germany.

• • •

On December 29, Skinnarland pored over an urgent message from London:

WE HAVE INFORMATION THAT HEAVY-WATER EQUIPMENT
MAY BE DISMANTLED AND SENT TO GERMANY STOP CAN
YOU VERIFY QUERY IN CASE THIS SO CAN THIS TRANSPORT
BE ABORTED QUERY VERY IMPORTANT THAT HEAVY WATER

CAN BE CONTAMINATED WITH CASTOR OIL BEFORE IT IS
SENT STOP IF THIS POSSIBLE PROCEED AS FOLLOWS STOP
PUT IN CASTOR OIL OR COD LIVER OIL SLOWLY INTO
CELLS OR INTO TRANSPORT CONTAINERS [BARRELS] STOP
AMOUNT REQUIRED IS EYEGLASS PER UNIT OR ONE
COFFEE CUP OF THIS OIL [WHOLE UNIT] STOP BE CAREFUL
AND PREFERABLY TRANSPORT BARREL STOP UPON
STARTING IN GERMANY OIL WILL HAVE EFFECT WHICH
COULD HAVE NATURAL EXPLANATION

London made it clear, however, that even after contamination the equipment and heavy water should be destroyed if possible before reaching Germany. Could this be done?

Through an underground contact living in the mountains, Skinnarland relayed the message to Gunnar Syverstad, a chemical engineer at the plant and brother-in-law of his brother Torstein. Syverstad's job was to analyze and determine the concentrations of heavy water, and was thus responsible for quantity and quality control. No production secret, therefore, could be kept from him. So when he was ordered to drain all the heavy water, whatever its concentration, into canisters falsely marked "potash lye," he knew that the whole plant was to be transferred to Germany. And what he knew he passed on to Skinnarland.

On December 31, Skinnarland radioed London:

EVERYTHING INDICATES IMI [HEAVY WATER] APPARATUS
WILL BE MOVED BECAUSE PREPARING DISMANTLE. . . . IT
IS DEFINITE THAT ALL WORK WITH IMI . . . WILL BE SHUT
DOWN. . . . WE HOPE TO GET MAJOR PORTION
CONTAMINATED IN WAY YOU ADVISE. . . . REGARDING
ABORTING TRANSPORT I CANNOT YET GIVE A PLAN
BECAUSE TIME AND MEANS NOT YET CLEAR

• • •

The man in charge of transport was Kjell Nielsen, who had survived the bombing in the cellar of the electrolysis building, as he had a few months earlier at Heroya. One day in early February, he was visiting some friends when the doorbell rang and a stranger asked for him. Outside, Nielsen was greeted by two men.

One of them was Rolf Sorlie, the former plant engineer who had secretly met with Claus Helberg just before the Gunnerside team launched its attack. He was the Rjukan contact who relayed Skinnarland's messages about Norsk Hydro to London and back. Sorlie, whose legs and hands had been crippled in his youth, had overcome this handicap and become a first-rate mountaineer and skier—skills that served him well as an underground fighter. The other stranger was a man Nielsen couldn't recognize. "He was awful to look at with a dense beard and marked by the tough life in the mountains," Nielsen would later say.

The bearded man, now known as "Bonzo," was Knut Haukelid, who had commanded the covering party in Gunnerside and had since been organizing Resistance groups in the mountains while maintaining constant contact with Skinnarland. Actually, his "awful" look was due not only to "the tough life in the mountains" but to a "hard blow" he had just received in a letter from his wife, which she had sent to him via the underground. She had not seen him for three years and never knew where he was. Now she wanted a divorce. Haukelid was miserable, but his country came first.

The three men went to Nielsen's room down the road, and Haukelid spewed out a barrage of questions that reflected his passionate devotion to a single cause: Was it true, London wanted to know, that the heavy water was to be shipped out? If so, how much? And would it be possible to destroy it all? If this could be done, "we would stop them for a year or two, perhaps for the rest of the war."

It probably could be done, Nielsen said. Canisters of heavy water would be sent by rail to Rjukan, then to Mael, where the train would be ferried across Lake Tinn to Tinnoset and chug on to the port of Heroya. There the canisters would be loaded on a ship bound for Germany. Somewhere along the line, the shipments could be blown up.

Nielsen paused, then added emotionally: But did they have any idea of the cost? How many civilians would die as a result of such action?

He had already seen the slaughter of too many. As a Red Cross volunteer in Finland during the Soviet invasion of that country, many had died in his arms. During the bombing of Heroya, he had watched while scores of his people were blown to pieces. And he had just wept over the bodies of women and children killed in the air attack on Vemork. Now, were more innocents to die for no good reason?

"Tell London," Nielsen urged, "that it isn't necessary to destroy the heavy water. In Germany they don't have the equipment necessary to convert all the diluted solutions to high concentration. Besides, there would be terrible reprisals against the people in Rjukan. Let them take it all."

The two visitors agreed, and Haukelid immediately went to telephone Skinnarland.

Haukelid had earlier devised a telephone code with him. He thus phoned a contact in the mountain village of Hovden and explained in code language the objections to an attack. The contact then rushed to Skinnarland with the message.

In the loneliness of his little hut, Skinnarland radioed London:

> BONZO REPORTS AS FOLLOWS COLON "OUR CONTACTS AT
> RJUKAN THINK GERMAN METHOD IS INFERIOR TO
> NORWEGIAN STOP THEY DOUBT IF RESULT OF OPERATION
> IS WORTH REPRISALS STOP WE OURSELVES CANNOT
> DECIDE HOW IMPORTANT THE OPERATIONS ARE STOP
> PLEASE REPLY THIS EVENING IF POSSIBLE

If the British accepted the recommendation, Skinnarland would send Haukelid, through Hovden, the message: "Ten kilos of fish will be delivered." If they rejected the advice, the answer would be five kilos.

. . .

London struggled to wrestle free from a painful dilemma. It had agreed under pressure to the American bombing of Vemork without consulting its close Norwegian allies and, while the results were indecisive, many civilians had died. Now, if it called for action to knock out the heavy-water shipment, many more civilians, as the report from

Norway indicated, would surely be killed—even though some British experts doubted that the Germans would win the nuclear race.

One such expert was SIS Chief Eric Welsh, who had reached this conclusion following the success of Operation Gunnerside and the breaking of the German code. But he was not a man to take chances. If the Germans realized that the highly accessible graphite could replace the scarce heavy water as a moderator for an atomic reactor, they could possibly produce a reactor, and then a bomb, far sooner than expected. Welsh had no way of knowing that a German scientist had mistakenly calculated that graphite would not work.

So, after weighing the consequences with Wilson and Tronstad, as well as with his superiors, Welsh pressed for an attack regardless of possible casualties. As an assistant to Welsh would tell scientist and author Arnold Kramish: "The Germans got into their head, and it was encouraged from the British side, that heavy water was absolutely necessary to produce the atom bomb.... We hoped to encourage this by blowing up the ferry."

The Germans would then perhaps see no need to turn to graphite.

Colonel Wilson agreed that an attack was necessary, and he managed to persuade the exiled Norwegian defense minister to go along, despite Tronstad's reservations. Thus, somewhat cynically, London sent a reply to Skinnarland only hours after receiving his query:

MATTER HAS BEEN CONSIDERED STOP IT IS THOUGHT
VERY IMPORTANT THAT THE HEAVY WATER BE
DESTROYED STOP HOPE IT CAN BE DONE WITHOUT TOO
SERIOUS CONSEQUENCES STOP OUR BEST WISHES FOR
SUCCESS STOP GREETINGS

Shortly, Haukelid received an unwelcome message over the telephone: He would be receiving five, not ten, kilos of fish.

• • •

Two days later, Haukelid, Sorlie, and Nielsen met again at Nielsen's house, this time with Syverstad present, to decide on how the heavy-water shipment should be destroyed. The atmosphere was gloomy and filled with dread. Were they not, they dared ask themselves, plotting in a sense the deaths of innocent civilians, perhaps members of their own families? Yet the cause came first, the sacred cause of freedom, perhaps even survival.

Should the heavy water and equipment be demolished before being shipped out?

Impossible, it was decided. That could be done only by twenty or thirty saboteurs from Britain, who would have to place a charge on each of the thirty-nine canisters being sent out to make sure all were destroyed. And there was no time to arrange this. Besides, after Operation Gunnerside, the Germans were edgy and on the alert against a similar attack. A special army detachment and the first company of the 7th SS Police Regiment had moved into the town, apparently to protect the heavy water. And the Army Ordnance Department had sent a lieutenant to Norway to make sure the operation went smoothly.

Should the train carrying the shipment from Vemork to Rjukan proper be blown up along the steep mountainside?

This would be a fairly easy task, since the railway tracks ran by Norsk Hydro's explosive dump, which was packed with forty-five hundred pounds of dynamite. But there would be problems. The explosion would have to occur at the exact moment the train passed the dump. And even if all the heavy-water canisters and equipment tumbled into the gorge, some might be salvageable.

Also, there was at least one guard at the dump. As Haukelid would lament, the saboteurs "did not know what precautionary measures the Germans would take" along the line that day. And they would have to know this, for it would take at least fifteen minutes to overcome the guard and place the detonator by the dump. The Germans might even send a scout car ahead of the train, detonating the explosive prematurely.

Should the train be blown up after it crossed Lake Tinn to Tinnoset and passed over a bridge en route to Heroya?

The train would be crowded with people boarding the ferry at Mael and all of them would probably be killed—in addition to those murdered in reprisals. And again, parts of the shipment might be salvaged.

Should the ferry be sunk?

Since Lake Tinn was nearly thirteen hundred feet deep at the spot where the explosion would occur, none of the shipment could be salvaged. But was it possible to place charges on board and be certain they would sink the ferry? Could the charges be detonated at the right moment? And could any of the civilian passengers aboard be saved from drowning?

"It is always hard to take a decision about actions which involve the loss of human lives," Haukelid would later write. "An officer often has to make such decisions in wartime, but in regular warfare it is easier; . . . his decisions as a rule have consequences only for soldiers, or at most for an enemy population. In this case, an act of war was to be carried out which must endanger the lives of a number of our own people—who were not soldiers."

Haukelid mulled over the alternatives and, in his turmoil, sought advice from other members of the Resistance in Rjukan. They were, he would say, "in despair at the thought of the misfortunes to which a fresh act of sabotage must lead."

Don't agree to it, they pleaded.

But Haukelid, who would lead any action, searched his soul, knowing that he would have to live forever with his decision. "I was the only person who had authority to make a decision," he would write. And "our orders from London left no room for doubt as to what was intended. It was vitally necessary for victory in the war that the Germans should not get the heavy water."

The plotters met again and again and with anguished resolve finally agreed to sink the ferry. If the craft went down near the opposite shore, where the water was deepest anyway, people living there might be able to help rescue at least some of the passengers. And perhaps the Germans would think that a boiler had exploded and not resort to reprisals against civilians. Surely they would not be eager to admit that saboteurs had slid past them once again.

On February 9, 1944, Haukelid sent a message to London via Skinnarland:

TIME SHORT STOP THEREFORE DIFFICULT TO EXECUTE
MILITARY ATTACK ON STORES WHICH GUARDED BY
GERMANS STOP WE CONSIDER MOST RELIABLE SOLUTION
IS SINKING OF FERRY ON LAKE TINN WITH ALL IMI
[HEAVY-WATER] CANISTERS ABOARD BY SABOTAGE. . . .
CAN WE HAVE PERMISSION DO THIS QUERY. . . . WE MUST
EXPECT REPRISALS

Hours later, London replied:

APPROVE SINKING OF FERRY WITH IMI CARGO IN DEEP
WATER. . . . SINKING MUST NOT FAIL OR ATTACK METHOD
WILL BE DISCLOSED. . . . STOP GOOD LUCK

The question now was, when would the shipment be leaving for Germany? Nielsen, in charge of transport, was shortly told to arrange for it to be loaded on the train to Rjukan during the week of February 13. The plotters met again to choose a propitious day for the sinking.

Everyone agreed that Sunday, February 20, would be best, for fewer passengers took the ferry on that day, and thus fewer were likely to be killed. Could Nielsen stall off shipment until then?

He would find a way, Nielsen assured his comrades.

Haukelid and Sorlie would be the chief saboteurs, but they needed an experienced helper. The Resistance would have to find someone swiftly. And it did . . .

• • •

At an outdoor cafe in Oslo, two men sat talking quietly over beer. One of them, Jon Dasnes, wearing dark glasses, was questioning his companion, Knut Lier-Hansen, a lean young man with an animated demeanor suddenly aglow. As a member of the Resistance, Lier-Hansen was always stirred by the prospect of a daring and dangerous mission. And now, it seemed, he would be sent on his most challenging mission yet.

Dasnes, one of the top Norwegian Resistance leaders, did not spell out the mission, but he told his companion that he would have to return to Rjukan, where he lived. Lier-Hansen had been called to Oslo to help operate a transmitting station, but his superiors now had something more important in mind. Dasnes frankly told him that a British-trained saboteur would have been his first choice for the job. But though Lier-Hansen had not received such training, he had been recommended as one of the best and bravest local guerrillas by a man who had—Einar Skinnarland. But just to make sure he was qualified, Dasnes fired questions at him about his background and experience.

The answers inspired confidence. A native of Rjukan, where his father had worked as an electrician for Norsk Hydro, Lier-Hansen, now twenty-seven, had served as a sergeant in the Norwegian infantry and fought against the Germans during the invasion. Captured by the enemy, he jumped off a truck while being driven to a prison camp and returned to battle shortly before Norway's surrender. He then made his way to Stockholm, but was sent back to Rjukan by Resistance leaders there to organize an underground unit while working for Norsk Hydro as a maintenance man. In this position, he was able, through his many connections, to gather information about the heavy-water operation and cache weapons in the mountains. And the bigger the risk, it seemed, the more he savored the task.

Just the man for this task, Dasnes concluded as he sipped his beer.

∎ ∎ ∎

The following day, February 10, Lier-Hansen was sitting with Haukelid and Sorlie in a mountain cabin not far from Rjukan, helping to plan the attack and poring over blueprints of the ferry that Syverstad had borrowed from company files. The train with its precious cargo would leave Vemork on Saturday, stay in Rjukan overnight, and roll on to Mael on Sunday morning, where it would grind aboard the ferry for the trip across Lake Tinn. The saboteurs would have to go to Mael and sneak aboard on Saturday night to set the charges.

Later, on a practice run, Haukelid put on worker's overalls and, armed with a Sten gun wrapped in his sleeping bag and a couple of hand grenades nestled in his rucksack, took a train to Mael. There he boarded the marked ferry, *Hydro*, to study its features and time the crossing. When this old screw-driven vessel reached the deepest point, its intended grave site, Haukelid glanced at his watch. It had taken twenty minutes. The bomb timer would have to be set accordingly, with precision to the second.

When no reliable timing device could be found, Sorlie finally came up with the answer: a simple alarm clock. He went to see a couple of underground friends and obtained a clock from each and electric detonators from one, who owned a workshop. Sorlie later returned to the shop with Haukelid, and the two men with the help of the owner fashioned nineteen pounds of plastic explosives into a twelve-foot-long, sausage-shaped bomb. It was large enough to ensure that the vessel would sink quickly.

Would the alarm clocks prove reliable? After returning to their mountain cabin in the morning, the two saboteurs decided to test the release system, connecting an electric detonator to each clock and going to sleep with the expectation that the alarm would awaken them. Several hours later, riflelike cracks split the air and Haukelid jumped out of bed and dashed outside, pistol in hand, while Sorlie ran to the window with his Sten gun. A German attack!

The plot, it appeared, was doomed, as were they. But as they scanned the peaceful wintry scene, ready to fire, the Germans were nowhere in sight.

What happened? Sorlie called down to Haukelid.

Haukelid paused for a moment, lowering his pistol.

The detonators work! he cried.

There was a moment of elation, but then reality cruelly sank in. Yes, they worked—and friends, neighbors, perhaps relatives would die as a result.

• • •

Tension over the question of massacre grew as the time drew near to test the soul as well as the bomb. Aside from the civilian ferry passengers, all high company officials were in grave danger, for the

Germans would surely suspect them of cooperating in the sabotage. Yet how could the feat be achieved without their help? Only from them could the saboteurs learn about the transport schedule and the nature of the cargo.

This meant that Nielsen, the transport arranger, and Syverstad, the chemical engineer, would be especially vulnerable. And they knew that the Gestapo had persuasive ways of extracting information from suspects. Should they flee or stay on the job and risk being forced to talk? Could they withstand the most horrible torture?

At one meeting of the plotters, Syverstad, pressed by Haukelid not to risk staying, finally decided to accompany him to Sweden after the bomb had been set in place. Sorlie would escape into the mountains and stay with Skinnarland, and Lier-Hansen would return to Oslo and burrow underground there.

Only Nielsen, though in the most precarious position of all, would not agree to run. Since the invasion, he had been sending industrial information to London mainly via Skinnarland and he didn't want to stop now. Someone had to remain behind with access to important data so Skinnarland could continue relaying it to the British.

But that would be suicide, the others argued.

Not necessarily, Nielsen replied. He had been having stomach pains recently. Probably his appendix. He would ask his sister, who lived in Oslo, to make an appointment for him with a "friendly" doctor he knew there. The doctor would remove his appendix, needed or not, on Saturday, the day before the explosion. Would the Germans suspect someone who was recovering from an operation at the time?

Nielsen had another idea, which, he felt, could throw the Germans off the trail of all of them.

Haukelid, he suggested, should take Chief Engineer Alf Larsen with him to Sweden. He would be the ideal scapegoat.

Actually, Larsen was not in the Resistance and apparently knew nothing about the plot. And Nielsen, while not questioning his loyalty, felt he obeyed German orders with unnecessary dedication.

But Larsen might agree to go—if he thought his masters would suspect him, however mistakenly, of some treacherous act.

A good idea, Haukelid agreed.

■   ■   ■

The next evening, February 17, Nielsen dined with Larsen in the company restaurant and, over coffee, broke the news.

"Something is going to happen on Sunday," he said, "and you will be vulnerable. You must go to Sweden for your own protection."

Larsen, according to Nielsen, "turned green. He could hardly talk." He knew Nielsen was alluding to some underground action. But what did he have to do with the Resistance?

"Take it easy," Nielsen said, feigning sympathy. "You will be guarded. Take a rucksack and skis, and leave your property and valuables in somebody's care."

Larsen now "almost fainted. He was almost out of his mind."

But he gurgled agreement.

On Saturday afternoon, just before he left for Oslo to have his appendix out, Nielsen, a violinist in the Rjukan symphony orchestra, played in a practice session. Afterward, he chatted with the orchestra director, Arvid Fladmoe, a well-known musician.

How did he plan to spend the weekend? Nielsen asked.

He was going to Oslo in the morning to keep a concert engagement.

Nielsen was shaken. The man would be taking the morning ferry to catch the train on the other side of the lake.

"It's beautiful skiing weather," he said. "Why not stay around and go skiing? You need the diversion."

No, Fladmoe replied, he had to be in Oslo the next day for a concert. (That evening, he would attend a dinner party held at the company guest house by Larsen, who would be accompanying the plotters in the morning but apparently did not know of the planned bombing.)

Nielsen feverishly debated with himself. Should he warn the man not to take the ferry? Could he let him simply sail off to his death? He decided he must. He could not risk telling anyone, not with victory over Hitler at stake. Shattered, he himself was shortly off to Oslo for his appendix operation.

Gunnar Syverstad was trapped in an even more excruciating predicament. His mother was also planning to take the marked ferry en route to Oslo, and he could not talk her out of going. Haukelid would later say: "I begged him to keep her at home somehow or other without saying anything, even if it meant knocking her down and locking her in a closet."

And Syverstad knew he could not let her go. He must find a way to save her, even if he had to follow Haukelid's suggestion. But he didn't have to. Not after he visited the bathroom. His eyes strayed to the medicine cabinet, and there on the shelf was a powerful laxative. On Saturday night, February 19, Syverstad saturated his mother's food with it, and, to his enormous relief, she was in no condition to travel the next morning.

Meanwhile, on Saturday, Lier-Hansen went to Mael to reconnoiter the wharf area one last time. "There were only about twenty or thirty guards in the area," he would tell me in the snack bar at the Norsk Hydro plant. "And they were in the railway station playing cards. I couldn't understand this."

Perhaps, he speculated, the Germans assumed that the ferry would be immune to attack because so many Norwegian civilians were aboard. Or perhaps that night, before he and his two comrades could set the charges on the ferry, Germans would still swarm into the area from Rjukan and heavily guard it.

That town was, in fact, "packed with German troops," according to Haukelid, who would report: "I cannot remember Rjukan being more tense." He would add that "our boys" had picked up a German telephone conversation from Oslo warning the troops in Rjukan to "keep a specially close lookout." The Germans had even decided to split the transport into two parts after the ferry landed at Tinnoset on the other side of the lake. Half the shipment would continue on by rail and the other half by road, so at least half might be saved in case of an attack.

An hour before midnight, February 19, Haukelid and Sorlie skied to the edge of the suspension bridge leading to the plant and saw, eerily bathed in hazy lamplight, two heavily guarded railway flatcars loaded with canisters. They would be rumbling toward Mael in a few hours. By that time, if all went well, the saboteurs would be in flight, miles away, reveling in their success—and agonizing over the death toll.

The two men were shortly skiing to a back street in Rjukan, where they would climb into a car with Larsen, Lier-Hansen, and the underground owner of the vehicle, who would drive the group to Mael.

It was time.

# 19

## THE FINAL BLOW

*February 1944*

**"I'M SORRY,"** the driver exclaimed in frustration, "but it won't go!"

And the fuel tank was full, too.

As the owner of the car, he was familiar with almost every wire, tube, and part, but though he lifted the hood and checked each one he couldn't find the culprit. The three saboteurs and Larsen were desperate. It was almost midnight and the minutes were slipping away. If they couldn't fix the car, where would they get another one, especially at this time of night? The Germans had confiscated almost every vehicle in town. And if the charges were not placed on the ferry in the next two or three hours, the train might pull into Mael packed with troops before the job could be done. The saboteurs might even be caught placing the charges and be killed. Worse, they would die in vain. For the heavy water and equipment would be on its way to Germany.

Unknown to them, London had a backup plan ready. If the sabotage attempt failed and the ferry completed its trip, other underground fighters would attack the train in the port of Heroya before the shipment could be transferred to a vessel bound for Germany. If that assault also failed, British planes and naval craft would bomb the ship at sea.

The saboteurs took turns tinkering with the car engine. To no avail. Was this faulty bit of machinery to determine the outcome of the German quest for a terrible secret weapon? Fingers turned black, foreheads grew sweaty, words waxed obscene. Suddenly they heard a grinding cough, then another, and, at last, a steady hum. A medley of sighs sent gusts of mist drifting into the frigid air as everyone piled into the car again. An hour lost, and a bit of confidence, too. That night they would have to set charges flawlessly in record time under the most perilous conditions. Yet a simple stalled automobile engine had stumped them for an hour.

The car sped several miles to Mael and drew to a halt under some trees about three-fourths of a mile from the ferry pier. The headlights flashed off and the three saboteurs, Haukelid would say, got out and told the driver, who would stay behind with Larsen, "to wait [and] be ready to start at a moment's notice, and if he heard shots . . . to drive off at once. In no circumstances was he to wait for more than two hours." If this period elapsed, Larsen would have to make his way to Oslo and "get to Sweden as best he could."

Haukelid, Sorlie, and Lier-Hansen then strode gingerly toward the ferry landing, their parkas bulging with Sten guns, pistols, and hand grenades. Haukelid looked almost like a hunchback with the long, sausage-shaped bomb hung around his shoulders.

"The bitterly cold night," Haukelid would report, "set everything creaking and crackling; the ice on the road snapped sharply as we went over it."

But not a whisper passed their lips as they moved forward. "We were preoccupied with the need to succeed," Lier-Hansen would tell me. "We had to believe we would."

As the three men edged stealthily past the railway station next to the ferry wharf, Lier-Hansen noted that nothing had changed since he had reconnoitered the area several hours earlier. About twenty or thirty guards were still playing cards inside the station. Nobody was outside guarding the ferry.

When the saboteurs reached the darkened vessel, Haukelid stole up the gangway while his comrades covered him. Not a soul on deck. But as he trod lightly toward the first-class quarters, the silence gradually evolved into a buzz of conversation marked by laughter from both sexes and other sounds of drunken merriment. German officers, it seemed, were wallowing in mirth. Meanwhile, almost the whole ship's crew was below playing poker.

Haukelid motioned to his companions to join him, and the three men crept down to the third-class section. Here they found a hatchway leading to the hold, where they would place the charges. Haukelid would later write:

> But before we had got the hatch open we heard steps, and took cover behind the nearest table or chair. The ferry watchman was standing in the doorway. . . . We hurriedly explained . . . that we had to hide and were looking for a suitable place. [He] immediately showed us the hatchway . . . and told us that several times [the passengers] had had illicit things with them on their trips.

Lier-Hansen told me a somewhat different story. Before the man appeared, he said, the saboteurs lifted the hatch cover, and when Haukelid and Sorlie had climbed down, he closed it and stood guard. Suddenly, he heard footsteps and found himself confronting the startled watchman, a Norwegian.

"What are you doing here?" the man asked.

"I just came down from the mountains," Lier-Hansen calmly replied. "I'm leaving on the ferry later, but since I had nowhere to stay for the night, I decided to come aboard early."

"You are not allowed to be here," the watchman said.

There was silence for a moment, and Lier-Hansen chilled at the thought that he might have to use violence against him. The man was, after all, a poor Norwegian like himself who was simply trying to earn a living.

"Well," the watchman finally said, "you can stay aboard, but don't tell anyone you spoke with me."

Lier-Hansen was thankful, but he wasn't sure why the man was so cooperative. Was he simply taking pity on him? Did he suspect that the intruder had reason to hide from the Germans and so was trying to help him? Or was he setting a trap? Whatever the reason, the saboteur felt, he couldn't take a chance. He had to keep the watchman from leaving until Haukelid and Sorlie had finished their work below, or the man might turn him in. In a leisurely manner, Lier-Hansen asked questions about life aboard the ferry.

"What's it like working on a boat?"

Well, the watchman replied, he was really a stoker's assistant, and there were problems.

"We have to use wood because there isn't enough coal," he explained. "But we haven't much wood, either, because we can't find enough people to cut down the trees. It's sabotage, you know, and there's a lot of it."

Lier-Hansen knew.

He continued engaging the man in conversation as if he were the most innocent of paupers.

. . .

Meanwhile, Haukelid and Sorlie, crouching in foot-deep brackish water, worked feverishly in the hold to set the charges before they were discovered. They fixed the plastic in a circle against the ship's hull, taped the detonator fuses, and connected the electric detonators to the fuses. Then they placed the nineteen-pound sausage-shaped charge in the water, laying it forward so that the rudder and propeller would rise above the surface when the water began to flow in. The railway cars would roll off the deck and help to pull the ferry down quickly. Haukelid had spent many hours calculating that a hole about eleven square feet must be blown out of the ship's side for the vessel to sink in less than five minutes so that it could not be beached.

Both their alarm clocks were wired to the charge, just to be safe. The hammer of each clock would short-circuit the current at 10:45 A.M.—based on the possibility that the train would be ten minutes late—for the ferry would presumably pass over the deepest part of the lake at that time. The problem was that barely a third of an inch separated the hammer and the alarm.

"There was one-third of an inch between us and disaster," Haukelid would later say.

Disaster, they feared, for the Allies.

. . .

Just above, on deck, Lier-Hansen was running out of conversation, but he kept talking, occasionally glancing at his watch. If the train came early, the place would be swarming with German soldiers and he and his comrades would be trapped. Finally, he said good-bye and the watchman moved off on his rounds.

Lier-Hansen tried to suppress a sense of guilt. The man had risked his job, maybe his life, by letting him remain aboard. And ironically, by doing so the fellow was facilitating a plot that might well result in his death. Lier-Hansen longed to call him back and warn him to leave the ship. He had done much fighting and seen many die, but never had war seemed so cruel.

Suddenly, there was a dreaded rumble in the distance. The train was coming! Just then, Haukelid and Sorlie burst out of the hatch. They had managed to place the charge without incident. The three men then ran up to the deck and down the gangway, with the rumble growing louder by the second. And within minutes, they were back at their car.

Sorlie put on his skis and, waving farewell, swooped up into the mountains where he would join Einar Skinnarland in his communications hut. The others raced toward Kongsberg, from where Haukelid and Larsen would take a train to Oslo, and then ski their way to safety in Sweden.

Haukelid urged Lier-Hansen to go with them to Oslo as originally planned and resume his underground work there. But Lier-Hansen refused. He must return to Mael, he said, to make sure the ferry left about 10 A.M., as scheduled. If there was more than a ten-minute delay, he would sneak aboard again and diffuse the bomb before it exploded prematurely at the dock, permitting the Germans to salvage much of their treasured shipment.

Outside Kongsberg, the driver let off Haukelid and Larsen and headed toward Rjukan, where he would remain with his car while Lier-Hansen skied back to Mael. The saboteur prayed he would find few passengers lined up at the pier.

• • •

At about nine that morning, February 20, a man knocked on the door of the Gulbrandsen home in Rjukan and it shortly creaked open. A middle-aged man smiled at the caller, a neighbor.

"Good morning," he said. "You're up early."

"I heard," the neighbor said, "that your daughter is going to Oslo this morning. I just thought you should know that something is expected to happen in the next day or two."

What? Where? the father asked, his smile now gone. A strong anti-Nazi himself, he understood well the language of the Resistance.

He couldn't say, the neighbor replied, though, it seems, he knew. He was apparently the car owner who had driven the saboteurs to Mael.

Eva Gulbrandsen was a "little frightened" when her father told her about the warning. But the man did not say where something would happen. It would probably be in Rjukan, she guessed, though she wondered what her trip had to do with it.

"Take your choice," her parents said. "Do you wish to stay or to go?"

Eva considered the choices and quickly reached a decision. It would probably be more dangerous staying in Rjukan than traveling to Oslo. She had always feared living in Rjukan, anyway. Ever since 1927, when an avalanche swept down the mountains and demolished several houses and a church nearby. The river might overflow at any time, and the vestiges of the bombed gas and chemical plant could explode. Yet despite her fears, she wouldn't mind staying longer, for as an expert skier she loved racing along the mountain slopes.

But her boss at the government office where she worked as a secretary had given her only a week off to visit her parents, and she had promised to be back on the job on Monday. It didn't seem right to use so vague a warning as an excuse to remain.

She would return to Oslo, she said.

Eva, twenty-one, was born in Rjukan, but had gone to Oslo shortly after the German invasion when her boss, the mayor, proved too friendly to his German masters. She despised the occupiers, and her hatred was fed by her father and her boyfriend, who was in the Resistance living somewhere in the mountains. And though she worried about her family's safety and her own, whatever the Resistance was planning, she hoped it would work.

After consuming a breakfast of cornbread and coffee made of burnt peas, Eva walked with her parents to the railway station in Rjukan, where she boarded the train to Mael. Soon it pulled into the station next to the ferry dock, and Eva noted that only two or three soldiers were guarding the area. Understandable. What was there to guard? But she was puzzled and a little concerned. Why had the neighbor worried about her going to Oslo?

When the train jerked to a halt, Eva stepped off and walked onto the ferry with other passengers. She descended a stairway to the second-class section and took a seat, glancing with a smile at the other nine people in the large compartment. She didn't know anybody. But she wasn't in the mood for conversation, anyway. Her vacation was over, and now she simply wanted to get back to her job in Oslo—and begin dreaming of her next vacation, she hoped with her boyfriend. If he came down from the mountains.

Impatient to leave, Eva glimpsed at her watch. It was after 10 A.M. Why hadn't the engines started?

• • •

Knut Lier-Hansen asked the same question as he sat on a hillside overlooking the wharf. He had arrived earlier and watched the railway flatcars piled high with crates bump into the great ferry cavern while the passengers, mainly civilians but also some German soldiers, streamed up the gangway. Men, women, children, even an infant. He agonized. Within half an hour, those people, more than fifty, would probably all be dead.

"If I had been a civilian and not a soldier," he told me, his eyes staring hypnotically into the past, "I think I would have tried to warn those poor Norwegians. But as a soldier I was very sensitive to security, and one couldn't be sure who was loyal and who was not. It was a bitter pill to swallow."

Lier-Hansen almost wished the ferry would be delayed long enough to give him an excuse to defuse the bomb. And, in fact, when his watch showed that the departure was several minutes late, he was about to head down to the pier. Just then, however, the whistle blew and the vessel began churning the water.

Lier-Hanson stood up and started for Rjukan, unsure whether to mumble "Thank God!"—or "Too late!"

• • •

As the ferry pulled away from the pier, Eva Gulbrandsen sat back and relaxed, wondering whether she should munch on some of the cornbread in her bag. There was little food at home because of the wartime shortage and she was hungry. But she decided to wait until she reached Oslo, for her fellow passengers might be even hungrier and it wouldn't be fair to eat in their presence.

Eva looked around, studying each of the nine other passengers. Two people sat in her row, and seven, including an elderly woman, a young couple and their baby, and two teenage sisters, twins, sat in rows perpendicular to hers. Eavesdropping on the conversations around her, Eva heard the sisters excitedly chatting about the clothes they had bought in Rjukan for their confirmation in Skien. The elderly woman was leaning over and proudly showing some photos to a younger woman next to her, apparently of her grand-children. The young husband, a musician who was returning home from the practice session of the Rjukan orchestra, sat in silence as his wife nursed their baby. Everyone seemed relaxed and there were comments about how good it felt to come out of the cold into a steam-heated compartment.

Suddenly, at about 11 A.M., a deafening explosion rocked the vessel and steam spurted out of the broken heating pipes, singe-ing Eva's hair. Simultaneously, water covered the floor and darkness shrouded the compartment, which had no portholes. The hiss of the steam blended with the panicky screams and prayers of the passengers.

"A bomb!" someone cried out. "We've been bombed!"

In the dark, no one could find the door, until Eva managed to slosh her way to it. Just outside, light beamed in from a small port-hole, and, as the water steadily rose, Eva banged her fists against the glass, hoping to shatter it and squeeze her way through the hole before the water inside engulfed her. But the glass was too thick. She then rushed to the steep, narrow stairway and, as the vessel listed sharply to port, she scrambled dizzily to the upper deck, which the water had not yet reached.

There was an eerie silence. No alarm sounded and no cry of "abandon ship" pierced the frosty air. Eva saw a young man running past and asked him to help her. Was the ship going down? Should she jump into the water?

"Don't ask me," he said breathlessly. "I can't help myself. I can't even swim." And he resumed running, apparently looking for a life preserver, though Eva was unable to see one anywhere.

Other passengers, she noted, had already leaped into the water and, without preservers, were swimming toward shore, about a quarter of a mile away. Only about three minutes after the explosion, the ship was clearly going down. Eva removed her long woolen coat but felt compelled to dive overboard before she could pull off her boots. She swam with desperate speed toward shore, fearing she might be hit by the propeller as the ferry sank.

When Eva finally looked back about a minute or two after jumping, the flatcars were rolling off and the stern was almost vertical, with the propeller grotesquely turning. It was going down with the twins who would never be confirmed; with the old woman who would never see her grandchildren again; with the mother who had nursed her baby for the last time. Eva hadn't spoken a word to them, yet the vision of each was indelibly etched in her mind, perhaps because she expected to share their destiny. Exhausted and barely able to move with her heavy clothes and boots, Eva was almost ready to submit to it.

• • •

At about this time, Knut Haukelid and Alf Larsen were speeding away from Oslo on a train that would take them close to the Swedish border. Larsen was still shaking from a near encounter earlier with the Rjukan Gestapo chief, Muggenthaler, at the Kongsberg railroad station. Norwegians were forbidden to travel more than fifteen miles from their home without permission, and if he were recognized he would probably be shot. Larsen had locked himself in a station lavatory and would leave only when his train to Oslo was about to pull out.

"Halfway to Oslo I looked at my watch," Haukelid would later write. "It was quarter to eleven. If everything had gone according to plan the ferry should just be sinking. . . . Larsen and I did not talk much on the journey. I was thinking of the past." Of the endless months of living in the snow and cold, always with danger; of friends in the mountains who so willingly risked their lives without knowing how vital their work was; of his Gunnerside comrades who had performed one of the most daring commando operations in the war; of his shredded personal life now marked by divorce, stemming from his single-minded devotion to the cause.

"What would happen now . . . ?" Haukelid asked himself. "How many Norwegian lives would be lost through this piece of devilry? . . . The English had sacrificed forty-one men with the gliders. Those men had known they would not be able to get away after they had done their work. The bombing had cost twenty-two lives. How many would it be this time?"

* * *

As Eva floundered helplessly in the water, she suddenly saw a rowboat drifting past jammed with first-class passengers—the only craft that survived the explosion. With her last strength, she paddled to it, but had to wait for another passenger to be pulled aboard—the orchestra director, Arvid Fladmoe. He had not taken Kjell Nielsen's advice to enjoy the weekend skiing in the mountains.

When Eva had been dragged aboard, she fainted, regaining consciousness minutes later when someone screamed: "My God, we're going down!"

As the overloaded boat swayed crazily and the water threatened to pour in, the survivors screamed at each other, some demanding that all luggage be thrown overboard and others clinging to their bags and refusing to give them up. The most fearful grabbed the bags and hurled them into the lake. Eva thought of the passengers she had left behind in her cabin deep in the hold. They were second-class passengers, not rich enough to travel first class like these people, who carried belongings they apparently deemed more valuable than life itself.

While several of the stronger men, grunting fiercely, wielded oars with shaky hands, the boat inched forward past floundering swimmers, who could only curse those who would not stop for them. Surely there was room for one more. Were they to be left to die?

Some at least were not, for by this time people ashore were rowing to the scene to rescue them.

Eva's boat finally reached shore and was greeted by a crowd of people. One woman helped Eva, who was barely conscious, to her house near the lake, and the girl soon found herself in a bedroom crowded with survivors. A few hours later she was aboard another vessel on a return trip to Mael, where her parents were waiting to embrace her.

Eva's nerves would never fully recover, and every time she would hear a loud noise, she found herself groping again in the blackness of a convulsed cabin, with screams and prayers ringing in her ears like a funeral dirge for dreams snuffed out.

Her cabin companions were among twenty-six passengers who died. Twenty-seven, including four German soldiers, survived. Hitler's bomb had taken another toll—even before it was built.

• • •

When Knut Lier-Hansen arrived back in Rjukan early Sunday afternoon en route to Oslo to resume his cover job there, he called his sister, who worked as a switchboard operator and leaked to him German plans as she learned of them from telephone conversations.

"Heard anything new?" he asked, knowing that his sister had no inkling of the sabotage attempt.

"Only that the Germans are rushing to the lake," his sister replied. "There was an explosion on a ferry this morning, apparently in the boiler room."

Lier-Hansen was silent for a moment. He hoped the Germans would have enough sense to try to rescue survivors from the Notodden side. If there were any. At least they seemed to feel that the boiler blew up and were not charging sabotage. Now there might not be reprisals after all. He suspected that the Germans knew it was sabotage, but that they were reluctant to admit to Berlin that commandos had outsmarted them once again—and perhaps invite reassignment to the Russian front.

. . .

In Oslo, on Sunday, Kjell Nielsen lay in a hospital bed stitched up from an operation the previous day to remove his perfectly functioning appendix when a nurse entered his ward. He knew her from Rjukan and they often talked of home.

"I thought you'd be interested to know," she said, "that a ferry has been blown up on Lake Tinn and some people were killed."

Nielsen stared at her, his face growing paler.

"What a tragedy!" he groaned.

The following day, February 21, the Germans traced him to the hospital and questioned him, but took no action. After all, he had been operated on the day the ferry went down. But since they had to arrest somebody, Nielsen would tell me, they chose his assistant, Arne Enger, whose brother happened to be the doctor who operated on him. Enger, however, was detained only temporarily.

A few other Norsk Hydro employees were also arrested, including the brother of Gunnar Syverstad. Gunnar himself dared to return to the plant the day after the sinking, hoping the Germans would not suspect him. But the company director was blunt. Syverstad must submit a detailed report on the makeup of the shipment and the identity of all those who had handled it. He would, said the director, "be subjected by the Gestapo to a thorough investigation."

Syverstad now fled to Sweden, as he had earlier planned, escaping only two hours before the Gestapo knocked on his door. But in March 1945 Syverstad and Leif Tronstad were shot to death by the brother of a treasonous magistrate from Rauland while they were interrogating the magistrate.

Other Norsk Hydro employees were warned not to leave. A Gestapo officer, swearing that "Rjukan would be made to weep this time," warned the head of the power station, who knew nothing about the plot: "If you escape I will blow up your villa with your wife in it."

Actually, however, the Germans did not carry out their threats. For though they probably knew the ferry had been sabotaged, they quietly accepted the explanation that the boiler had exploded, as the commandos had hoped. To launch reprisals would be to admit to military incompetence again.

Furthermore, General von Falkenhorst, who, with the other German leaders, had rushed once more to the scene to view the damage, greatly admired such artful enemy initiatives. And perhaps out of respect for such art, he was reluctant to kill those whom he identified with the artists. Even so, a British court would convict him after the war of committing war crimes and sentence him to death, though he would be pardoned in 1953.

# CONCLUSION

UNTIL HIS CAPTURE, General von Falkenhorst was baffled by the enemy's obsession with heavy water. He knew it was an ingredient for a powerful explosive, but how important could it be? He was apparently no more puzzled, however, than Adolf Hitler, who was misled by his scientists into believing that a bomb-building project was probably impractical.

Certainly the German nuclear program faced many obstacles. Germany had fewer top-rate nuclear scientists than the Allies had, ironically because many of the greatest minds had fled Europe to escape Nazi persecution. Money and resources were in shorter supply than in America. And the huge plants that would have been required to build a bomb would surely have been prime objectives of Allied bombers, though, as the U.S.–led attempt to destroy Iraqi nuclear facilities in the Persian Gulf War showed, bombs cannot always find well-hidden targets.

But whatever the barriers to a German bomb, the Allies had to assume that Hitler might build one before they did. And since the heavy-water operation at Norsk Hydro was the only concrete evidence that he was making the effort, the Allies had no choice but to attack it at any cost, whether the threat was real or not. And indeed, reports about Norsk Hydro were a driving force behind the frantic attempt by Allied scientists to build a nuclear weapon.

Actually, Allied anxiety was not misplaced. Hitler might have won the nuclear race if luck had not ruled against him. At a time when the race might have gone either way, two fateful accidents of history prevented a German chain reaction: Heisenberg's carelessness in allowing his uranium heavy-water reactor to explode, and Bothe's conclusion that graphite could not replace heavy water as a neutron moderator, an error all the more disastrous coming after Szilard reached the opposite conclusion.

Without these critical blunders, the microscopic chaos of atoms splitting might well have given the scientists the courage to stop keeping Hitler's expectations low and persuade him there was good reason to invest large sums of money in a full-scale nuclear project. Surely money that was funneled into rocket development would have been diverted to the bomb and augmented almost without limit if Hitler thought such a weapon could be built before the war ended.

Even with the two mishaps, the Germans, according to Jomar Brun, might have set off a chain reaction early enough to produce a wartime bomb with the heavy water they were turning out at Rjukan-Vemork in ever greater volume—if Allied sabotage had not interrupted the flow. It has been said that while Heisenberg and his colleagues might have sparked a chain reaction, they did not know how to build an atomic bomb. Perhaps, but before Allied scientists were given all the money they needed for experimentation, they weren't sure how to build one, either.

In any event, the Allied attacks on Norsk Hydro apparently constituted the coup de grâce that finally doomed the German nuclear program. As Kurt Diebner, a German atomic scientist, would lament after his country's surrender:

> When one considers that right up to the end of the war . . . there was virtually no increase in our heavy-water stocks in Germany, and that . . . there were in fact only two and half tons of heavy water available, it will be seen that it was the elimination of German heavy-water production in Norway that was the main factor in our failure to achieve a self-sustaining atomic reactor before the war ended.

And William Casey, an OSS official who would head the Central Intelligence Agency under President Ronald Reagan, appeared to agree when he wrote: "In April 1945, the dismantled high-concentration plant was found in Bavaria, together with uranium and heavy water on the brink of going critical, lacking about seven hundred liters of additional heavy water."

# EPILOGUE

ALMOST UNTIL THE DAY Germany surrendered in 1945, General Groves feared it would make an atomic bomb before the Allies did. While feeling enormous relief when that day finally came, he continued to drive his scientists. He now found himself in a new race: to make a bomb before an invasion of Japan could claim many more lives and, in a personal sense, before the war ended without the world knowing what blinding power General Groves had created. The war, of course, ended with a cataclysmic display of this power.

Leo Szilard, who had so vigorously pressed the government to build a bomb, lobbied just as vigorously against its use once Germany had surrendered, arguing that the United States could set a precedent that might ultimately lay waste to the world. But his voice was drowned out by the explosions over Hiroshima and Nagasaki.

Werner Heisenberg and his German colleagues were captured by the Allied forces when the war ended and were sent to Britain, where they were detained, incommunicado, in Farm Hall, Godmanchester, from July to December 1945. Heisenberg claimed he had deliberately sabotaged Germany's bomb development, though it is not clear that this is true. Later, he and the other German atomic scientists returned to Germany and resumed their research. Heisenberg became director of the German Research Council in Göttingen, contributing to theoretical physics until forced by illness to retire in 1970. He died in 1976.

The Norwegian saboteurs became national heroes in Norway after the war. Even today, many Norwegians feel that their courageous exploits helped greatly to rescue the world from Nazi domination. Vemork has become a nationalist mecca, where an elaborate museum spells out every move the saboteurs made in their attacks. After the war, the heroes returned home and most resumed their work in business or on the farm, while spending much time on their skis exploring the mountains that haunt them with memories of a mission that could not fail. Kasper Idland emigrated to Long Island and Einar Skinnarland to Toronto to work as an engineer. In recent years, Idland, Knut Haukelid, Arne Kjelstrup, and Hans Storhaug have died.

The survival of the saboteurs, while joyously celebrated by the Norwegian people, has, at the same time, deepened the public chagrin, especially in southern Norway, over the tragic fate of the British commandos in Operation Freshman. Their gravesites and a monument near the area where they were murdered are visited not only by their families but by Norwegian tourists paying homage to them—though there is no grave bearing the name of Jimmy Cairncross and three comrades whose bodies lie on the ocean floor. However, a separate memorial to these men, paid for by the grateful citizens of Stavanger, was erected in 1985. Syd Brittain, whose heart had been rooted in the area since he learned of his comrades' fate, unveiled the stone and presented to a Norwegian sports club a trophy in memory of all the victims. The inscription engraved on it, "The Washington Cup," tells their story.

John M. Bennett, the green flight commander in the air attack on Norsk Hydro, would receive the Silver Star medal for heroism after leading a daring daylight raid on Berlin in 1944. After the war he returned to Texas and divided his time between his ranch and his bank. He died in 1973. Cowboy Roane, who accompanied Bennett on the Rjukan raid, recovered from his stomach ailment when Bennett left the "Bloody 100th" Bombardment Group, ending their love-hate relationship. After the war Roane returned to his Texas home with a chestful of medals and became a school administrator. His students harbored little doubt that he was a war hero.

# NOTES

*Full data on sources can be found in the Bibliography.*

## PROLOGUE

1  *A mysterious crash*: Interview: Martin Selmer Sandstol.

## 1. "A DELIGHTFUL PLAYTHING"

6  *Urey and heavy water*: Richard G. Hewlett and Oscar E. Anderson, *A History of the United States Atomic Energy Commission, The New World, 1939–1946*; Isidor Kirshenbaum, George M. Murphy, Harold C. Urey, eds., *Production of Heavy Water*; Richard Rhodes, *The Making of the Atomic Bomb*; George B. Pegram, *Columbia University Quarterly*, 3/34 (incl. quotes "one of the most delightful playthings," p. 65, and "It is the most expensive murder on record," p. 68); Urey, *Columbia University Quarterly*, 9/34; *New York Times*, 3/28/34, 11/13/34, 11/16/34 (incl. quote "be valuable in understanding more of living processes"), 12/9/34; Urey, "Some Thermodynamic Properties of Hydrogen and Deuterium," Nobel lecture, Stockholm, 2/14/35.

7  *Groves's fear of German bomb*: Leslie R. Groves, *Now It Can Be Told* (incl. quote "Our chief danger . . . ," p. 187).

8  *Houtermans's letter to Szilard*: Described in memo from Leo Szilard to Arthur H. Compton, 6/1/42 (incl. quote "It might be argued, of course . . ."), Office of Scientific Research and Development (OSRD), S-1, Industrial and Social Branch, National Archives, Washington, DC.

8  *Compton's letter to Bush*: Dated 6/22/42 (incl. quote "We have just recognized how a chain reaction . . ."), OSRD, S-1, Industrial and Social Branch, National Archives.

8 *Bush's letter to Strong*: Dated 8/31/42 ("A plant at Vemork . . ."), OSRD, S-1, Industrial and Social Branch, National Archives.
9 *Weizsaecker on Heisenberg-Bohr meeting*: Int. Carl von Weizsaecker.
9 *Heisenberg on meeting*: Robert Jungk, *Brighter Than a Thousand Suns*, pp. 102–4.
9 *Groves's personality and background*: Stephane Groueff, *Manhattan Project*; Groves; Hewlett and Anderson; Jungk; Robert De Vore, *Collier's* 10/13/45; Groves's personal papers, incl. memoirs by his wife, Grace, and his daughter, Gwenn, Modern Military Branch, National Archives; diaries of Chaplain Groves (the general's father), Modern Military Branch, National Archives; int. Luis Alvarez, Hans Bethe, Richard Groves (the general's son), Kenneth Nichols, Isidor I. Rabi, Robert Serber, Edward Teller, Victor Weisskopf, Eugene P. Wigner.
10 *Groves's visit to University of Chicago*: Groueff; Groves's personal papers, Hailey interviews (incl. quote "You may know that I don't have a Ph. D . . .").
11 *Groves tries to turn Wigner against Szilard*: Groves's personal papers, Hailey interviews (incl. quote "Within ten minutes . . .").
11 *Groves, Conant, and Szilard*: Groves's personal papers.
11 *Szilard's personality and background*: Szilard, Gertrud Weiss, and Kathleen R. Windsor, eds., "Reminiscences" in *Perspectives in American History* (Vol. II); Weiss and Weart, eds., *Leo Szilard: His Version of the Facts* (incl. quote "The devil shows Adam . . ."); H. G. Wells, *The World Set Free*; Alice Kimball Smith, "The Elusive Dr. Szilard," *Harper's*, 7/60; Eugene Rabinowitch, eulogy to Szilard, *Bulletin of the Atomic Scientists*, 10/64; int. Bethe, Allan Forbes (incl. quote "When Szilard fled . . ."), Ralph E. Lapp, Rabi, Serber, Teller, Egon A. Weiss, Weisskopf, Wigner.
14 *Szilard's meeting with Einstein*: Weiss and Weart (incl. Albert Einstein letter to Franklin D. Roosevelt); int. Weiss, Wigner.
15 *Szilard tries to obtain money from Union Carbide and Uranium Committee*: Weiss and Weart (incl. quotes); Szilard papers, University of California at San Diego; int. Weiss, Weisskopf, Wigner.
17 *Compton's warning about German bomb*: Compton letter to Bush, 6/22/42, OSRD, S-1, Industrial and Social Branch, National Archives.
17 *Strong memo to Eisenhower*: Dated 9/8/42, Modern Military Branch, National Archives.

## 2. THE JOURNEY OF PRODUCT Z

19 *Allier meets with Eriksen*: Maurice Goldsmith, *Frédéric Joliot-Curie*; *France-Soir*, Paris, 2/10/48; Jacques Allier report, 2/45, Centre d'Études, Fontenay aux Roses, France; Norsk Hydro letters to I.G. Farben, 1/24/40, 2/7/40, and Farben letter to Norsk Hydro, 1/30/40, Centre d'Études; int. Bertrand Goldschmidt.
20 *Szilard message to Joliot-Curie*: Jungk; Weiss and Weart.
22 *Allier meeting with Dautry and Joliot-Curie*: Goldschmidt, *Atomic Rivals*;

Goldsmith (incl. quote "It is not necessary to have hope . . . ," p. 17); *France-Soir*, 2/10/48; Allier report, 2/45; int. Goldschmidt.

23 *Allier's secret trip to Norway*: Goldschmidt; Goldsmith; Allier report, 2/45; Allier memos to Dautry from Norway, Centre d'Études; int. Goldschmidt.

25 *The transfer to Paris*: Ibid.

27 *The race to Clermont-Ferrand*: Goldschmidt; Goldsmith; Jungk; Arnold Kramish, *The Griffin*; Henri Moureux report, "Un episode peu connu de la bataille de l'eau lourde" (incl. quotes), 12/6/50 (unpublished), Centre d'Études; int. Goldschmidt.

29 *Escape to England*: Ibid.


## 3 · THE TURNING POINT

31 *Heisenberg builds atomic reactor*: David Irving, *The German Atomic Bomb* (incl. quote "We have at last succeeded . . . ," p. 118).

32 *Harteck and heavy water*: Ibid. (incl. quote "As the burden . . . ," p. 59); Paul Harteck papers on heavy water, 12/41, 1944, Oak Ridge, TN.

35 *Casimir and Heisenberg*: Hendrik Brugt Gerhard Casimir, *Haphazard Reality*; Kramish (incl. quote "History legitimizes Germany . . . ," p. 118).

35 *Heisenberg answers political and military leaders*: David Charles Cassidy, *Uncertainty*; Irving (incl. quotes on size of bomb, p. 120); Kramish; Thomas Powers, *Heisenberg's War*; int. Carl von Weizsaecker.

38 *Heisenberg-Doepel reactor blows up*: Ibid., Jungk.

39 *Heisenberg and Fermi*: Cassidy; Laura Fermi, *Atoms in the Family*; Irving; Kramish; Powers; int. Bethe, Weizsaecker.

40 *Bothe's blunder*: Irving; Kramish (incl. Bothe's love affair, pp. 174–75—Kramish in possession of love letters); Powers; *Cf. Zeitschrift für Physik*, Vol. 22.


## 4 · DIVIDED THEY STAND

42 *Welsh and heavy water*: Kramish; Powers (incl. quote "Heavy water? . . ."); int. Kramish.

43 *Peierls seeks information on Heisenberg*: Int. Rudolf Peierls (incl. quote "someone with knowledge of physics . . ."

43 *The Dahl deception*: Kramish; int. Kramish.

45 *Tronstad and British intelligence*: Ibid.; Powers; Leif Tronstad diary, Leif Tronstad, Jr.'s possession; int. Leif Tronstad, Jr.

46 *Churchill visits Roosevelt*: Winston Churchill, *The Hinge of Fate* (incl. quotes), pp. 374–82.

47 *Bush's memo to Roosevelt*: Groves, p. 10, 6/17/42, OSRD, S-1, Industrial and Social Branch, National Archives.

48 *"We have no idea as yet . . ."*: Memo to Secretary of State Cordell Hull, 9/29/44,

Germany Treatment, World War II Conferences, Freeman Matthews Files, Record Group 59, Department of State Files, National Archives.

49 *U.S. officials oppose cooperation with British*: Groves (incl. quote "might well be influenced . . . ," p. 129); Vincent C. Jones, *Manhattan: The Army and the Atomic Bomb*; Rhodes; int. Robert R. Furman.

50 *Stalin, heavy water, and the bomb*: Holloway, *Stalin and the Bomb*; A. P. Alexandrov, *Bulletin of the Atomic Scientists*, 12/67; Igor Golovin, *Bulletin of the Atomic Scientists*, 12/67; Alan Moorehead, *Saturday Evening Post*, 5/24, 31, 6/7, 14/52.

51 *Stimson urges Roosevelt to go it alone*: Reginald Victor Jones, *The Wizard War* (incl. quote "along for the present . . . ," p. 229).

51 *Akers asks for cooperative effort*: Ibid.

52 *Halban's heavy water experiment*: Letters, James B. Conant to C. J. Mackenzie 1/1/43, Conant to Mackenzie 1/2/43, Urey to Conant 3/11/43, Urey to Conant 4/2/43, Conant to E. V. Murphree 4/6/43, Conant to Urey 4/7/43, Urey to Conant 4/16/43, Conant to Urey 6/29/43, OSRD, S-1, Industrial and Social Branch, National Archives.

53 *Starheim and Skinnarland escape to Britain*: Int. Einar Skinnarland.

55 *Skinnarland returns home*: Ibid.

55 *Brun's career*: Jomar Brun, *Brennpunkt Vemork 1940–1945*; Kramish; int. Kramish, Kjell Nielsen, Per Pynten.

56 *Nine-stage heavy-water process*: Irving; int. Nielsen, Pynten.

57 *Castor oil slows process*: Int. Nielsen, Pynten.

57 *Germans seek to increase production*: Irving; Kramish; Powers; int. Skinnarland, Weizsaecker.

58 *Tronstad wants heavy water sent to Britain*: Kramish; Powers; int. Kramish, Skinnarland.

59 *favor assault on Norsk Hydro*: Irving; Kramish; Powers; Richard Wiggan, *Operation Freshman*; Operation Freshman file, Public Records Office, Kew, Richmond, Surrey, England.

### 5. "TO THE LAST MAN"

60 *"Grouse's mission is of great importance . . ."*: Poulsson, *Aksjon Vemork Vinterkrig Pa Hardangervidda* (*Luck Was My Companion*, unpublished English translation, p. 37); int. Jens Anton Poulsson.

60 *Wilson and the SOE*: Kramish; Poulsson (English translation); Powers; John S. Wilson, *The Heavy-Water Operations in Norway*; int. Kramish, Skinnarland.

61 *How should plant be attacked?*: Ibid.

62 *"One never knows how one will react under fire . . ."*: Poulsson (English translation), p. 24.

62 *"The majority of the boys . . ."*: Ibid., p. 18.

63 *"The great majority of Norwegian people . . ."*: Jacob Stevenson Worm-Muller, *Norway Revolts Against the Nazis*, p. 9.

63 *"They had ... a certain squeamishness ..."*: William Warbey, *Look to Norway*, pp. 192–93.
64 *Poulsson Haugland briefed on mission*: Poulsson (English translation); int. Knut Haugland, Poulsson.
65 *Poulsson's Grouse team*: Int. Claus Helberg, Arne Kjelstrup.
67 *Brun flees to Britain*: Thomas M. Gallagher, *Assault in Norway*; int. Skinnarland.
68 *Falkenhorst's court-martial argument*: E. H. Stevens, ed., official record, *The Trial of Von Falkenhorst* (incl. quotes, pp. 223, 108).
69 *Falkenhorst and Terboven*: Ake Fen, *Nazis in Norway*; Tore Gjelsvik, *Norwegian Resistance, 1940–1945*; Jens Christian Hauge, *Resistance in Norway 1940–1945*; Stevens; Paul G. Vigness, *The German Occupation of Norway*; Worm-Muller (incl. quote "great revival, ... a mighty reaction in spirit ...," p. 32).

6. THE WASHINGTON CUP

72 *Syd Brittain prepares for Operation Freshman*: Saga (Oslo), 4/25/85; int. Syd Brittain.
73 *Cairncross goes to war*: R. A. de G. Sewell (brother of Cairncross), letter to author, 1/2/94.
74 *Injured Brittain cut from mission*: Int. Brittain (incl. quotes).
75 *Henniker goes on test flight*: Mark Henniker report (incl. quotes), n.d.; Operation Freshman file, Public Records Office.

7. AT LAST A GIRL

78 *Grouse team trudges to base near Rjukan*: Poulsson (English translation); int. Haugland, Helberg, Kjelstrup, Poulsson.
82 *Haugland flees Nazis*: Int. Haugland.
83 *Clearing the way for Operation Freshman*: Poulsson (English translation); int. Haugland, Helberg, Kjelstrup, Poulsson.
83 *Freshman doesn't land*: Ibid.
84 *"Glider in sea"*: Operation Freshman file, Public Records Office.
84 *Brittain prays for comrades' safe return*: Int. Brittain.
84 *Sandstol learns of second crash*: Int. Sandstol.

8. "THIS FILTHY BUSINESS"

85 *Nygaard and British survivors*: Int. Tor Nygaard (incl. quotes).
86 *The Hovlands and the survivors*: Int. Torbjorn Hogstad (incl. quotes), Bergit Hovland.
88 *Rescue group climbs to crash site*: Wiggan; Norwegian eyewitness accounts, Norges Hjemmefrontmuseum, Oslo; Operation Freshman file, Public Records Office; int. Jostein Berglyd.

89 *Fylgjesdal and the survivors*: Knut Stahl, *De Lange Arene 1940–1945*; int. Bruse Espedal, Thorvald Fylgjesdal.

90 *At the Haaheller farm*: Ibid.

92 *Hjordis and the harmonica*: Ibid.

93 *Hjordis to supervise burial*: Ibid.

93 *Henniker clings to hope*: Wiggan; Operation Freshman file, Public Records Office.

94 *Falkenhorst's moral dilemma*: Stevens (incl. quotes, pp. 22–23).

## 9. THE METHODS OF MURDER

96 *Behren's moral dilemma*: Karl Maria von Behren court-martial records, Public Records Office.

97 *Bornschein witnesses executions*: Int. Fritz Bornschein (incl. quotes).

100 *Behren makes deal with Wilkens*: Behren court-martial records, Public Records Office.

101 *Rediess reports to Berlin*: Ibid.

102 *Wilkens urges Seeling to kill prisoners*: Werner Fritz Seeling court-martial records (incl. quotes), Public Records Office.

105 *Waiting for the poison to work*: Ibid.

106 *Death by strangulation, stamping, injection*: Ibid.

106 *The doctor's last patient*: Ibid.

107 *The drip of honey at Grini*: Operation Freshman file, Public Records Office.

108 *The deadly deception*: Ibid.

## 10. TRAINING TO DIE

110 *Pondering a new mission*: Wiggan; Wilson; Operation Freshman file, Public Records Office.

111 *"You can't do that!"*: Wiggan.

112 *"This was some devious British scheme . . ."*: John A. Bross, *Secret Operations*.

112 *Ronneberg's new assignment*: Gallagher; Joachim Ronneberg report, Public Records Office; Norges Hjemmefrontmuseum, Oslo; int. Ronneberg (incl. quotes).

113 *American reactor ushers in nuclear age*: Ronald W. Clark, *The Birth of the Bomb*; Rhodes; Groueff; Groves; Dan Kurzman, *Day of the Bomb*; Weiss and Weart; int. Weisskopf, Wigner.

115 *Ronneberg's background*: Int. Ronneberg.

116 *Haukelid's background*: Haukelid, *Skis Against the Atom* (incl. quote, p. 19).

117 *Kayser's background*: Int. Fredrik Kayser.

117 *Storhaug's background*: Haukelid.

118 *Idland's background*: Int. Ronneberg.

118 *Brun knew all the answers*: Ibid.; int. Kayser, Ronneberg.

119 *"A number of servicewomen kept the house in order . . ."*: Haukelid, p. 76.

119 *"You should realize that the Germans . . .":* Ibid.
120 *Men given cyanide pill:* Ibid.

## 11. REUNION IN PARADISE

121 *"Evil brew" saves Haugland's life:* Int. Haugland.
122 *Rediess warns Berlin about British target:* Stevens; Wiggan.
122 *Generals demand stronger guard:* Stevens; Operation Freshman file, Public Records Office.
122 *"London's radio message about the glider disaster . . .":* Int. Poulsson.
123 *Poulsson bags reindeer for Christmas Eve dinner:* Ibid.; int. Poulsson.
124 *"The mountains were big . . .":* Poulsson (English translation), p. 67.
124 *Tronstad's farewell remark:* Haukelid; int. Kayser, Ronneberg.
124 *"The hum of the powerful engines . . .":* Haukelid, p. 15.
125 *British plane fails to land:* Poulsson (English translation); int. Haugland, Helberg, Poulsson (incl. quotes).
125 *"Our pilot was unable to find the reception committee":* Haukelid, p. 30.
126 *Gunnerside uncertain where landed:* Ibid. (incl. quotes, p. 83); int. Ronneberg, Kayser.
127 *The search for Grouse:* Ibid.; Ronneberg report.
128 *The capture of Kristiansen:* Ibid.; Haukelid (incl. quotes, p. 85).
130 *"There's someone on skis over there . . .":* Int. Ronneberg.
130 *Exchange between Haukelid and Ronneberg re two figures:* Ibid.; int. Ronneberg (incl. quotes).
131 *Gunnerside meets Grouse:* Ibid.; int. Kayser.

## 12. PRELUDE TO GLORY

132 *The newcomers could "have the meat . . .":* Haukelid, p. 89.
132 *"Jens put a few wet sticks into the stove . . .":* Ibid., p. 94.
133 *Skinnarland, the secret "safety valve":* Int. Skinnarland.
133 *Deciding Kristiansen's fate:* Haukelid; int. Ronneberg.
134 *Commandos plan attack:* Ibid.; Ronneberg report; int. Haugland, Helberg, Kjelstrup, Ronneberg.
136 *Helberg's background:* Int. Helberg.
137 *" 'In Rjukan,' Poulsson would later say . . .":* Poulsson (English translation), p. 69.
137 *"Where trees grow . . .":* Int. Ronneberg.
138 *Helberg skeptical about climb to plant: Yearbook of the Norwegian Mountain Touring Club,* 1947 (Helberg memoir); int. Helberg, Ronneberg.
138 *Helberg's exploratory mission:* Helberg memoir (incl. quote "Local people . . ."); Int. Helberg.
140 *Commandos debate route of attack:* Ibid.; Ronneberg report (incl. quote "I felt that the attack . . ."); int. Kayser, Kjelstrup, Poulsson, Ronneberg (incl. quote "Okay, we'll withdraw . . .").

141 *Idland takes Ronneberg aside*: Gallagher; int. Ronneberg (incl. quotes).

142 *Commandos threaten unexpected visitor*: Poulsson (English translation, incl. quotes, p. 69); int. Helberg, Poulsson, Ronneberg, Lellean Tangstad.

## 13. ASSAULTING THE CASTLE

144 *"The hum of the machinery ..."*: Haukelid, p. 105.

144 *Skiing toward the target*: Int. Helberg, Kayser, Kjelstrup, Poulsson, Ronneberg.

145 *"It was only by a hair's breadth ..."*: Haukelid, p. 107.

146 *"I'll test it out ..."*: Int. Helberg.

146 *Climbing the cliff*: Gallagher; int. Helberg, Kayser, Kjelstrup, Poulsson, Ronneberg.

148 *"Do you understand your orders?"*: Int. Ronneberg.

149 *"Knut," he said, "you and Kjelstrup advance alone ..."*: Ibid.

149 *"To one of the most important military objectives in Europe"*: Haukelid, p. 108.

149 *Advance into the yard*: Ibid.; Gallagher; Ronneberg report; int. Helberg, Kayser, Kjelstrup, Poulsson, Ronneberg.

150 *"Damn it! Locked!" he mumbled*: Ronneberg report; int. Ronneberg.

150 *Ronneberg sees heavy-water cells*: Ibid.

150 *"This must be the tunnel"*: Int. Ronneberg.

150 *Creeping through the tunnel*: Ibid.

151 *"Put your hands up!"*: Int. Kayser.

151 *"We're British soldiers"*: Ibid.

152 *Placing the charges*: Int. Kayser, Ronneberg (incl. quote "be careful").

152 *"The time seemed long to us ..."*: Haukelid, p. 110.

152 *"What was it like for the Chicken ..."*: Ibid., p. 112.

153 *"We waited and waited ..."*: Ibid., p. 112.

153 *"You must remember to call out ..."*: Ibid., p. 112.

153 *"We had surrounded a section of Germans ..."*: Haukelid, p. 112.

153 *"The time passed extremely slowly ..."*: Poulsson (English translation), p. 27.

153 *Stromsheim breaks through window*: Int. Kayser, Ronneberg.

154 *"Damn it!" Ronneberg cried ..."*: Int. Ronneberg.

154 *"Take care not to short-circuit ..."*: Haukelid, p. 109.

154 *Johansen can't find his glasses*: Int. Ronneberg (incl. quotes).

155 *"Someone is coming down the stairs!"*: Ibid.

156 *"At last there was an explosion ..."*: Haukelid, pp. 112–13.

156 *"There was a bang"*: Poulsson (English translation), p. 77.

156 *Haukelid and Poulsson hide from German*: Ibid.; Haukelid (incl. quotes, p. 113).

157 *Kjelstrup and the password*: Int. Kayser, Kjelstrup (incl. quotes).

## 14. THE HEAVENS CELEBRATE

159 *"When we were down in the bottom of the valley ..."*: Haukelid, p. 114.

160 *"The German cars went toward Vemork ..."*: Helberg memoir.

160 *The trek to Svensbu*: Haukelid; Poulsson; int. Helberg, Kayser, Kjelstrup, Poulsson, Ronneberg.

161 *"We felt great satisfaction ..."*: Helberg memoir.

161 *Larsen and Nilssen learn of attack*: Gallagher.

162 *"On the night of 27th–28th February 1943 ..."*: Wilhelm Rediess report, Norges Hjemmefrontmuseum, Oslo.

162 *Falkenhorst inspects damage*: Haukelid (incl. quotes, pp. 126–27); int. Skinnarland.

164 *"I'll meet you guys in Svensbu ..."*: Helberg memoir; int. Helberg.

164 *"One mass of driving snow"*: Ronneberg report.

165 *"In order to breathe ..."*: Haukelid, p. 117.

166 *Saboteurs split up*: Haukelid; Ronneberg report; int. Kayser, Kjelstrup, Poulsson, Ronneberg.

166 *"When everything was packed ..."*: Haukelid, p. 119.

167 *Poulsson stops at inn*: Poulsson (English translation, incl. quote "The temptation was too great," p. 75); int. Poulsson (incl. other quotes).

169 *Kristiansen and chocolate*: Gallagher.

170 *Haukelid and Kjelstrup inform London of triumph*: Haukelid (incl. quotes, p. 121); int. Haugland.

170 *Ronneberg's group skis toward Sweden*: Ronneberg report (incl. quotes); int. Kayser, Ronneberg.

## 15. FLIGHT OF THE GLADIATOR

173 *Poulsson reunites with Helberg*: Poulsson (English translation); Helberg memoir; int. Helberg, Poulsson.

173 *"Take care of yourself, Claus ..."*: Int. Helberg.

173 *Helberg's flight*: Ibid. (incl. quotes); Helberg memoir.

181 *"What is being done for these brave men ... ?"*: Report, Gunnerside attack, Norges Hjemmefrontmuseum, Oslo.

## 16. THE ANGELS ARE WAITING

182 *"The sabotage of the Norsk Hydro plant ..."*: *Svenska Dagbladet*, 3/14/44.

183 *"The first reports on this action were most encouraging"*: Groves, p. 188.

183 *Groves learned of plan for attack from Akers*: General George Marshall memo to Field Marshal Sir John Dill, 4/3/43, Modern Military Branch, National Archives.

183 *"The juice story still of highest big policy importance ..."*: Tronstad diary, 3/20/43.

183 *" 'Heavy water,' derived by an electro-chemical process ..."*: *New York Times*, 4/3/43.

184 *"I am quite sure that [heavy water] cannot be used ..."*: Urey letter to Watson

Davis, Science Service, Washington, D.C., 4/8/43, OSRD, S-1, Industrial and Social Branch, National Archives.

184 *"The latest information . . ."*: Marshall memo to Dill, 4/3/43, Modern Military Branch, National Archives.

185 *"As nothing has been heard of this raid . . ."*: Dill cable to RAF Chief Charles Portal, 4/3/43, Modern Military Branch, National Archives.

185 *"SOE state that after one unsuccessful attempt . . ."*: Portal cable to Dill, 4/6/43, Modern Military Branch, National Archives.

185 *"As a result of information I have received . . ."*: Portal cable to Dill, 4/7/43, Modern Military Branch, National Archives.

185 *Groves challenges British experts*: Int. Kramish (incl. quote "You may be right . . .").

186 *"It now seems extremely probable . . ."*: Conant report to Groves, 7/1/43, OSRD, S-1, Industrial and Social Branch, National Archives.

186 *Plant expected "to reach full production . . . again from August 15"*: Skinnarland radio message to London, 8/8/43, Skinnarland's possession and Norges Hjemmefrontmuseum, Oslo.

186 *"Partial production of the 99.5% heavy-water concentrate started in June . . ."*: Ibid., 8/3/43.

187 *"Dr. Bush and General Groves consider it of highest importance . . ."*: Strong memo to Marshall, 8/13/43, Modern Military Branch, National Archives.

187 *Bush "received the very distinct impression . . ."*: Strong memo to Marshall, 8/13/43, Modern Military Branch, National Archives.

187 *Eaker given "specific direction on the highest level . . ."*: Strong memo to Marshall, 8/13/43, Modern Military Branch, National Archives.

188 *"When the weather favors attacks in Norway . . ."*: Ira Eaker order as Commanding General, 8th Air Force, 10/22/43, Eaker papers, Library of Congress.

188 *Roane and Bennett prepare for Rjukan raid*: John M. Bennett, *Letters from England*; Harry H. Crosby, *A Wing and a Prayer*; int. Harry H. Crosby, Owen Roane.

189 *Bennett's personality*: Bennett; Crosby (incl. quotes involving Bennett and himself, pp. 206–8); int. Crosby, Thomas M. Hatfield, Roane.

189 *Roane's background*: Edward Jablonski, *Double Strike*; Martin Middlebrook, *The Schweinfurt-Regensburg Mission*; *Denton* (Texas) *Record-Chronicle*, 11/90; *Fort Worth Star-Telegram*, 8/5/90; *Houston Post*, 12/22/91; int. Roane.

190 *Bennett's background*: Bennett; Hatfield, *Austin-American Statesman*, 11/17/90; *Houston Chronicle*, 5/17/93.

191 *"As leader of a group . . ."*: Bennett.

192 *"Even in broad daylight . . ."*: Ibid.

193 *"The success of our take-off . . ."*: Ibid.

193 *Confusion in the sky*: Bennett; int. Roane.

## 17. THE COFFINS ARE FULL

194 *Julia visits Boilestad*: Int. Birger Boilestad.

195 *"To stay in that bomb shelter . . ."*: Ibid.

195 *Frantsen leaves work for home*: Int. Dagfinn Frantsen.

196 *"Give them my love"*: Ibid.

196 *"This was really a beautiful sight"*: Bennett, p. 15.

197 *Bennett's dilemma*: Ibid.

197 *"Make a large circle . . ."*: Ibid., p. 17.

197 *"It'll probably be a milk run"*: Ibid., p. 13.

197 *"Milk run! Shit!"*: Int. Roane.

198 *One aircraft shot down*: Bennett.

198 *Roane finds way to attack*: Int. Roane.

199 *B-24s diverted to Rjukan*: Int. Kenneth G. Jewell.

199 *The planes kept switching positions . . ."*: Jewell letter to Forrest S. Clark, n.d.

199 *"Soon, all the planes were talking freely . . ."*: Ibid.

199 *Wright's homemade bomb*: Int. Robert Wright (incl. quote).

200 *Gilbert and the 392nd*: Lawrence Gilbert report (incl. quotes); int. Lawrence Gilbert.

201 *Nielsen survives attacks on Heroya and Vemork*: Kjell Nielsen report; int. Nielsen (incl. quotes).

202 *"My God, what's happened to my family?"*: Ibid.

203 *Boilestad searches for loved ones*: Int. Boilestad (incl. quote).

203 *Moe's wife dies in shelter*: Int. Nielsen.

204 *Boilestad blames those who "cared only about making weapons and money and war"*: Int. Boilestad (incl. quote).

205 *Frantsen searches for loved ones*: Int. Frantsen (incl. quote).

206 *Bennett and Roane reproached on return to base*: Int. Roane (incl. quotes).

207 *Roane and his stomach problem*: Ibid.

207 *"Cowboy is a top pilot"*: Bennett, p. 15.

## 18. AN AGONIZING DECISION

209 *"Vemork completely destroyed . . ."*: Skinnarland radio message to London, 11/30/43, Skinnarland's possession and Norges Hjemmefrontmuseum, Oslo.

209 *Damage assessment*: Reports, Groups of 1st and 3rd Bomb Divisions, 8th Air Force, National Archives, Suitland, Md.

209 *British doubt Germans could build bomb*: Int. Kramish.

210 *Raid "was carried out without any advance notice . . ."*: Norwegian government protest to British and American military officials, 11/17/43, Modern Military Branch, National Archives.

210 *Germans worry about more air attacks*: Int. Nielsen.

210 *"We have information that heavy-water equipment . . ."*: London message to Skinnarland, 12/29/43, Skinnarland's possession and Norges Hjemmefrontmuseum, Oslo.

211 *Syverstad knows plant to be transferred to Germany*: Int. Nielsen.

211 *"Everything indicates IMI . . . apparatus will be moved . . ."*: Skinnarland message to London, 12/31/43, Skinnarland's possession and Norges Hjemmefrontmuseum, Oslo.

212 *Nielsen meets with Sorlie and Haukelid*: Haukelid; int. Nielsen.

212 *Haukelid's wife wants divorce*: Haukelid.

213 *"Tell London . . . that it isn't necessary . . ."*: Int. Nielsen.

213 *"Bonzo reports as follows . . ."*: Skinnarland message to London, 2/15/44, Skinnarland's possession and Norges Hjemmefrontmuseum, Oslo.

214 *"The Germans got into their head . . ."*: Int. Kramish.

214 *"Matter has been considered . . ."*: London message to Skinnarland, 2/15/44, Skinnarland's possession and Norges Hjemmefrontmuseum, Oslo.

214 *Haukelid ordered to destroy heavy water*: Haukelid.

214 *Haukelid, Sorlie, Nielsen, Syverstad meet*: Haukelid; int. Nielsen.

216 *"It is always hard to take a decision . . ."*: Haukelid, p. 187.

216 *Haukelid mulls over alternatives*: Haukelid (incl. quotes), pp. 186–87.

217 *"Time short . . . Therefore difficult to execute military attack . . ."*: Skinnarland message to London, 2/9/44, Skinnarland's possession and Norges Hjemmefrontmuseum, Oslo.

217 *"Approve sinking of ferry . . ."*: London message to Skinnarland, 2/9/44, Skinnarland's possession and Norges Hjemmefrontmuseum, Oslo.

217 *Plotters plan sinking*: Haukelid; int. Nielsen.

217 *Lier-Hansen recruited for attack*: Int. Lier-Hansen.

218 *Lier-Hansen meets with Haukelid and Sorlie*: Ibid.

218 *Haukelid boards ferry disguised*: Haukelid.

219 *Haukelid and Sorlie fashion bomb*: Ibid.

219 *Haukelid and Sorlie test release system*: Ibid.

220 *Nielson plans hoax to avoid arrest*: Int. Nielsen.

220 *Plan to make Larsen the scapegoat*: Ibid. (incl. quotes).

221 *Nielsen decides not to warn Fladmoe of attack*: Ibid.

222 *Syverstad finds way to keep his mother home*: Ibid.; Haukelid.

222 *Lier-Hansen reconnoiters wharf area*: Int. Lier-Hansen (incl. quote).

222 *"I cannot remember Rjukan being more tense"*: Haukelid, p. 189.

222 *Haukelid and Sorlie observe flatcars with heavy water*: Ibid.

## 19. THE FINAL BLOW

224 *"I'm sorry . . . but it won't go!"*: Int. Lier-Hansen.

224 *Saboteurs tinker with car*: Ibid.; Haukelid.

225 *Haukelid tells driver to wait for saboteurs*: Haukelid.

225 *"The bitterly cold night . . ."*: Ibid., pp. 191–92.

225 *"We were preoccupied with the need to succeed"*: Int. Lier-Hansen.

225 *Haukelid steals aboard ferry*: Ibid.; Haukelid.

226 *"But before we had got the hatch open . . ."*: Haukelid, p. 192.

226 *Watchman confronts Lier-Hansen*: Int. Lier-Hansen (incl. quotes).

227  *Haukelid and Sorlie set charges*: Haukelid.

228  *Lier-Hansen bids watchman good-bye*: Int. Lier-Hansen.

228  *Saboteurs flee scene*: Ibid.; Haukelid.

229  *Gulbrandsen decides to take ferry*: Int. Eva Gulbrandsen (incl. quotes).

230  *Lier-Hansen waits for ferry to leave*: Int. Lier-Hansen.

231  *Eva studies fellow passengers*: Int. Gulbrandsen.

231  *Eva tries to escape after explosion*: Ibid. (incl. quote).

232  *Haukelid and Larsen head for Swedish border*: Haukelid (incl. quotes).

233  *Eva is dragged aboard lifeboat*: Rjukan Arbeiderblad, 2/21/44; int. Gulbrandsen (incl. quote "My God, we're going down!").

234  *Lier-Hansen arrives back in Rjukan*: Int. Lier-Hansen (incl. quotes).

235  *Nielsen has operation*: Int. Nielsen (incl. quotes).

235  *Syverstad returns to work, then flees*: Syverstad report (incl. quote "be subjected by the Gestapo . . ."), Norges Hjemmefrontmuseum, Oslo; int. Nielsen.

235  *"Rjukan would be made to weep . . ."*: Int. Nielsen.

## CONCLUSION

238  *Brun thought sabotage blocked German bomb*: Brun.

238  *"When one considers that right up to the end of the war . . ."*: Gallagher, p. 229.

239  *"In April 1945, the dismantled high-concentration plant . ."*: William J. Casey, *The Secret War Against Hitler*, p. 44.

# BIBLIOGRAPHY

## BOOKS

Allen, Thomas B., and Norman Polmar. *World War II: America at War, 1941–1945.* New York: Random House, 1991.

Baden-Powell, Dorothy. *Operation Jupiter: SOE's Secret War in Norway.* London: Robert Hale, 1982.

Baxter, James Phinney III. *Scientists Against Time.* Boston: Little, Brown, 1946.

Bennett, John M., Jr. *Letters from England.* San Antonio: privately published, 1945, 1986.

Bernstein, Jeremy. *Hans Bethe: Prophet of Energy.* New York: Basic Books, 1980.

Beyerchen, Alan D. *Scientists Under Hitler.* New Haven: Yale University, 1977.

Biquard, Pierre. *Frederic Joliot-Curie.* London: Paul S. Eriksson, 1962.

Bohn, Per. *Imi: Norsk Innsats i Kampen Mot Atomkraften.* Trondheim: F. Brun, 1946.

Bower, Tom. *The Paperclip Conspiracy: The Hunt for the Nazi Scientists.* Boston: Little, Brown, 1987.

Brissaud, Andre. *Canaris.* London: Weidenfeld & Nicolson, 1973.

Bross, John A. *Secret Operations: Some Reminiscences.* Privately printed.

Brown, Anthony Cave. *Bodyguard of Lies.* New York: Harper & Row, 1975.

———. *The Last Hero: Wild Bill Donovan.* New York: Times Books, 1982.

Brown, Anthony Cave, and Charles B. MacDonald, eds. *The Secret History of the Atomic Bomb.* New York: Dial, 1977.

Brun, Jomar. *Brennpunkt Vemork 1940–1945.* Oslo: Universitetsforl., 1985.

Bush, Vannevar. *Pieces of the Action.* New York: Morrow, 1970.

*By Air to Battle—The Official Account of the British Airborne Divisions.* London: HMSO, 1945.

Casey, William J. *The Secret War Against Hitler.* New York: Regnery, 1988.

Casimir, Hendrik Brugt Gerhard. *Haphazard Reality: Half a Century of Science.* New York: Harper & Row, 1983.

Cassidy, David Charles. *Uncertainty: The Life and Science of Werner Heisenberg.* New York: W. H. Freeman, 1992.

Christensen, Chris A. R. *Dad: Mad Livet Some Innsats i Krigatodems Noorge.* Oslo: Tanum, 1965.

Churchill, Winston S. *The Gathering Storm.* Boston: Houghton Mifflin, 1948.

———. *The Hinge of Fate.* Boston: Houghton Mifflin, 1953.

Clark, Ronald W. *The Birth of the Bomb.* New York: Horizon, 1960.

———. *Einstein.* New York: World, 1971.

———. *The Greatest Power on Earth.* New York: Harper & Row, 1980.

Compton, Arthur Holly. *Atomic Quest.* New York: Oxford University Press, 1956.

Crosby, Harry H. *A Wing and a Prayer.* New York: Harper Collins, 1993.

Cruickshank, Charles Greig. *S.O.E. in Scandinavia.* New York: Oxford, 1986.

———. *Deception in World War II.* New York: Oxford, 1979.

Curie, Eve. *Madame Curie.* New York: Doubleday, Doran, 1937.

Curtis, Monica, ed. *Norway and the War, Sept. 1939–Dec. 1940, Documents on International Affairs.* London: Oxford University Press, 1941.

Dahl, Helge. *Rjukan: Bind II.* Rjukan: n.p., 1984.

Derry, Thomas Kingston. *The Campaign in Norway.* London: HMSO, 1952.

———. *A Short History of Norway.* London: G. Allen, n.d.

Drummond, John D. *But for These Men.* London: Allen, 1962.

Eifler, Carl F., and Thomas N. Moon. *The Deadliest Colonel.* New York: Vantage, 1975.

Eklof, Per. *Sabotorer i Telemark eller Kampen Om Det Tunga Vattnet.* Flem: n.p., 1975.

*European Resistance Movements, 1939–45, Proceedings of the First International Conference on the History of the Resistance Movements.* New York: Pergamon Press, 1960.

*European Resistance Movements, 1939–45, Proceedings of the Second International Conference on the History of the Resistance Movements.* New York: Pergamon Press, 1964.

Fen, Ake. *Nazis in Norway.* Harmondsworth: Penguin Books, 1943.

Fermi, Laura. *Atoms in the Family.* Chicago: University of Chicago, 1954.

Ferrell, Robert H. *George C. Marshall.* New York: Cooper Square, 1966.

Fjeldbu, Sigmund. *Et Lite Sted Pa Verdenskartet: Rjukan 1940–1950:* Oslo: n.p., 1980.

Foot, M. R. D. *S.O.E.: The Special Operations Executive, 1940–46.* London: British Broadcasting Corporation, 1984.

Freeman, Roger A. *The Mighty Eighth: Units, Men and Machines.* London: Macdonald, 1970.

French, A. P., and P. J. Kennedy, eds. *Niels Bohr: A Centenary Volume.* Cambridge, Mass.: Harvard University, 1985.

Frisch, Otto. *What Little I Remember.* Cambridge, England: Cambridge University, 1979.

Gallagher, Thomas Michael. *Assault in Norway.* Harcourt, Brace, Jovanovich, 1975.

Gilbert, Martin. *The Second World War.* New York: Holt, 1989.

Gjelsvik, Tore. *Norwegian Resistance, 1940–1945.* Montreal: McGill-Queen's University, 1979.

Goebbels, Joseph. *The Goebbels Diaries, 1942–43.* London: Hamilton, 1948.

Goldschmidt, Bertrand. *Atomic Rivals.* New Brunswick, N.J.: Rutgers University, 1990.

Goldsmith, Maurice. *Frederic Joliot-Curie: A Biography.* London: Lawrence & Wishart, 1976.

Goudsmit, Samuel Abraham. *Alsos.* Los Angeles: Tomash, 1947, 1983.

Gowing, Margaret. *Britain and Atomic Energy 1939–1945.* New York: St. Martin's Press, 1964.

Groueff, Stephane. *Manhattan Project: The Untold Story of the Making of the Atomic Bomb.* Boston: Little, Brown, 1967.

Groves, Leslie R. *Now It Can Be Told,* New York: Harper, 1962.

Hahn, Otto. *My Life: The Autobiography of a Scientist.* New York: Herder & Herder, 1970.

Hart, B. H. Liddel. *The German Generals Talk.* New York: Morrow, 1948.

Hauge, Jens Christian. "Resistance in Norway 1940–1945." Unpublished.

Haukelid, Knut. *Skis Against the Atom.* London: Collins, 1973.

Heilbron, J. L. *The Dilemmas of an Upright Man: Max Planck as Spokesman for German Science.* Berkeley: University of California, 1986.

Heisenberg, Elisabeth. *Inner Exile.* Boston: Birkhauser, 1984.

Heisenberg, Werner. *Encounters with Einstein.* Princeton, N.J.: Princeton University, 1989.

———. *Physics and Beyond: Encounters and Conversations.* New York: Harper & Row, 1971.

Hershberg, James. *James B. Conant: Harvard to Hiroshima and the Making of the Nuclear Age.* New York: Knopf, 1993.

Hewins, Ralph. *Quisling, Prophet Without Honor.* London: W. H. Allen, 1965.

Hewlett, Richard G., and Oscar E. Anderson. *A History of the United States Atomic Energy Commission, The New World, 1939–1946.* University Park, Pa.: Pennsylvania State University, 1962.

Hinsley, Francis Harry. *British Intelligence in the Second World War.* London: HMSO, 1979.

Holloway, David. *The Soviet Union and the Arms Race.* New Haven: Yale University, 1983.

———. *Stalin and the Bomb.* New Haven: Yale University, 1994.

Howarth, David. *The Shetland Bus.* London: Thomas Nelson, 1951.

Hoye, Bjarne, and Trygve Ager. *Norwegian Church Against Naziism.* New York: Macmillan, 1943.

Humble, Richard. *Hitler's Generals.* London: Barker, 1973.

Irving, David. *The German Atomic Bomb.* New York: Simon & Schuster, 1968.

Jablonski, Edward. *Double Strike.* Garden City, N.Y.: Doubleday, 1974.

Johnson, Amanda. *Norway, Her Invasion and Occupation.* Decatur, Ga., 1948.

Jones, Reginald Victor. *The Wizard War: British Scientific Intelligence, 1939–1945.* New York: Coward, McCann, and Geoghegan, 1978.

————. *Reflections on Intelligence*. London: Heinemann, 1989.

Jones, Vincent C. *Manhattan: The Army and the Atomic Bomb*. Washington, D.C.: Center of Military History, United States Army, 1985.

Jungk, Robert. *Brighter Than a Thousand Suns: A Personal History of the Atomic Scientists*. New York: Harcourt, Brace, 1958.

Kahn, David. *Hitler's Spies: German Military Intelligence in World War II*. New York: Collier, 1985.

Kaplan, Fred M. *The Wizards of Armageddon*. New York: Simon & Schuster, 1984.

Kaufman, Louis, Barbara Fitzgerald, and Tom Sewell. *Moe Berg: Athlete, Scholar, Spy*. Boston: Little, Brown, 1975.

Keegan, John, ed. *Who Was Who in World War II*. London: Arms and Armour, 1978.

Kevles, Daniel J. *The Physicists*. New York: Knopf, 1978.

Kirshenbaum, Isidor, George M. Murphy, and Harold C. Urey, eds. *Production of Heavy Water*. New York: McGraw-Hill, 1955.

Kistiakowsky, George B. *A Scientist at the White House*. Cambridge, Mass.: Harvard University, 1976.

Kjelstadlis, Sverne. *Hjemmestyrkene*. N.p., 1959.

Kramish, Arnold. *The Griffin: The Greatest Untold Espionage Story of World War II*. Boston: Houghton Mifflin, 1986.

Kurzman, Dan. *Day of the Bomb*. New York: McGraw-Hill, 1985.

Lawren, William. *The General and the Bomb: A Biography of General Leslie R. Groves, Director of the Manhattan Project*. New York: Dodd, Mead, 1988.

Lloyd, Alan, and Leo Cooper. *The Gliders*. London: Secker & Warburg, 1982.

Lovell, Stanley P. *Of Spies and Strategems*. Englewood Cliffs, N.J.: Prentice-Hall, 1963.

Michel, Henri. *The Second World War*. New York: Praeger, 1975.

Middlebrook, Martin. *The Schweinfurt-Regensburg Mission*. New York: Scribner's, 1975.

Midgaard, John. *A Brief History of Norway*. Oslo: Tanum, 1963.

Mitcham, Samuel W., Jr., and Gene Mueller. *Hitler's Commanders*. Lanham, Mich.: Scarborough House, 1992.

Moore, Ruth. *Niels Bohr: The Man, His Science and the World They Changed*. Cambridge, Mass.: Massachusetts Institute of Technology, 1966, 1985.

Moorehead, Alan. *The Traitors*. London: Hamish Hamilton, 1952.

Moran, Lord (Sir Charles Wilson). *Churchill: Taken from the Diaries of Lord Moran*. Boston: Houghton Mifflin, 1960.

National Academy of Sciences. *Biographical Memoirs: Leo Szilard*, Vol. 40. New York: Columbia University, 1969.

*Norsk-Hydro 1905–1955*. Oslo: Norsk Hydro, 1955.

Olsen, Kr. Anker. *Norsk Hydro Gjennom 50 ar*. Oslo: Norsk Hydro, 1955.

*Operation Epsilon: The Farm Hall Transcripts*. Berkeley: University of California, 1993.

Pais, Abraham. *Niels Bohr's Times*. Oxford: Oxford University, 1991.

Paneth, Philip. *Haakon VII, Norway's Fighting King*. London: Alliance Press, 1944.

Parton, James. *"Air Force Spoken Here": General Ira Eaker and the Command of the Air.* Bethesda, Md.: Adler & Adler, 1986.

Pash, Boris. *The Alsos Mission.* New York: Award House, 1969.

Peierls, Ruydolf. *Bird of Passage.* Princeton, N.J.: Princeton University, 1985.

Petrow, Richard. *The Bitter Years: The Invasion and Occupation of Denmark and Norway, April 1940–May 1945.* New York: Morrow, 1974.

Pflaum, Rosalynd. *Grand Obsession: Madame Curie and Her World.* New York: Doubleday, 1989.

Pilat, Oliver. *The Atom Spies.* New York: Putnam, 1952.

Poulsson, Jens Anton. *Aksjon Vemork Vinterkrig Pa Hardangervidda.* Oslo: n.p., 1982.

Powers, Thomas. *Heisenberg's War.* New York: Knopf, 1993.

Rhodes, Richard. *The Making of the Atomic Bomb.* New York: Simon & Schuster, 1986.

Rigden, John. *Rabi: Scientist and Citizen.* New York: Basic Books, 1987.

Riste, Olav, Johannes Andenaes, and Magne Skodvin. *Norway and the Second World War.* Oslo: Tanum, 1966.

————. *Norway and the Second World War.* Oslo: Tanum, 1970.

Royal Norwegian Government. *The Gestapo at Work in Norway.* London: Distributed by Hodder & Stoughton, 1942.

Segre, Emilio. *Enrico Fermi: Physicist.* Chicago: University of Chicago Press, 1970.

Shirer, William L. *The Challenge of Scandinavia.* Boston: Little, Brown, 1955.

————. *The Rise and Fall of the Third Reich.* New York: Simon & Schuster, 1959.

Smith, Alice Kimball. *A Peril and a Hope: The Scientists' Movement in America, 1945–1947.* Cambridge, Mass.: Massachusetts Institute of Technology, 1971.

Smith, Richard Harris. *O.S.S.: The Secret History of America's First C.I.A.* Berkeley: University of California, 1972.

Snyder, Louis L. *Louis L. Snyder's Historical Guide to World War II.* Westport, Conn.: Greenwood, 1982.

Spiro, Edward (E. H. Cookridge). *Set Europe Ablaze!* London: Pan Books, 1969.

Stahl, Knut. *De Lange Arens 1940–1945.* Stavanger, Norway: Stabenfeldt Forlag, 1964.

Stevens, E. H., ed. *The Trial of Von Falkenhorst, War Crimes Trial Series,* Vol. 6. London: William Hodge, 1949.

Teller, Edward. *Better a Shield Than a Sword.* New York: Free Press, 1987.

U.S. Department of State. *Foreign Relations of the United States.* Washington, D.C.: U.S. Government Printing Office, 1940–1943.

Urey, Harold C. *I'm a Frightened Man.* New York: Crowell-Collier, 1946.

Vigness, Paul G. *The German Occupation of Norway.* New York: Vantage, 1970.

Walker, Mark. *German National Socialism and the Quest for Nuclear Power, 1939–1949.* Cambridge: Cambridge University, 1989.

Walker, Roy. *A People Who Loved Peace: The Norwegian Struggle Against Naziism.* London: Victor Gollancz, 1946.

Warbey, William. *Look to Norway.* London: Secker & Warburg, 1943.

Warlimont, Walter. *Inside Hitler's Headquarters 1939–45*. Novato, Calif.: Presidio, 1964.

Weiss, Gertrud, and Spencer R. Weart. *Leo Szilard: His Version of the Facts*. Cambridge, Mass.: Massachusetts Institute of Technology, 1978.

Weiss, Gertrud, and Kathleen R. Windsor, eds. "Reminiscences" by Leo Szilard. In *Perspectives in American History*, Vol. 2. Cambridge, Mass.: Harvard University, 1969.

Weisskopf, Victor F. *The Joy of Insight*. New York: Basic Books, 1991.

Wells, H. G. *The World Set Free*. London: Macmillan, 1914.

West, Nigel. *M16: Britain's Secret Intelligence Service Operations, 1909–45*. London: Weidenfeld & Nicolson, 1983.

Wiggan, Richard. *Operation Freshman*. London: William Kimber, 1987.

Wilson, John S. *The Heavy Water Operations in Norway*. London: privately published, 1942–1944.

Worm-Muller, Jacob Stevenson. *Norway Revolts Against the Nazis*. London: Drummond, 1942.

Wyller, Trygve, Knut Stahl, et al.. *Stavanger Under Okkupasjonen, 1940–45*. N.p., n.d.

York, Herbert. *The Advisors: Oppenheimer, Teller, and the Superbomb*. Stanford, Calif.: Stanford University, 1989.

### PERIODICALS, PAMPHLETS, BOOKLETS

Alexandrov, A. P. Article on Igor Kurchatov. *Bulletin of the Atomic Scientists*, Dec. 1967.

Anderson, Herbert L. "The Legacy of Fermi and Szilard." *Bulletin of the Atomic Scientists*, Sept. 1974.

"The Atomic Bomb Secret—Fifteen Years Later." *Bulletin of the Atomic Scientists*, Dec. 1966.

Berglyd, Jostein. "Operation Freshman." Rogaland Fylkeskommune, Stavanger, n.d. (booklet).

Blakeslee, Howard W. "Germans Lost Race to Develop Atom Bomb Under Nazi System." *Evening Star*, Washington, D.C., Aug. 24, 1945.

Bruckner, D. J. R. "The Day the Nuclear Age Was Born." *New York Times*, Nov. 30, 1982.

Cahn, Robert. "Behind the First Atomic Bomb." *Saturday Evening Post*, July 16, 1960.

De Hoffmann, Frederic. "Pure Science in the Service of Wartime Technology." *Bulletin of the Atomic Scientists*, Jan. 1975.

De Vore, Robert. "The Man Who Made Manhattan." *Collier's*, Oct. 13, 1945.

"Enrico Fermi." *Bulletin of the Atomic Scientists*, Jan. 1955.

Frisch, Otto R., and John A. Wheeler. "The Discovery of Fission." *Physics Today*, Nov. 1967.

"Geschichte des Infanteriregiments 355, 1936–1945, eine Dokumentation," West Germany, 1973.

Goldschmidt, Bertrand. "The Supplies of Norwegian Heavy Water to France and the Early Development of Atomic Energy." *Definitif* (Paris), April 1993.

Golovin, Igor. "Father of the Soviet Bomb." *Bulletin of the Atomic Scientists*, Dec. 1967.

Goudsmit, S. A. "How Germany Lost the Race." *Bulletin of the Atomic Scientists*, Mar. 15, 1946.

Groves, Leslie R. "The Atom General Answers His Critics." *Saturday Evening Post*, June 19, 1948.

Gubbins, Colin. "Resistance Movements in the War." *Journal of the Royal United Service Institution* (London), May 1948.

Heisenberg, Werner. "Research in Germany on the Technical Application of Atomic Energy." *Nature*, August 16, 1947.

————. "The Third Reich and the Atomic Bomb." *Bulletin of the Atomic Scientists*, June 1968.

Helberg, Claus. "The Hardanger Mountain Plateau During the War." *Yearbook of the Norwegian Mountain Touring Club*, 1947.

"Igor Kurchatov, 1903–1960," *Bulletin of the Atomic Scientists*, Dec. 1967.

Industriarbeider Museet. "The Drama of Heavy Water, Rjukan—Telemark 1942–1943" (Rjukan pamphlet).

Irwin, Theodore. "The Legend That Is Dr. Szilard." *Pageant*, Dec. 1961.

Kjestadli, Sverre. "The Resistance Movement in Norway and the Allies, 1940–45." *European Resistance Movements, 1939–45*. Proceedings of the Second International Conference on the History of the Resistance Movements. New York: Pergamon Press, 1964.

"Leif Tronstad." *Nature* 56 (July 21, 1945), p. 74.

Lerner, Max. "Jekyll-Hyde Klaus Fuchs." *New York Post*, Feb. 13, 14, 15, 1950.

Moorehead, Alan. "Traitor Klaus Fuchs: He Gave Stalin the A-Bomb." *Saturday Evening Post*, May 24, 31; June 7, 14, 1952.

Norges Hjemmefrontmuseum. "Norges Hjemmefrontmuseum." Oslo, 1982 (booklet).

"Operation Freshman." *After the Battle*, Number 45 (British periodical).

Oppenheimer, J. Robert. "Niels Bohr and Atomic Weapons." *New York Review of Books*, Dec. 17, 1964.

Pegram, George B. "Professor Urey and the Nobel Prize." *Columbia University Quarterly*, New York, Mar. 1934.

Petersen, Aage. "The Philosophy of Niels Bohr." *Bulletin of the Atomic Scientists*, Sept. 1983.

Rabinowitch, Eugene. Eulogy to Szilard. *Bulletin of the Atomic Scientists*, Oct. 1964.

————. "The Virus House: The German Atomic Bomb Project." *Bulletin of the Atomic Scientists*, June 1968.

Royal Norwegian Government Information Office. *Norwegian Monthly Review*, 1941–1945.

Ryne, Linn. "Vemork Industrial Museum." *Norway Now* 8, Oslo, 1991.

Smith, Alice Kimball. "The Elusive Dr. Szilard." *Harper's*, July 1960.

"Soviet Atomic Espionage." *Bulletin of the Atomic Scientists*, May 1951.

"Spies in U.S. Told Russia All." *U.S. News & World Report*, Apr. 6, 1951.

Urey, Harold C. "Deuterium." *Columbia University Quarterly*, Sept. 1934.
Zeisel, Hans. "On Szilard." *Bulletin of the Atomic Scientists*, Sept. 1970.

## NEWSPAPERS

*Austin American-Statesman*, 11/17/90
*Dalane Tidende* (Stavanger, Norway) 7/16/74, 6/28/82, 1/10/86
*Denton (Texas) Record-Chronicle*, 11/11/90
*Fort Worth Star-Telegram*, 8/5/90
*France-Soir* (Paris), 2/10/48
*Gloucester Journal* (England), 5/4/84
*Hawick News* (Scotland), 12/28/84
*Houston Chronicle*, 5/17/93
*Houston Post*, 12/22/91
*New York Post*, 2/13/50, 2/14/50, 2/15/50
*New York Times*, 3/28/34, 11/13/34, 11/16/34, 12/9/34, 12/11/34, 4/3/43, 4/4/44
*Norfolk & Suffolk Express Series* (England), 7/10/92
*Rjukan Arbeiderblad* (Norway), 2/21/44, 2/22/44
*Rogalands Avis* (Norway), 11/18/67, 11/20/67
*Saga Weekly* (Oslo), 4/25/85, 8/25/85
*Stavanger Aftenblad* (Norway) 11/1/67
*Svenska Dagbladet* (Stockholm), 3/14/44
*Varden* (Rjukan, Norway), 11/13/93, 11/15/93

## DOCUMENTS AND OTHER UNPUBLISHED MATERIAL

Allier, Jacques. Report to Minister of Armaments Dautry. "Rapport sur la mise à disposition du gouvernement français du stock d'eau lourde de la société norvegienne de l'azote (mars 1940)," Dec. 1944, Centre d'Études, Fontenay aux Roses, France.

———. Unpublished memoir. "L'Affaire de l'eau lourde," February 1945, Centre d'Études.

American intelligence agencies' and scientific organizations' report. How Russia Became a Nuclear Power: The Untold Story of the Soviet Atomic Bomb, Modern Military Branch, National Archives, Washington, D.C.

Behren, Karl Maria von. Court-martial records, Public Records Office, Kew, Richmond, Surrey, England.

British Cabinet, Foreign Office, and Prime Minister, Official papers. Includes the Prime Minister's Operational File, which contains the record of atomic energy discussions between Churchill and Roosevelt, Public Records Office.

British and Foreign State Papers, 1940–1944. HMSO, London, 1953.

Brittain, Syd. Operation Freshman briefing notes.

Bush-Conant files, OSRD, S-1, Industrial and Social Branch, National Archives.

Bush, Vannevar. Papers, Library of Congress.

Clark, Forrest S. 44th Bomb Group, 8th Air Force. Letters to author re air attacks on Rjukan and Kjeller.

Compton, Arthur H. Papers, Washington University, St. Louis, Mo.

Dautry, Raoul. Official papers re Norsk Hydro, Centre d'Études, Fontenay aux Roses, France.

Dobson, Edward M. 392nd Bomb Group, 8th Air Force. Letter to author re attack on Rjukan.

Eaker, Ira. Papers, Library of Congress.

8th Air Force. Official records, National Archives, Suitland, Md.

Einstein, Albert. Papers, Princeton University Library.

Federation of American Scientists and related organizations files. Special Collections, Harper Memorial Library, University of Chicago.

Files on Allied attacks on Norsk Hydro. Norges Hjemmefrontmuseum, Oslo.

German records on atomic research. USAEC Technical Information Service, Oak Ridge, Tenn., and Military Records Center, Alexandria, Va.

Gilbert, Lawrence. Report on Rjukan bombing, National Archives, Suitland, Md.

Groves, Chaplain Leslie R. Diaries, National Archives.

Groves, General Leslie R. Official files, Modern Military Branch, National Archives.

———. Personal papers, Modern Military Branch, National Archives, Washington, D.C.

Harteck, Paul. Papers, including "Die Produktion von schwerem Wasser," December 1941, and "Bericht uber den Stand der SH.200 Gewinnung," 1944, USAEC Technical Information Service, Oak Ridge.

Henniker, Mark. Report on test flight to Norway, n.d., Operation Freshman file, Public Records Office.

Himmler, Heinrich. Files, Modern Military Branch, National Archives.

Holloway, David. "Entering the Nuclear Arms Race. The Soviet Decision to Build the Atomic Bomb, 1939–1945," working paper presented at International Security Studies Program colloquium at the Woodrow Wilson International Center for Scholars, Washington, D.C., July 25, 1979.

Joint Chiefs of Staff. Papers, Modern Military Branch, National Archives.

Manhattan Engineering District. Files, including general records of the Manhattan Project, material of "Top Secret—Special Interest to General Groves," and the Harrison-Bundy Collection, Stimson, Secretary of War Henry, Modern Military Branch, National Archives.

———. Office of the Commanding General, files, memo from General George Marshall to Field Marshall Sir John Dill, April 3, 1943, Modern Military Branch, National Archives.

Moreux, Henri. Directeur du Laboratoire, Municipal de Paris, memoir, "Un Episode peu connu de la bataille de l'eau lourde: Clermont-Ferrand et la prison de Riom," December 6, 1950, Centre d'Études, Fontenay aux Roses, France.

National Committee on Atomic Information. Files, Library of Congress.

Nazi murderers of Operation Freshman captives. Court-martial records, Public Records Office.

Nielsen, Kjell. Reports, American bombing of Rjukan on November 16, 1943, and of Heroya on July 24, 1943.

Norsk Hydro letters to I. G. Farben Industry, January 24, February 7, 1940; letter from Farben to Norsk Hydro, January 30, 1940, Norges Hjemmefrontmuseum, Oslo.

Norwegian government protest to British and American officials, 11/17/43, Modern Military Branch, National Archives.

Office of Scientific Research and Development, S-1, files, Industrial and Social Branch, National Archives.

OSS Report, Director's Office, to January 1944, Modern Military Branch, National Archives.

Operation Freshman, official records, Public Records Office.

Operation Grouse, official records, Public Records Office.

Operation Gunnerside, official records, Public Records Office.

Operation Swallow, official records, Public Records Office.

Rediess, Wilhelm. Report on British attack of Feb. 27, 1943, Norges Hjemmefrontmuseum, Oslo.

Release of Records Relating to Special Operations Executive (S.O.E.) Activity in Scandinavia, 1940–1945, June 2, 1994, Public Records Office.

Ronneberg, Joachim. Report, Public Records Office.

Roosevelt, Franklin D. Papers, Franklin D. Roosevelt Library, Hyde Park, New York.

Sachs, Alexander. "Early History Atomic Project in Relation to President Roosevelt, 1939–1940," Franklin D. Roosevelt Library and Mrs. Alexander Sachs.

Szilard, Leo. Papers, University of California at San Diego Library.

Tronstad, Leif. Diary, Leif Tronstad, Jr., Oslo.

U.S. Department of State. Files, National Archives.

Urey, Harold C. "Some Thermodynamic Properties of Hydrogen and Deuterium," Nobel lecture, Stockholm, February 14, 1935.

Wirtz, Karl. Includes "Die elektrolytische Schwerwassergewinnung in Norwegen," 1942, and report on visit to Rjukan in 1942, USAEC Technical Information Service, Oak Ridge.

## INTERVIEWEES

Bruce Alshoure, flyer, 100th Bombardment Group
Luis Alvarez, nuclear scientist
Arne Bang-Andersen, Stavanger policeman
Mary Bell, sister of British Corporal James Cairncross
Jostein Berglyd, Norwegian historian
Hans Bethe, U.S. atomic scientist
Fritz Bornschein, German soldier
Birger Boilestad, Rjukan resident
Syd Brittain, British flyer
Forrest S. Clark, flyer, 44th Bombardment Group
Harry H. Crosby, flyer, 100th Bombardment Group
Bruse Espedal, Stavanger resident

André Finkelstein, French scientist
Allan Forbes, friend of Szilard
Dagfinn Frantsen, Rjukan resident
Liv Fransten, Dagfinn's wife
Robert R. Furman, U.S. military intelligence agent
Thorvald Fylgjesdal, Norwegian farmer
Lillian Gabrielsen, Rjukan resident
Lawrence Gilbert, officer, 392nd Bombardment Group
Bertrand Goldschmidt, French scientist
Richard H. Groves, son of General Leslie Groves
Eva Gulbrandsen (Berg), Rjukan resident
Jonas Haaheller, Norwegian farmer
Thomas M. Hatfield, history professor, University of Texas
Knut Haugland, Norwegian saboteur
Claus Helberg, Norwegian saboteur
Amanda Hetland, Helleland resident
Ivar Hetland, Helleland resident
Reichin Hogstad, Torbjorn's wife
Torbjorn Hogstad, Norwegian farmer
Bergit Hovland, sister of Helleland Sheriff Hovland
Thomas Jeffrey, 8th Air Force officer
Kenneth G. Jewell, 44th Bombardment Group
Arne Johansen, son of Norsk Hydro guard
Fredrik Kayser, Norwegian saboteur
Arne Kjelstrup, Norwegian saboteur
Arnold Kramish, U.S. nuclear scientist
Grethe Langeland, Rjukan resident
Ralph E. Lapp, U.S. nuclear scientist
Knut Lier-Hansen, Norwegian saboteur
Aase Moe, Rjukan resident
Monrad Moe, Rjukan resident
Kenneth Nichols, assistant to General Groves
Kjell Nielsen, Norsk Hydro engineer
Tor Nygaard, Helleland resident
Rudolf Peierls, British nuclear scientist
Warren Polking, officer, 392nd Bombardment Group
Bergljot Poulsson, wife of Jens Anton Poulsson
Jens Anton Poulsson, Norwegian saboteur
Per Pynten, Norsk Hydro engineer
Isidore I. Rabi, nuclear scientist
Owen Roane, pilot, 100th Bombardment Group
Joachim Ronneberg, Norwegian saboteur
Martin Selmer Sandstal, Norwegian farmer
Robert Serber, U.S. nuclear scientist
R. A. de G. Sewell, brother of British pilot Gerard Walter Sewell de Gency

Einar Skinnarland, member, Norwegian Resistance
Svein Sorensen, nephew of ferry captain
Birger Stromsheim, Norwegian saboteur
Jack Swartout, pilot, 100th Bombardment Group
Torgeir Syverstad, son of Gunnar Syverstad
Lellean Tangstad, Rjukan resident
Edward Teller, U.S. nuclear scientist
·Leif Tronstad, Jr., son of scientist Tronstad
Gertrud Weiss, sister of Szilard
Victor Weisskopf, U.S. nuclear scientist
Carl Friedrich von Weizsaecker, German nuclear scientist
Eugene Wigner, U.S. nuclear scientist
Robert Wright, flyer, 93rd Bombardment Group


## MUSEUMS AND LIBRARIES

Centre d'Études, Fontenay aux Roses, France
Columbia University, New York
Delane Folkemuseum, Slettebo, Egersund, Norway
Franklin Delano Roosevelt Library, Hyde Park, N.Y.
Industriarbeider Museet, Vemork, Norway
Library of Congress, Washington, D.C.
Ministry of Defence Library, London
New York Public Library, New York
National Archives, Washington, D.C., and Suitland, Md.
Norges Hjemmefrontmuseum, Oslo
Norwegian Defence Historical Archives, Oslo
Office of Air Force History, Washington, D.C.

# INDEX